MADAME DE LAMBALLE

MADAME DE LAMBALLE

BY

GEORGES BERTIN

Translated into English by
ARABELLA WARD

With Portrait, an Introduction and Historical Notes
by the Translator

NEW YORK
GODFREY A. S. WIENERS
1901

30 72889 B

Introductory Note

In offering to the public an English version of Monsieur Georges Bertin's "Madame de Lamballe," I feel that the title alone will arouse interest.

The life of Madame de Lamballe is well known. The story of her intimacy with Marie Antoinette, and of her unceasing devotion to the royal family, is one of the most interesting and pathetic chapters in the history of the French Revolution.

The present volume is largely made up of unpublished documents and of articles taken from the newspapers of that day. The French, therefore, from a literary standpoint, is often open to criticism. Although I have kept as closely as possible to the original, I have been obliged, in some places, to deviate slightly, in order to conform to the English idiom.

For historical references I have consulted Taine's " Ancien Régime," Morris's " French Revolution," Carlyle's " French Revolution," Guizot's " History of France," Madame de Campan, and "Secret Memoirs of the Royal Family of France," first published from the journal, letters, and conversations of the Princesse de Lamballe, and brought out in Philadelphia in 1826.

I should like to avail myself of this opportunity to extend my thanks for the valuable suggestions made to me in regard to the present work, as well as for the gift of the accompanying illustration.

ARABELLA WARD.

June, 1901.

Table of Contents

CHAPTER VI

TABLE OF CONTENTS

CHAPTER VII

CHAPTER VIII

TABLE OF CONTENTS

CHAPTER IX

TABLE OF CONTENTS

CHAPTER XII

TABLE OF CONTENTS

CHAPTER XIII

CHAPTER XIV

CHAPTER XV

CHAPTER XVI

CHAPTER XVII

Conflict between the king and the Assembly.—Decree for the
deportation of priests, etc.—The Tuileries invaded.—The
dauphin.—Courage of Madame de Lamballe.—Pétion.—Roederer.—Pétion and Manuel suspended.—The Mayor of Paris
restored to office.—Fête of the Federation.—The king and the
royal family at the Champs-de-Mars.—Merlin, Chabot, and
other patriots murdered.—Arms in the cellars of the château.
—The king contemplates flight.—The people wish to attack
the Tuileries.—Camp around the château.—The battalions of
the National Guard hasten to the protection of the king.—The
faubourgs in arms.—Preparations for defence at the château.
—Princesse de Lamballe, Madame de Lâge de Volude, and the
Comtesse de Ginestous.—Arrival of the Marseillais.—Condemnation of Girard.—The Comtesse de Lâge in Paris.—Visit
of the princess.—Situation of the royal family and the princess.
—The king resolved to oppose with arms any attack on his
house.—Scepticism of Madame de Lâge de Volude.—Madame
de Lâge de Volude leaves Paris.—Agitation in the faubourgs.
—The Tuileries about to be attacked.—The Swiss from Courbevoie and Rueil.—Officers and soldiers passing through Paris.
—The tocsin sounds.—Impressions at the château.—Assas-

TABLE OF CONTENTS

CHAPTER XVIII

CHAPTER XIX

TABLE OF CONTENTS

CHAPTER XX

Madame de Lamballe

Madame de Lamballe

CHAPTER I

A little town, quaintly nestling on a fertile plateau, boasting no vanity from its choice site, but preserving all the modesty of its surroundings—such is Nangis.

Nevertheless, like others, it has had its day in the past, and, like them, can claim a place in history. Thus we see it as a frame to the picture which naturally has its place in the beginning of the study we are about to undertake.

Scarcely had day dawned on the 31st of January, 1767, a memorable date in its annals, when Nangis broke through its ordinary calm and awoke to active life.

On that day its inhabitants were to have as guests the Prince de Lamballe and his future wife, the Princesse de Carignan, and this royal union was to be blessed in the old church, of which the town was justly proud, a fine specimen of Gothic architecture, with its beautiful lines and remarkable purity of style. The

3

people on this occasion acted as always under similar circumstances.

At the entrance of Nangis they erected a triumphal arch on which they raised an enormous escutcheon with the coat-of-arms of the town, the azure shield with six besants of silver. By their hands every house was adorned with flags, and poles to which oriflammes were suspended were placed at equal distances along the streets.

Notwithstanding the attention demanded by these preparations, anxiety and curiosity reached a high pitch. At the least noise, at the rolling of a carriage, the gates were immediately opened and the windows were filled with heads, eager to question the road from Montereau.

The agitation was no less apparent in the streets. Citizens went and came, attracted by the unusual presence of horsemen who had passed and repassed at full speed since morning, and whose duty it was to announce the arrival of the Princesse de Carignan's carriages. When the equipage of the Duc de Penthièvre appeared the crowd was in an uproar. The good duke, so universally beloved and respected, was radiant; this marriage carried out his most cherished wishes, and the joy depicted on the face of his son added to his happiness.

In order to follow a gallant custom, or rather from a very natural feeling of the heart, which in his legitimate desire to become acquainted at last with her who was to be his companion for life he could not resist, the Prince de Lamballe had gone the day before to Montereau, where the princess was staying. He had been introduced as a simple gentleman, and had paid her a compliment in offering her a bouquet in the name of his master. The few moments in which he had been able to look at her had sufficed for him to appreciate mademoiselle's charms, and the infatuation caused by his happiness, but poorly dissimulated, well-nigh disclosed who he really was.

His emotion was such that upon his return to Nangis he had no need to acknowledge the state of his affections; every one was convinced that it would be a love match.[1]

As soon as the carriages appeared the Duc de Penthièvre stepped out, followed by the Prince de Lamballe and the Comte and Comtesse de La Marche. Mademoiselle Carignan, with her suite, did likewise, and advanced, escorted by Monsieur de Lastic, her chief usher.

The presentation took place at once; the duke embraced the princess, after which it was the turn of the Prince de Lamballe, who held her long in his arms.

Then all this brilliant assemblage returned to the carriages and went back to Nangis.

In the Prince de Lamballe Mademoiselle de Carignan had no difficulty in recognizing the gallant messenger of the previous evening, who had caused her no little anxiety. Timidly she reproached him for not having made himself known. During the journey he showed her the most assiduous attention, and the duke did not cease to thank her for the pleasure which he owed to her. On her side, the princess acknowledged every care given her during the journey.

At the gates of the city the crowd increased, became denser, and the people craned their necks in order to see the better. Raised in the midst of a severe court, which had carefully kept her apart from all luxury, the princess at first seemed confused by the magnificent preparations for her marriage; but this feeling was only a passing one, and soon disappeared in the joy and happiness which seemed to reign everywhere.

The clergy were assembled before the church to receive the royal wedding procession and conduct it to the chapel of the Marquis de Nangis. The little chapel, situated at one side of the church, was filled with souvenirs of this noble family; their arms ornamented the high altar, the frescoes portrayed their deeds of valor. Conducted with perfect art, the ordinarily severe, even mournful, aspect of the ceremony was lost. Flowers were scattered about in profusion, and, by the diversity of their coloring, added brightness to the whole effect. The benediction was pronounced by the Cardinal de Luynes.

On this point we disagree with Fortaire, who makes the royal couple leave in the afternoon, and who gives the details of a supper which must have taken place the same evening at the Hôtel de Toulouse. Fortaire

6

afterwards states that perhaps his memory is at fault, and we cannot prefer his version to the one in the " Gazette de France," a daily paper; the more so, as we think that the recent loss in the Duc de Penthièvre's family would have necessitated a private wedding.

From the church they went with great pomp to the Château de Nangis, kindly put at the disposal of the Duc de Penthièvre by the Guerchy family.

Is it necessary to add that the young couple hurried through the collation which was given them ? Before all else they wished to talk without restraint, away from tiresome staring. Nothing could have been more propitious to sweet interchange of thought, nothing could have been better suited to a delightful *tête-à-tête* than this beautiful estate of Nangis. Thanks to the deep forests everything there was a mystery, and in their then state of feelings might not our lovers have fallen under the charm of the deepest passion ?

The château itself, which was very old and entirely surrounded by vast moats filled with water, and which they saw from afar, lighted by the uncertain rays of winter, like a fantastic tableau, attracted them and added still more to the impression already produced.

Several days passed in this way, entirely given up to love and poetry, would perhaps have turned the prince's growing passion for his young wife in a very different direction, and shed its happy influence on this union. Had they been ordinary mortals, no thought of conventionality could have hindered them from thus passing those days of happiness; but princes born, princes of the same blood, politics alone presided over their nuptials, and could not help ruling their life. Their return to Paris had been arranged in advance, and it was impossible to change the plan.

The day closed with a great feast, to which all the Duc de Penthièvre's friends had been invited. The fête was held in the large drawing-room of the château, which was illuminated by a thousand lights.

According to Michelin, this same room had been used for the banquets at the wedding of Marie of Saxony, daughter of the King of Poland, with the dauphin, and also for that of Joseph de Bourbon-Conti and Fortunée Marie d'Este, Princess of Modena.

The following day Nangis returned to its wonted calm, the château and the park resumed their everyday appearance, and all the lords went back to Paris.

Of the seven children born from the union of Marie Félicité d'Este with the Duc de Penthièvre, the Prince de Lamballe and Mademoiselle de Bourbon alone remained. So, from his son's childhood, the duke had resolved to marry him, in the sweet hope of seeing him perpetuate his race. Was it not premature? Was it very prudent to bind in wedlock, somewhat against his will, this youth of nineteen, whose conduct had already caused him more than one pang?

The duke, in his wisdom, had certainly weighed all the consequences of his resolution. He himself had married at the same age, and the example of his happiness was there to strengthen his decision. Was it, then, so rash on his part to believe that the influence of a woman young, full of attractions, and of a pleasing personality would be more efficacious than his paternal authority, and that she would succeed in averting unhappy temptations from the prince, whose character was weaker than his disposition was vicious ?

The Duc de Penthièvre had not sought in this marriage a fortune for his son; his own was sufficient, and he knew that the court of Sardinia was not rich enough for him to aspire to a large dowry.

The inventory of the possessions of the Princesse de Lamballe gives us a hint as to the marriage contract, signed at Turin, the 17th of January, 1767, before the State minister and royal notary of the king of Sardinia. From this inventory we see that the princess had a dowry of one hundred and fifty thousand livres from the Prince and Princesse de Savoie Carignan, her father and mother, Piedmont money, worth in French money one hundred and eighty thousand livres, with an income at four per cent., besides a trousseau worth eighteen thousand livres. For this the princess gave up all claim of inheritance from her father and mother, in favor of her brothers, or their heirs in the male line. The Duc de Penthièvre gave to his daughter-in-law seventy-five thousand livres' worth of diamonds and other precious stones.

Furthermore, it was stipulated that if the princess

survived her husband, she should have, in addition to her dowry, sixty thousand livres, in French money, thirty thousand livres income for life, besides sixteen dresses and other articles for her use, to the amount of seventy-five thousand livres. The king, to whom the Duc de Penthièvre had told his plans, approved of them, and offered him the hand of Mademoiselle de Savoie Carignan.

The preliminaries were arranged according to the following account in the " Gazette de France ":

" VERSAILLES, January 10, 1767.

" On the seventh of this month the king announced the marriage of the Prince de Lamballe and Marie Thérèse Louise, Princesse de Carignan, fourth daughter of Louis Victor Amédée Joseph de Savoie, Prince de Carignan, and of Christine Henriette de Hesse Rheinfels."

The following day, the 8th of January, according to the same authority, the French ambassador presented the official announcement in the name of the king:

" TURIN, January 14, 1767.

" Last Thursday, Baron de Choiseul, ambassador of France to this court, had a private audience with the king, in which he presented to his Majesty the request for Princesse Marie Thérèse de Carignan from the Prince de Lamballe; at the same time he gave the king the letter which her very Christian Majesty wrote to him on this occasion. To-day the king announced the marriage to the royal officers, to the chevaliers of

the Annonciade, and to the principal courtiers who
have admittance to his cabinet; the signing of the contract and the celebration of the marriage are arranged
for Saturday, the 17th, and the same day the young
princess will leave for France." [2]

Following is the itinerary of the young princess's
journey, by which she took fifteen days to reach Paris:

" VERSAILLES, February 11, 1767.

" The Princesse de Lamballe left Turin the 17th of
January in the carriage of the Prince de Carignan, her
father, and reached the Pont de Beauvoisin the 24th,
where she was met by the Chevalier de Lastic, acting
for the Duc de Penthièvre and the Prince de Lamballe.
The latter presented to the princess the ladies who
were to be in her suite and the officers who were to
serve her. On the 25th the princess left the Pont de
Beauvoisin, in the Prince de Lamballe's carriage, and
reached Montereau the afternoon of the 30th."

The Prince and Princesse de Lamballe left Nangis
the 1st of February, arrived the same day at Paris, and
went to the Hôtel de Toulouse. It is probable that
in the evening the young couple were presented to the
royal princess, and that the supper of thirty covers
took place, of which Fortaire speaks. In the meantime appeared the wedding song dedicated to the Prince
de Lamballe:

" Crown with wreaths thy brow immortal, Hymen,
Wave high thy torch that shines with heav'nly hue.
Upon my bank a triumph that is new
Now summons thee, and Love calls thee again.

MADAME DE LAMBALLE

Two hearts, each pierced with Cupid-given pain,
Seek happy union in a lasting chain.
Why tarry you? Haste to my banklets low,
And see increase your ever fair empire
Of wedded ones, in whom we all admire
The rarest gifts that Heav'n can e'er bestow."
Thus spoke the Nymph, the goddess of the Seine,
To Hymen, God of Wedlock, who replied :
" Fair Queen of Waters, which forever glide
About thy sovereign city, not in vain
You speak ; no other dwelling and no other sun
Where I receive from mortals homage meet
Is sought by me, or cherished, but the one
Which your banks give, and which to me is sweet ;
Nor elsewhere do I ever see, as here,
My altars thronged with those I hold most dear ;
My power invoked most zealously by each,
And the dependence that my laws must teach.
The city honors me by greatest zest,
E'en Love himself, my rival, at my best
Ne'er throws a shadow o'er my power quite ;
United, both, we share our strength and might.
He wishes to be happy but through me ;
Through him I'd rule, and to his laws agree.
And yet, alas ! Love's enemy and mine,
An adversary bold and full of shame,
Upon thy banks to-day in silence came ;
He broke my laws, he overstepped their line,
And left to crime an open path so fine
That Hymen's lovely Innocence and Peace
Please less, and direful crimes increase ;
That, without shame, thy people outrage sore,
And—" Hymen ceased, and said no more.
Nor could he, for his voice was choked.
The Nymph, in pity, thus invoked :
" Why cherish thus thy every deepest grief ?
Why vainly add to sorrow's weight ?
If some wrong mortals find relief

In scorning right, if virtuous laws they hate,
Yet all the rest still have their firm belief
In thee ; they love and know thy rights are great.
Thy altar smokes again with incense sweet,
A Prince, son of Penthièvrus, doth entreat——"
Then, all beside himself, god Hymen spoke :
" O sweetest hope, that ever was so fair,
O best beloved, in my great despair,
Seek you, O Nymph, with flattery to cloak
My anger ? Is't true, a son ? " She spoke :
" Yes, yes, a son, his father's image, he,
Proud, generous, tender, strong, kind for humanity,
Who finds the empire sweet that laws from thee must give ;
Who wishes but by thee in happiness to live."

Then Hymen's heart rejoiced indeed ;
No longer was he weighed with care.
To France's fields he longed to speed ;
Wave there his torch, his bright crown bear,
Call to him Laughter, Joy, and Grace,
Who, full of strength, sprang up apace.
They all burst forth in merry glee ;
They part, take wing, and hither flee
To our green banks. Ne'er Love before
Began his course on lighter wing,
E'en when in mischief he would soar,
When fresher thoughts his mother'd bring,
Than when, another heart to score,
He left Cytheria, Paphos' shore,
And sweet repose from two hearts tore.
Thus this most faithful, god-sent boy
Olympus scales, its mighty height,
And, speeding hence on wings of light,
Stands on our banks in beaming joy.

Four days later Madame de Lamballe was presented,
by the Comtesse de La Marche, to the king and to
the royal family.

Louis XVI., who forgot nothing in his diary, mentions the fact in these words:

" February 5th, '67, the presentation of Madame de Lamballe."

The following day the royal family paid a visit to the princess, whereupon Louis XVI. again writes:

" February 6th, visited Madame de Lamballe."

CHAPTER II

Let us now make the acquaintance of her in whom the Duc de Penthièvre had placed his fondest hopes, whom he considered capable of reforming the Prince de Lamballe, and whose influence his son could not, in his opinion, resist.

Born at Turin, the 8th of September, 1749, Marie Thérèse Louise de Savoie Carignan in her eighteenth year was not exactly what we call pretty. Her features somewhat lacked the regularity which is the accompaniment of true beauty; but the brilliancy of her complexion was remarkable. Although her large, light blue eyes were rather expressionless, her face was none the less interesting, thanks to her blond hair of an adorable golden hue, which increased still more the sweetness of an *ensemble* full of charms and attractions. Add to this a remarkably beautiful figure, and it is easy to see that the Princesse de Lamballe was really very charming.[1]

Morally, she was good. Nothing of a coquette, she was very sweet and almost ingenuous. Though but little blessed with natural wit, her gayety was none the less frank and full of spontaneity. She was not an enemy to pleasure ; but she preferred it simple and without ostentation. Criticism has often been levelled at the frivolous side of her character, but never did it succeed, even in its sharpest attacks, in citing a wrong action on her part. Such was the delightful child whom politics had united with Louis Alexander Joseph Stanislas de Bourbon Lamballe.

The Duc de Penthièvre had therefore good reason for appearing satisfied with this marriage. Not only on this occasion did he receive many congratulations, among others a letter from his old friend De Lamoignon, for whom for many years he had professed a special regard, but he could see for himself both the improvement in his son's behavior and the increasing influence which the young princess seemed to gain over him.

On the 10th of February our young heroine was present *in fiocchi* at the representation of " La Gouvernante " given upon the return of Molé.

Some time after, a wealthy stranger came to Paris and spoke of his various meetings with noble personages. He told how he had been presented by the Marquis de Besseville to the Duc de Penthièvre and to the Prince de Lamballe, while the lady-in-waiting to the princess, the Comtesse de Guébriant, presented him to Madame de Lamballe.

That which further confirms the good opinion of the duke regarding the improved morals of his son, is this letter from the Prince de Lamballe, written at Versailles, March 25th, in which, doubtless in order to devote himself wholly to his wife, the prince declares that "the desire which he had had to raise a small pack of hounds for hunting deer was entirely gone."

We read of the king's holding a grand review on the Field of Marly, July 1st. It was a magnificent fête, say the contemporary documents; the queen was there, as well as the Comtes de Provence and d'Artois, Mesdames Adélaide, Victoire, Louise, and Sophie, the Duc de Bourbon, Madame de Lamballe, and the entire court.

The king rode about among the troops, followed by a brilliant *cortège*, at the head of which was the Duc de Chartres, the Prince de Condé, and the Prince de Lamballe. But marriage, unfortunately, did not succeed in reforming this prince. He was decidedly incapable of appreciating the charm of his young wife, and the hope that the poor duke had conceived of rescuing his *blasé* son was strangely disappointed.

In short, only five months after his marriage, Monsieur de Lamballe had Mademoiselle de la Chassaigne, from the Comédie Française, for his mistress.

Private memoirs tell us of it in the following words:

"Mademoiselle de la Chassaigne, a young actress of the Comédie Française, a niece of Mademoiselle de la Mothe, former chorus-leader in this theatre, is to-day the object of the gossip and the jealousy of all her friends. Although not very pretty, and possessed of very little talent, she has been honored with the attention of a young prince (Lamballe), but lately married.

The father of the young man is very conscientious, and has taken every precaution to prove the necessary facts relating to the truth of the case. He has assured the actress of his protection, and a sum of money has been settled upon her and her prospective child."

Three months later, the same author tells us, on September 26th a still graver deed was committed, and the prince communicated to his wife the result of his misconduct. He was then intimate with one of the cleverest courtesans of the city, and his need of money made him commit an abominable act, for, not content with deceiving his wife, he carried off her diamonds with which to pay for his debaucheries.

"They have spoken," Bachaumont says further, "of the flight of Mademoiselle La Forest, to the great regret of a young prince but lately married, who had conceived for her a dangerous passion. The motive for this hasty flight is known positively. The lover had made her a present of a rather large share of the princess's diamonds. The woman learned that an investigation was being made, and thought best to disappear. Better advised, however, she presented herself, after a short time, before the Duc de Penthièvre, the young prince's father, brought back the diamonds, and threw herself on her knees, asking for consideration. The duke appeared satisfied with this proceeding, and told her that an estimate should be made of the diamonds, and that their value should be paid to her; that she need have no anxiety; that his son alone was to blame; that her child should be cared for, since she said she expected one, and that in any case she

should not suffer; but he demanded that she should
not see the young prince, her lover, again."

As a result of the inconstancy of the prince, whom
she loved and who so recently had vowed to be faithful to her, Madame de Lamballe was taken very ill.

" A bright, amiable young princess, married last
winter to a husband also young, has not been able
to suffer his repeated acts of infidelity, and, however
disastrous they may have been to her love for this
modern Theseus, she could not without a feeling of
positive jealousy see his estrangement and desertion.
She became envious of the most despicable objects
whom the prince honored with his attentions, and has
given way to profound melancholy and hysteria. Since
the fashionable physicians have been unable to remedy
the trouble, which is more mental than physical, she
has placed herself in the hands of one Pittara, a charla-
tan now in vogue, who applies plasters to his patients.
Several ladies of the court have tried him, and the
Duchesse de Mazarin having spoken of him to the
princess the latter sent for him a short time ago."

The prince, who had lost every feeling of decency, no longer sought to save appearances, and no
doubt thinking himself too closely watched in the
Hôtel at Toulouse, left it.

" It is said that the Prince de Lamballe went away
without letting any one know where he was, and that
the Duc de Penthièvre has sought everywhere for him.
He has been found in a furnished hotel, under treat-

ment for a severe illness, the result of a too hazardous gallantry.

" They describe him as being in a most deplorable state, and they add that perhaps he will be sadly mutilated."

In spite of the disgust which his son's conduct caused him, the Duc de Penthièvre strove to save him and had him carried to his own home to be cared for. He had not yet lost all hope of reforming him, but, first of all, he wished to send away Mademoiselle La Cour, and thanks to a large sum which he offered the latter he succeeded. Unfortunately, however, his efforts to help his son were without avail. Insensible to the paternal affection and to the attention of the princess, Monsieur de Lamballe fled again, scarcely one month before his death.

" Monsieur le Prince de Lamballe," our inexhaustible chronicler again relates, " is on the D'Antin road, at Monsieur de Wargemont's; he is in a most deplorable state, aggravated by his having hurt himself on horseback."

For the second time the duke sought his son and had him brought back to Lucienne, where the physicians hoped for a speedy cure in the country air. But the malady only increased ; every day brought a new trouble, and three weeks later the unhappy prince could no longer be deceived as to his condition. Realizing his wrongdoings, and won over, perhaps, by the example of his family, who did not address a single word of reproach to him, the prince desired to receive the sacraments of the Church. Some days after, his condition became hopeless, and the members of his family could not enter his room.

" The Prince de Lamballe is completely without hope of recovery, and is living only by fever. The princesses no longer come into his room. He is sure to succumb to the numberless remedies which have been given him. It is known, from an apothecary, that he has taken seven pounds of mercury, not to mention the Keyser pills and other mixtures of the charlatans in whose hands his Highness placed himself at the beginning of his illness. The Princesse de Conti and the Comtesse de La Marche are at Lucienne with the disconsolate family. For the rest, the prince is ending his life well; Father Imbert, the monk, is his confessor.
" The Prince de Lamballe has just died."

This " ending his life well," from a spiritual point of view at least, as Bachaumont tells us, was none the less terrible, and the last moments of the unhappy man, whose sufferings were frightful, were a cruel atonement for the wrongdoings of his wretched life.

Doubtless a kindly notice was requested by the Duc de Penthièvre, for the " Gazette de France," from which we gather the details of this event, was careful not to pass over in silence the repentance and piety shown by the dying man.

" Louis Alexander Joseph Stanislas de Bourbon,

Prince de Lamballe, first huntsman of France, died at the Château de Lucienne, near Versailles, the 6th of this month, at half-past eight o'clock in the morning, aged twenty years and eight months. He was born the 6th of September, 1747. He was married the 17th of January, 1767, to Marie Thérèse Louise de Carignan. We cannot too highly commend the sentiments of piety and resignation and the courage which this prince showed during his long illness, up to the last moments of his life. On account of his death the court will wear mourning for ten days.

The funeral took place the next day but one.

"Last Sunday the funeral of the Prince de Lamballe was held without ostentation. The procession left Lucienne about half-past eleven o'clock in the evening. It consisted first of three carriages, in one of which was the body of the dead prince; in the second, the minister and the vicar of the parish of Lucienne, with a chaplain; and in the third the Marquis de Besseville and the Viscount de Castellane, first equerries, bearing the crown; secondly, two gentlemen on horseback; thirdly, four pages and an outrider; fourthly, a large number of valets on foot bearing torches; and, finally, one hundred poor people. The procession reached Rambouillet at six o'clock in the morning, and was there met by the minister, the vicar, and a large number of the clergy.'

This sad event was a cruel blow to the princess: her sorrow was deep, her grief indescribable. Nothing, in short, was more real than the love she had professed for her unworthy husband, upon whom, in spite of his misconduct, she never ceased to the last moment to lavish the most touching affection.

Then, alone in her grief, undecided, incapable of reflection, she thought of retiring to the Abbey of Saint Antoine, where, within the shadow of the severe walls of the cloister, she could bury her regrets.

In what a terrible position this frightful bereavement placed her! What should she do? How act as a widow, so young, without experience, in the midst of a world with which she was unacquainted, in an adopted country, whose customs were scarcely known to her?

It was at this point that the Duc de Penthièvre appeared, an angel of goodness, endowed with every virtue, and begged the princess not to leave him.

With a nature so essentially susceptible to generous feelings, the princess could not, without being strongly affected, see the havoc which the son's death had caused in her father-in-law, and she felt that she had duties to fulfil and consolation to render; then, at length, more mistress of herself, in possession of all the reason that had for a time been wandering, she saw in him a guide and support, and his request alone was needed to induce her to go to Rambouillet.

CHAPTER III

It is at Rambouillet that we see her passing the first days of her widowhood, with the Duc de Penthièvre and Mademoiselle de Bourbon, her sister-in-law, who never ceased to lavish upon her the tenderest care, and who, the following year, by her marriage with the Duc de Chartres, brought a healthful diversion to the grief of the family. This country life, to which at first she was only resigned, since at the time quiet and solitude alone suited her state of mind, after a while pleased her immensely, and the beautiful trees of the park, which appealed so strongly to reverie, had a particular charm for her. At Rambouillet she found again the calmness of mind which she sought, and that free and easy life which was one of her favorite dreams; for, although the house was filled with every luxury which the position of her hosts demanded, the Duc de Penthièvre, with his modest tastes, had banished from it formality and etiquette. Could it have been the remembrance of these happy days which suggested to Marie Antoinette the idea of the beautiful Trianon, where the queen so loved to go, to be free from the obligations of the court?

The year 1769 opened with the solemn announcement of the marriage of the Duc de Chartres with Mademoiselle de Bourbon Penthièvre.[1] This marriage contract had been made over and over again many times by the whims of the Duc d'Orléans, but was finally concluded the 4th of January, as we read in the " Gazette de France ".

" On the morning of day before yesterday, the king announced the marriage of the Duc de Chartres, son of the Duc d'Orléans, first prince of the blood, and Mademoiselle de Penthièvre, daughter of the Duc de Penthièvre."

It was in every respect a fine match. Mademoiselle de Penthièvre, according to Bezenval, did not have a dowry, it is true, of more than fifty thousand crowns income; but, at the death of the Prince de Lamballe, she would inherit the entire fortune of her father, estimated at an income of three millions at least.

On the other hand, Mademoiselle de Penthièvre was deeply in love with the Duc de Chartres, who at the time was very attractive, and she did not hesitate to declare that she would never marry any one but him.[2]

Nevertheless the wedding was not celebrated at Versailles until the 5th of the following April. Why all this delay ? Was it to allow the young prince to become fully acquainted with her who loved him after having seen him but once at Madame de Modène's, " where the Duc de Chartres had offered her his hand to lead her to her carriage " ? This marriage, which was not announced under more auspicious circumstances than that of the Princesse de Lamballe, could scarcely be more happy.

To believe Bachaumont, who tells us a pretty anecdote about the occupations of the young *fiancé*, is to suppose that the Duc de Chartres gave to Mademoiselle de Penthièvre only a brief courtship. What he mentions on this point is of sufficient interest to have a place in our story:

" At the wedding of the Comte de Fitz James, the Duc de Chartres gave him a supper at his little house, called the *Souper des Veuves*. There were present the mistresses of this prince, and of different lords who were married or about to become so. Everything was draped in black. The women were in mourning, also the men. The candles of Love were extinguished and were replaced by those of Marriage. These two gods were in a continual state of rivalry at this fête; in a word, everything there characterized the Fall of Pleasures and the Empire of Reason. They say there is a question of renewing this farce in a still more solemn manner on the occasion of the approaching marriage of the Duc de Chartres."

Once married, the Duchesse de Chartres acquired a passion for the theatre, and was often seen there, accompanied by her sister-in-law, Mademoiselle d'Orléans, and by the Comtesse de La Marche. The Prince de Conti gave his niece a pretty fête in the Park d'Issy. "A delightful affair," says Bachaumont.

" There was no crowd; it was almost a family gathering. '

In spite of her mourning, the Princesse de Lamballe did not fail to attend a celebration at the end of the year at Saint Denis; then she returned, without doubt, to her father-in-law. Our gracious princess always became wearied when she was obliged to appear at any court reception. To leave her favorite occupations, even for a few days, seemed to her a cruel ordeal, and it needed much of the Duc de Penthièvre's gentle and at times even paternal authority to make her do so. She seldom left her father-in-law, especially as, in addition to his kindly acts, he uttered sweet words of sympathy, which came from a heart eminently kind and generous. Nothing can better express his charity than these lines of Florian:

> " Disguised his birth, 'neath garments meek,
>   Penthièvre at times the poor doth seek ;
> And from his priceless palace rare
>   Renews the widow's scanty fare."

Thus Madame de Lamballe lived quietly during the last part of that year and the beginning of the following. But in 1770 a great event occurred, the results of which were seriously to influence the future of our charming heroine. The dauphin married the Archduchess of Austria, Marie Antoinette, and the whole court was invited to assist at the magnificent fêtes, the splendor of which surpassed, they say, those of all preceding royal marriages. Madame de Lamballe was present at every ceremony, and the dauphiness, to whom she was presented, was charmed with her and overwhelmed her with attentions which the spectators did not fail to notice. More than one saw even then the dawn of an intimacy which later was to give so much trouble to the two friends.

Probably the princess stayed at Versailles only the necessary time and then returned to her beloved occupations in the country. Then, either for distraction or because of her health, which was still somewhat poor, the Duc de Penthièvre took her to the seashore.

"The Duc de Penthièvre has taken Madame de Chartres, Madame de Lamballe, and Madame de La Marche to Havre de Grace. The Duc de Chartres is going also; he will probably start the 10th of September."

Unfortunately this trip was postponed, owing to an unexpected illness on the part of the Duc de Penthièvre during a stay in the Château of Crécy. Little by little the princess recovered her spirits, and through the soothing influence of her father-in-law she again faced the world, for we see her in February, 1771, doing the honors of the Hôtel de Toulouse for the royal Prince of Sweden and for his brother, Prince Adolphus, as well as for the King of Denmark.

It was at this time that she became intimate with the dauphiness, a fact of secondary importance at the time, but which Mercy Argenteau, who will be a great help to us, was nevertheless careful to note and report to Marie Thérèse on the 17th of March, designating the intimacy as "an unusual affection." He foresaw rightly, for this was the beginning of that great friendship which later was to be of such interest to Mercy and to his august sovereign.

At that time Madame de Lamballe was almost constantly at court. During the year 1771 we see her assisting at every ceremonial. The "Gazette de France" mentions her presence in the chapel at high mass on Holy Thursday, at which the king was present accompanied by the royal family, the Duc de Bourbon, and the Duc de Penthièvre. In May she went to Fontainebleau, was there presented by the king to the future Comtesse de Provence, and attended the supper. Then, in June, she accompanied the Holy Sacrament in the procession of Corpus Christi.

The Duc de Penthièvre could not but congratulate himself on his efforts in bringing back calmness of mind to his daughter-in-law and in making her by degrees take up the duties of society. Another happiness was in store for him, for his daughter, the Duchesse de Chartres, was about to bear a child, and her husband's attentions, if we may believe Bachaumont, were more than assiduous.

"They speak," he says, "only with the greatest admiration of the care which the Duc de Chartres takes of his august wife. He never leaves her and redoubles his tender attentions. Far from giving himself up to the mistakes of his early youth, which would seem more excusable under circumstances in which his passions would be likely to carry him away, he uses the kindest and most deferential manner towards the princess, and this causes great joy to the Duc de Penthièvre.''

But, in spite of all the care with which she was surrounded, in spite of every attention, the Duchesse de Chartres gave birth to a still-born child on the 10th of October. This was a great grief to the family, a grief shared by the young dauphiness, who wrote to her mother on the 13th of October, 1777:

'' You surely know, my dearest mother, the sorrow of the Duchesse de Chartres, who has just given birth to a still-born child.''

Then the daughter, knowing the secret longing of her mother, went on to say:

'' I wish I had some news to tell you concerning myself, but as yet there is apparently none.''

After this event the lack of documents causes us to lose sight of the princess, whom we do not again find until January, 1772, when she is one of a sleighing party.

We read in the '' Gazette de France '' that—

'' Madame the Dauphiness and the Comtesse de Provence, accompanied by the Princesse de Lamballe, took a sleigh ride on the 30th of last month. Madame, the dauphin's wife, afterwards gave a dinner to the Princesse de Lamballe, who had the honor of being with her on this drive." [3]

In August of the same year the Duchesse de Chartres went to Forges les Eaux. Unfortunately, we cannot analyze the description given by Bachaumont, and which, if we are to believe it, does not lack a certain interest. Was the princess on the trip? We are not positive. However, we append the paragraph from Bachaumont:

" At the time of the journey of the Duc and Duchesse de Chartres to the waters of Forges there was edited in Normandy a paper called the ' Gazette Normande.' It was a journal modelled after the supplements of the ' Gazette de France '; that is to say, it was evil, untruthful, calumnious, with, however, some few good points, as it should have."

The princess does not appear again until the following year, when her father-in-law saw his dearest hope realized in the person of his little grandson, the Duc de Valois, afterward Louis Philippe I., born the 6th of October, 1773.

It was on the occasion of this great event that the duke received from his young page, Florian, who had not yet reached the age of eighteen, the curious letter signed " Polichinelle," in which he describes minutely the good qualities of his protector:

" FONTAINEBLEAU, October 29, 1773.

" MY LORD: Your serene Highness will receive many compliments on the birth of the Prince de Va-

lois. Those who mean the best often express themselves in the poorest manner and I am of this number,
my lord. I have begun a thousand letters before writing one which would express to you all the joy I feel
at this happy event. I have had the honor to serve
Madame la Duchesse de Chartres, your daughter, and
it is only right for me to rejoice at that which surely
crowns the happiness of both of your serene Highnesses. I should not dare to reveal to you my sentiments if you had not allowed me, my lord, to love you
and to tell you so, and this, without my losing the
deep respect which I should have for your august
person, even though you were not a royal prince. It
is, therefore, with every reason that I dare to assure you
of it, my lord, as well as of the everlasting gratitude
with which, throughout my life, I shall be,

"Your serene Highness's most humble and most
obedient,

"POLICHINELLE."

At the head of the letter this note may be found:
"Deliver the subjoined answer; this letter is from
little Florian, who has been my page." Below is the
answer, written by the hand of the Duc de Penthièvre.
It reads thus:

"I was very sure that Polichinelle would share my
joy, and I thank him for it. I always wish to empha-
size to Polichinelle my desire to be of use to him."

Both the princess and the Duc de Penthièvre were
presented to the Comtesse d'Artois, and were present
at a supper at Choisy the same evening.

The year 1774 was an important one, both on account of the death of the old king and of the dauphin's accession to the throne. This same year is the one in which Madame de Lamballe appears to enjoy the entire favor of Marie Antoinette. She became, in truth, from this time, the inseparable companion of the queen, and was perhaps happier than at any other period.

" Madame the Dauphiness," says the " Gazette de France," " the Comte de Provence, Madame la Comtesse d'Artois, and the Princesse de Lamballe were sleighing together, the 4th of the month, in the park of Versailles, and in the city. Madame the Dauphiness afterwards gave a dinner to the court ladies who had the honor of accompanying her on this drive."

The princess lost none of the pleasures of the court, and from the moment Marie Antoinette appeared in public, her place was by the side of the dauphiness. Bachaumont, always on the lookout for news, speaks of the representation of " Iphigenia " by Gluck, a favorite of the dauphiness.[4] This opera made quite a sensation, thanks to the particular attention paid the composer by the daughter of Marie Thérèse. Bachaumont says simply that it was a brilliant spectacle, and that " the dauphin and the dauphiness, the Comte and Comtesse de Provence arrived at half after five." He adds: " The Duchesse de Bourbon was already present, as well as the Princesse de Lamballe."

The "Nouvelle de Paris et de Versailles," from which we gather these details, is more explicit, and does not hide from us the fact that the dauphiness and her suite sought by their own enthusiasm to awaken the applause of the audience.

"Yesterday's spectacle—namely, the long-expected representation of the opera of 'Iphigenia' by Monsieur Gluck—was as brilliant as can be imagined.

"His Highness the Dauphin, Madame the Dauphiness, the Comte and Comtesse de Provence, the Duchesse de Chartres, the Duchesse de Bourbon, the Princesse de Lamballe, the princes, ministers, and entire court were present on this great musical occasion. Madame the Dauphiness never ceased to applaud during the performance, and those in the boxes followed her example."

Several days later, the 10th of May, Louis XV. died and there began for the dauphin that long ordeal so dreaded on account of his youth and inexperience—an ordeal which was finally to lead to his execution.

The news of the king's death greatly affected the Duchesse de Chartres, whom Madame de Lamballe brought to the Duc de Penthièvre with a view to giving her grief some distraction. Was this the real reason for the sorrow of the duchess? Were there not other causes for it? That which makes us incline toward the latter hypothesis (although in this respect we cannot found our personal impressions on any given historical fact) is that the Baroness Oberkirch, generally to be relied on, tells us that June 6th—that is, less than a month after the event just mentioned—there was a supper given on her estate of Vanves to the Duchesse de Chartres and Madame de Lamballe.

The great grief of the Duchesse de Chartres did not seem to be shared by those surrounding her, for the young king's first thought, as soon as he was able, was to give the queen Trianon, afterwards so much talked about, and already at that time nicknamed "Little Vienna"—Trianon, which the queen had so long wanted, and which she received with good grace, placing, however, certain conditions on her royal husband which another less good-natured man might not have accepted so complaisantly.

"The queen, when wife of the dauphin," says our inexhaustible Bachaumont, "made known her wish to have a pleasure-house of her own in which she could do just as she pleased. His Majesty, who had been told of this, said to her a few days ago: 'Madame, I am ready to satisfy your wish. I beg you to accept for your own use the large and the small Trianon. These beautiful palaces have always been the residence of kings' favorites, therefore they should belong to you.'

"The queen greatly appreciated this gift and especially the gallant compliment which accompanied it. She answered the king, laughingly, that she would accept the Petit Trianon, on condition that he would come there only when invited."

Marie Antoinette at once began to furnish the Trianon according to her tastes and to make it the gay and attractive hiding-place in which the best moments of her life were passed. Mercy even found that this occupation absorbed her too much and wrote to Marie Thérèse:

" The queen's time is at present completely given up to the laying out of an English garden."

Further on he continues:

" This amusement would be a very harmless one if it left her time for serious thought."

Marie Thérèse approved of Mercy, but extravagance was her constant thought and she wrote in reply:

" I am more and more convinced that I am not deceived in my daughter's character, which for a long time I have thought inclined towards frivolities."

Although giving a large share of thought to the " frivolities " of her daughter, Marie Thérèse evidently occupied herself chiefly with the queen's friendships; for Mercy, well trained and fully equal to his task, announced that Madame de Lamballe was greatly in favor and that the queen " often received her in her boudoir." To add piquancy to the affair he traced for his mistress the portrait of her daughter's friend—a portrait which was far from poor, since he said: " She adds to much sweetness and affability a very truthful character, far removed from intrigue or anything unseemly "; he even adds that, " although a Piedmontese, the princess is in no way intimate with madame or with Madame d'Artois"; in a word, Mercy found " the choice excellent."

In spite of this fine description, Mercy took care to add that he had made some observations on this intimacy, in order, he said, to prevent trouble.

It was not until September, 1775, that the princess became superintendent of the royal household, yet already long before that it was hinted at. Then, after a while, they did not hesitate to speak openly of it; it became the subject of all conversation; intrigue mingled with it and the report acquired such strength that Madame de Noailles took umbrage and asked Mercy for an explanation. The latter was careful to reassure her, though he realized that the growing favor of Madame de Lamballe would arouse the greatest feelings of animosity. For the rest, he did not trouble himself about it, because, in his opinion, the queen dominated Madame de Lamballe, while the latter was without influence. In spite of every effort of this astute person, the queen had wished at different intervals to appoint her friend to a position, and especially upon her departure for Brittany. So he did not leave Marie Thérèse in ignorance of the different phases of this new intimacy, sometimes holding out hope, sometimes humbly acknowledging the futility of his remonstrances.

CHAPTER IV

The Duc de Penthièvre, strongly urged by Louis XVI., who feared the bad result caused by the dissolution of Parliament and the troubles which this might bring about, accepted the delicate mission of presiding over the Estates of Brittany. No choice could have been happier. Alone, perhaps, of all the gentlemen of France, the duke, by his breadth of view and his upright character, at once firm and dignified, was capable of bringing to a good end so difficult a task, and, by his tact and moderation, of stepping out of one of the most delicate situations with honor. Sure that his daughter-in-law would follow him, that she would help him with her beauty and her affectionate devotion in accomplishing his noble undertaking, and convinced of the usefulness of his services towards the king, Monsieur de Penthièvre did not delay his reply and at once prepared to start.

The separation was very hard for the two friends, but the queen could not feel bitter towards Madame de Lamballe for wishing to accompany her father-in-law. Moreover, it would have been poor taste to oppose her going. Having taken leave of the royal family, the Duc de Penthièvre started on the 14th of December and on the evening of the 17th our worthy travellers reached their journey's end. Always simple in his tastes, carefully avoiding all ostentation and everything that might seem to bring him into notice, the noble duke asked that his entrance into Rennes be incognito and without any of the display he might have had.

Three days later the Estates opened. We find in the archives of Ille and Vilaine the following reference to our charming princess:

" TUESDAY, 20th December, 1774.

" The Estates opened at five o'clock this evening. The entrance of Monsieur the Marquis of Sérent and Monseigneur the Bishop of Rennes was marked by general applause, as was also the case when the Princesse de Lamballe entered the court.''

The arrival of the duke and his daughter-in-law at Rennes was recognized by all. Every one saw in the Comte de Toulouse's son one who would quell discord and restore confidence.[1]

Madame de Lamballe was considered as the most favorable bond of union for the duke's clearly expressed projects of conciliation.

Nothing better explains the situation at that time than the following words, uttered on the arrival of these illustrious visitors: " Now all politics look smiling.'' Public feeling showed itself in a gift to Madame de Lamballe, intended to keep in perpetual remembrance her arrival:

39

" MONDAY, January 9, 1775.

" The deputies who first welcomed the Duc de Penthièvre and Madame de Lamballe at the opening of the Estates, offered to his Serene Highness a gift of one hundred thousand livres, and begged the princess to accept a diamond of equal value.''

Neither the duke nor the princess felt that they could receive such gifts and they declined them with one accord, as the records of the following Wednesday show :

" WEDNESDAY, January 11, 1775.

" The deputies who offered the gifts to the Duc de Penthièvre and the Princesse de Lamballe were received with courtesy and thanks, but were asked to beg the Estates to be good enough to allow them to decline the gifts.''

The actors, also, according to Métra, were desirous of celebrating the arrival of our two visitors by presenting an allegorical piece, called " The Coronation of a King.'' The play delighted the audience, but the duke was ill-pleased at the " unkind allusions to the memory of Louis XV.,'' for whom he " had had a profound veneration.''

At first he thought he would punish the author of the piece, but contented himself by " forbidding a second representation.''

At the end of about two months, during which time she " won the heart of every one in the province,'' the princess decided to leave, and returned a few days in advance of her father-in-law. She yielded, no doubt, to the urgent solicitation of Marie Antoinette, who, in her impatience to see the princess again, wrote the latter to come immediately to her upon her return, no matter what happened. The princess did so, and was rewarded by the pleasant surprise of seeing, on a mirror in the queen's apartment, her portrait, which Marie Antoinette had had painted during her absence. This was, indeed, a touching mark of affection. To cap the climax, by some strange and perhaps wished-for coincidence, the princess arrived in time to attend a private fête given by the queen in the Salon d'Hercule, in honor of her brother, the Archduke Maximilian.

At that time popular ambition was fixed upon the position of superintendent of the royal household, sought after by various persons at court. Every one spoke with envy of the coming nomination of Madame de Lamballe, for the queen had many times made known her intention in the matter. Even the newspapers reported the rumor as a fact, in spite of the claims of real princesses of the blood, as Bachaumont tells us. As yet these were only reports, but they suddenly acquired such strength that Mercy took care to inform Marie Thérèse of what was going on.

At the time when the princess left for Brittany he wrote that the queen still had some "vague ideas" of having Madame de Lamballe for superintendent of the royal household. He even pretended that for two years he had kept Marie Antoinette from carrying out the idea.

Marie Thérèse feared undue haste on the part of her daughter in making the appointment, but the faithful ambassador reassured her, and even imagined that he had succeeded, at least for the time being, in dissuading the queen from this idea. One month later he is more explicit, and is no longer doubtful of the success of his measures.

" The idea of making Madame de Lamballe superintendent of the royal household," he writes, " has not gained in the last few weeks. I trust that things will remain as they are; and, indeed, it looks now as if the Duchesse de Cossé would postpone the date on which she had planned to retire from court life."

In reply to Mercy's letters of reassurance, Marie Thérèse, who was more skeptical, could not hope that her daughter would do otherwise than carry out her own ideas. Her only consolation was that the date of Madame de Cossé's retirement from court was not yet fixed. In his heart of hearts Mercy knew that Marie Thérèse was right; but he would not acknowledge his defeat and sought again for new arguments to confirm his words. Now it was Madame de Lamballe's health which was at stake. This was a last straw for the poor drowning diplomat and he caught at it eagerly.

" The Princesse de Lamballe is subject to a nervous trouble, which often causes weakness and convulsions. If her condition does not alter she runs one less chance of becoming superintendent, and I notice that the queen is still undecided on this point.''

Mercy's scheming did not succeed, however. Marie Thérèse did not let herself be deceived by it. Naturally strong herself, she attached little importance to Madame de Lamballe's nervous attacks, which she called simply '' twitchings,'' and she hoped that Madame de Cossé would still continue to hold the position which the princess sought. Now, let us leave the empress and Mercy to exchange their hopes and fears, and for a while turn to the family of the princess, which came to Paris in the early part of June, as we see by the '' Gazette de France '':

'' The Prince de Carignan with his sons, Prince Victor and Prince Eugène, who have been travelling under the names of the Marquis de Marène, Comte de Salussole, and Comte de Villefranche, were presented on the same day by Comte de Viry, court ambassador from Sardinia, to the king, the queen, and the royal family. They were introduced by Lord La Live de la Briche, court presenter.''

For some time the princess had wished to establish one of her brothers in France, and, prevailing upon her friendship with the queen, she at last obtained the promise that her desire should be fulfilled. The Countess d'Artois also used her influence in bringing this about.

Marie Thérèse, on the other hand, blamed her

daughter's " enthusiasm " in favoring the establishment of the young Prince de Carignan, fearing that
he would strengthen the Piedmont party, which was
already sufficiently numerous.

In the meantime, after some remonstrance which he
thought it was his duty to offer on this subject, Mercy
did not hesitate to draw the queen's attention to the
growing power of this party. Marie Antoinette knew
that he was right, but excused herself by saying that
" she had not been able to blind herself to her personal
feelings," which for the future she promised to resist.

This appointment was refused by the ministers, but,
thanks to the queen, was obtained through the usual
complaisance of the king. So Marie Antoinette could
announce the joyful news to her friend, and thus prove
to her that absence had not altered her feelings.

Without consulting his ministers the king granted
to the princess's brother thirty thousand livres income
and the command of a regiment of national infantry.
The object of the journey of the Princes de Carignan
was merely to present the young colonel and to thank
the royal family.

Meanwhile, the coronation took place at Reims.
Notwithstanding our investigation, we have not been
able to find any mention of the princess at the fêtes
given at this time. We presume that she spent the
time with her sister-in-law, who shortly after gave
birth to the Duc de Montpensier, and that, as soon as
the duchess had sufficiently recovered, the two prin-

cesses retired to Anet, to be with the Duc de Penthièvre. A courier was despatched to the Duc de
Chartres with news of this birth.

Now to go back to the argus-eyed empress and the
indefatigable Mercy, who was all eyes and ears in
order to satisfy the smallest wish of Marie Thérèse.
He well knew how to flatter her by telling her every
detail, every smallest action, every peccadillo of the
queen's. We left the empress satisfied in the belief
that Madame de Cossé no longer thought of retiring
from court; but the time had come for Mercy to dis-
abuse her and to admit to her that, since her return
from Reims, Madame de Cossé had begged the queen
to dismiss her, both on account of her own health and
that of her son.

Then, more explicit still, he announces definitely
the departure of the Comtesse de Noailles, and in spite
of his efforts at diplomacy, the secret appointment of
the princess. In order to make the best of his failure,
and to avoid the reproaches of his mistress for his lack
of foresight, he adds that, in spite of Madame de Lamballe's youth, " it remains to be seen if in her new
position she will preserve the sweet and simple disposition she has shown until now.'

In her letter to the Comte de Rosenberg, Marie Antoinette is less positive. In speaking of the changes in
her household caused by the retirement of Madame de
Cossé and the Maréchale de Mouchy, she hints lightly
at the fact of her having asked the king for Madame

de Lamballe. "Judge of my delight," she continues; "I shall make my intimate friend happy, and I myself shall be even happier than she." She recommends the strictest silence as to the news, so far as the empress is concerned. "The emperor alone knows it. Beg him not to mention it, for you know what the consequences would be." Taken unawares, Mercy resigned himself to advising the queen; but he saw that promises had been exchanged. Then he turned to the empress, and persisting in his original statements told her that "he finds that the arrangement is of no help to him and may even harm him." Finally, as a climax to his efforts at consolation, he says that Madame de Lamballe has lost much of her favor with the queen, whose friendship vacillates between the Comtesse de Dillon and the Comtesse de Polignac.[2] He admits, however, that the latter is, without doubt, the favorite. Mercy is charming at this point: "These various friendships are causing much trouble and inconvenience." All this is very plausible. While the scheming and corresponding about Madame de Lamballe was going on, the latter was travelling in Holland with the Duchesse de Chartres. "A most delightful trip," says Madame de Genlis.[3]

Fearing that her mother might make trouble for her, Marie Antoinette did not tell her of the changes she was making in her household until the 15th of September—that is, three days before the official nomination.   In this way all interference was impossible on the part of the empress, who was strongly opposed to her daughter's plans.   In this letter, in order to save herself trouble, the queen did not refer to all the difficulties she had had to surmount.   These she passed over in silence, as she did the opposition of the ministers and that of the king himself.   She wrote merely that the king had given her the super-intendent of her choice.   Taking the bull by the horns, she says:

" I hope that what my dear mother hears of Madame de Lamballe will convince her that there is abso-lutely nothing to fear from the latter's association with my sister-in-law.   Her reputation has always been good, and she has nothing of the Italian in her.   She, as well as her brother, are settled here for life.   I trust they will both feel that France is now their country. "

Marie Thérèse was always incredulous, but was re-assured about Madame de Lamballe by Monsieur de Breteuil, who " greatly praised the good traits of the princess."   Even Mercy himself found that this praise conformed to his own ideas.   But he made certain qualifications, saying that it was easy for people to hold favorable opinions about one who so lately had attained a position at court.

The princess was appointed on September 16th, and took the oath on the 18th.   We publish in full the official certificate of her appointment:

" *Provisions for the Superintendent of the Royal Household,
Madame la Princesse de Lamballe:*

" Louis, by the grace of God, King of France and
of Navarre, to all who read this: Greeting.

" The queen, our very dear consort and companion,
having made known to us her wish that our very dear
and well-loved cousin, the Princesse de Lamballe, should
be appointed to the position and the office of chief adviser and superintendent of the royal household, our
love for the aforesaid queen and our recognition of the
admirable qualities of our cousin have induced us to
defer to her wishes.   Moved by these causes and by
other important considerations, we have given and
granted, and by this present letter, signed by our hand, we
do give and grant to our very dear and well-loved cousin,
Marie Thérèse Louise de Savoie Carignan, widow of
our very dear and well-loved cousin, the Prince de
Lamballe, the position and office of chief adviser and
superintendent of the royal household, in order that our
aforesaid cousin may have, hold, and exercise the same,
enjoy and make use of the honors, power, functions, authority, privileges, prerogatives, and distinc-
tions which appertain thereto, to the same degree and
in the same manner as the late Mademoiselle de Clermont[1] enjoyed, or had a right to enjoy them, together with the revenues, conditions, maintenance,
allowance, decorations, and other rights, revenues, and
emoluments appertaining thereto in the court of the
aforesaid queen, be the same herein particularly speci-
fied or not, and this to continue during our royal
pleasure.

" We notify our very dear and well-beloved cousin,
the Sire Comte de Saulx, chevalier of our orders, and
gentleman-in-waiting to the aforesaid queen, the first

master-in-ordinary and quartermaster in her hôtel, the controllers-general of her house, and all others whom it may concern, that after our aforesaid cousin shall have taken the required oath from the hands of the aforesaid queen, they will cause to be registered this letter, the documents in her mansion and apartments, and the revenues, that our said lady cousin may fully and peacefully enjoy the privileges thereof, and we desire the aforesaid persons to obey her in all things and to see to it that all concerned may understand the nature of the above appointment.

" We notify, also, the treasurer-general of the household of the aforesaid queen, that the said position, remunerations, maintenance, and other rights shall be paid to her at the next term and in the usual manner, following the orders which shall be despatched in regard thereto, on her simple receipts, and that they shall return this present letter, or a copy thereof, duly certified once only; and that all that will have been paid to her on this occasion shall be passed on and allowed in the expenses of these accounts by our beloved and faithful councillors.

" The keepers of our accounts at Paris are ordered to do this without question, for such is our pleasure, in witness whereof we have caused our seal to be put to these presents.

" Given at Versailles, 16th day of September, the year of grace 1775, and of our reign the second."

The love with which, by her sweetness of temper and her beauty, the gentle princess had inspired the Bretons during her stay at Rennes, was still so great that the Estates decided to extend to her their warmest congratulations upon her appointment as superintendent of the royal household.

This is her reply:

"PARIS, October 8, 1773.

"GENTLEMEN: I greatly appreciate the mark of attention you have shown me concerning my appointment to the position of superintendent of the royal household. I beg you to accept my thanks. The province of Brittany would not be doing me justice if it doubted my feelings for it. I shall always desire to give it proof of my sentiments. I beg you, gentlemen, to believe the sincere esteem I have for you.

(Signed) "M. L. F. DE SAVOYE.

" *To the Delegates of the Estates of Brittany.*"

CHAPTER V

As soon as the matter of superintendent had been settled, Mercy,[1] who already in his letter of September
18th had hinted to the empress as to the difficulties
which would result from it, considering the fact that
" nothing had been decided or determined on, either
as to the amount of the salary or the degree of authority she was to exercise over the royal household,"
again expressed his fears as to the trouble and quarrels
which the continuation of this position would entail.
His first idea was to have a list of rules drawn up which
should exactly define the nature of the position, and
determine its rights and privileges. The Abbé de Vermond[2] was careful to make a very simple and clear
statement, which, because of the suppression of certain
abuses and expenditures, would without doubt be approved by the ministry. The queen was pleased to accept it, and with her own hand added a recommendation.
Unfortunately, it lost its good qualities in the light of
day. The queen had not the necessary strength to
impose her wishes, and the result was that Madame de
Lamballe " gently and tearfully " told her that the
Duc de Penthièvre refused to have her accept a position which seemed " to have forfeited a part of its

ancient prerogatives.'' Furthermore, the princess threatened to resign from the position '' if it were not made just as it used to be.''

Our unfortunate ambassador had not yet finished with his trouble. For, although the question of salary had not been raised, the superintendent evidently meant that hers should be the same as that of Mademoiselle de Bourbon. And, in Mercy's opinion, it was far from likely, not to say well-nigh impossible, that the ministry, bent on being economical, would grant her fifty thousand crowns.

However, in spite of everything, the princess received the salary which had originally been determined on, and the king, unable to refuse the queen anything, signed the order with no apparent objection.[3]

'' *Order for fifty thousand crowns salary for Madame la Princesse de Lamballe:*

'' To-day, the 20th October, 1775. The king, being at Fontainebleau, having chosen Madame la Princesse de Lamballe to fill the position of superintendent of the royal household, his Majesty wishes at the same time to make known the esteem and special affection with which the queen honors her, by granting to the aforesaid Princesse de Lamballe the means to support herself in this important position with the dignity suitable to a princess of her rank. To this end his Majesty has declared, and does now declare, wish, and intend that, beginning with the first of last September, Madame la Princesse de Lamballe shall enjoy, as superintendent of the royal household, apart from a salary which is due her from the royal estate, so long as she shall occupy the aforesaid position, the sum of fifty thousand crowns, to be paid annually on her simple receipts without any deductions now or in future; the sum to be set aside for this purpose by the keeper of the royal treasury, now and in future, according to the conditions or directions which shall be drawn up concerning it, without, however, the granting of this favor, which is a personal one to the Princesse de Lamballe, to those who may succeed her in the aforesaid position; and, as a pledge of his will, his Majesty has signed with his own hand the present document, and has ordered it countersigned by his secretary of state and of the fiscal board.''

With this warrant for the position of superintendent, Madame de Lamballe reached the highest point in her career. We are about to see her for a time in the fulness of favor. Then, by one of those phenomena so often seen in court life, she will enter on her downward path. Before the favorite friend of the queen there arose suddenly an ambitious rival. In short, Madame de Polignac is about to appear.

But we have not yet reached that point. Let us leave the princess to enjoy unreservedly the brilliant days she had yet to pass with her august mistress.

'' The queen,'' says Bachaumont, '' has the greatest friendship for the young princess, who is perfectly congenial to her. It is known that her Majesty often makes up parties with her to the Petit Trianon or Petit Vienne, and that she admits to her suite only a few ladies and no man. There she abandons herself to all the innocent follies of her age.''

This sojourn in the Trianon inspired also various kindly acts on the part of the queen. We are glad to note the following:

" I shall induce her to come, and, without any suspicion on her part that we know all her love affairs, we will soften her woes, lessen her anxiety for her mother, and, if it seem wise, speak to the king of our beautiful marriage project for this dear child. Let her come all alone, and we shall enjoy the pleasure of compensating her later. The happiness of others does some good everywhere, but it seems to me that it is still greater among the surroundings of simple nature, far from the noise in which we are condemned to live."

It was the fashion of the times to find recreation without the society of men. Apropos of this we might well relate an incident which happened to the Duchesse de Chartres and the Princesse de Lamballe at the home of the Duchesse de Bourbon, where, by a trick which disarmed the anger of the ladies, the Duc de Chartres, with inordinate curiosity, succeeded, in company with some friends, in obtruding himself upon their cosy gathering of women.

As we have already stated, Madame de Lamballe was especially fond of outdoor fêtes, small parties at which she could do and say what she pleased. But, for all that, there was no lack of official functions, for the " Gazette de France " mentions her presence at a ball in the hall in which plays were given on the occasion of the marriage of the king's sister.

One day she and her royal friend set out to walk to Sceaux, and as nothing escaped the vigilant eye of the "parish," Bachaumont is careful to note on his tablets: "Her Majesty finally went to Sceaux with the Princesse de Lamballe, and spent the day there alone with her." Another time the court was to pass a few days at Choisy before the removal from Fontainebleau. In the first place, there happened to the two friends one of those adventures which, although tragic for an instant, had no serious results, and to which, for that matter, the princess will henceforth accustom us.

"At Choisy," says Mercy, "the queen planned a sail on the river. Up to that point nothing had occurred. But some bargemen, seeing the gondoliers from afar, plunged into the river in token of their joy. Thinking that the imprudent men were drowning, the queen became ill, and was the indirect cause of the princess's fainting. Both women were promptly attended to, and recovered quickly enough to avoid any serious result."

A similar adventure happened to the princess when she was at Fontainebleau, sailing on the lake. Métra describes the incident to us:

"The queen experienced an accident which showed how she was loved. She was sailing in one of her gondolas; a window fell in, hit the queen, and caused a slight bruise on the arm of the Princesse de Lamballe, who fainted. However, thanks to a bleeding, all evil consequences were avoided, and the princess discovered how dear she was to our queen, who showed the most tender solicitude for her.''

It was about this time that Baculard d'Arnaud dedicated to Madame de Lamballe his well-known lines accompanying a copy of the '' Épreuves du Sentiment '' :

> In a few faithful touches,
>   Unspoiled by flatterer's art,
> Both sentiment and nature
>   I deftly could impart.
> If my brush, bold to venture,
>   Should try (Apelles' shade !)
> To paint most perfect beauty,
>   I know the model maid.

Every proof of friendship which Madame de Lamballe received from the queen led her, if we are to believe Mercy, to attempt to impose a little too much on her Majesty's good will. Thus, on the separation of the Comte and Comtesse de La Marche, is it not curious to see her greatly occupied in having '' the countess given the pension of a princess of the blood,'' which usually was granted only to widows, and only on the pleasure of the king ?

By her efforts the princess was on the point of accomplishing the undertaking. The king hesitated, and finally almost consented. But Mercy was there on the watch, and he soon convinced the queen how impolitic it would be for her to yield to such a demand. Marie Antoinette, it seems, admitted that she realized the danger, but dared not oppose her friend.

In the face of such an admission, Mercy made a positive accusation.

"I have proved," says he, "that the Princesse de Lamballe costs the state annually more than one hundred thousand crowns, including the salary her brother obtains here, and the number of additional expenses caused by the revival of the position of superintendent, and that the object of these wholly useless expenses is merely to satisfy an affection of the queen for one for whom she wishes to procure a brilliant and useful position. But this same person should be circumspect enough not to take advantage of the kindness of the queen, especially on occasions which in no wise affect this superintendent, who exceeds her duties by soliciting favors manifestly contrary to the true service of her sovereign, bringing upon herself the odium of making people believe that her credit is used only to effect superfluous expenditures."

"All my remonstrances," he continued, "have not prevented the queen from almost yielding several times to the reiterated importunities of the Princesse de Lamballe; and yet I have succeeded in so far as her Majesty is still undecided, and at least there will result the advantage of making her see to what point one may go in abusing her kindness and generosity."

In a letter to her mother Marie Antoinette appears to be defending herself and says:

"I could not refuse the petition made for the Comtesse de La Marche, but I have spoken only once of it, and have made no great point of it."

In spite of his every effort, Mercy was obliged to admit that the Comtesse de La Marche would have the pension; but he tried to prove that the influence of the queen would avail nothing in the matter.

The intrigues with which Mercy concerned himself, and which he carefully records, have carried us somewhat away from our subject. Let us now return to it.

As soon as she was appointed superintendent, the princess took possession of a dwelling reserved for the holder of that position. At first she occupied an apartment on the first floor of the south wing, facing the Rue de la Surintendance, consisting of twelve rooms, which later she was to give up to the Comtesse de Provence. Then she occupied the four rooms on the ground floor of the Pavillon d'Orléans, below the apartments of the Duc de Chartres, Louis Philippe. At the same time she had an apartment of twelve rooms and a suite above the ground floor on the Rue de la Surintendance.

It was considered fashionable to live outside the château when one's term of service had expired, perhaps because, as Madame Campan tells us, "one felt at home only when in the simplest dwelling, ornamented with English gardens." The princess wished to have her private house and bought from her father-in-law the Hôtel du Maine, which was situated by the side of that of the Duc de Penthièvre, and for which she paid seventy thousand livres.

It was the beginning of a new year. Was it to be as exciting and as full of pleasure as the preceding ?

This seemed likely, for they were preparing to dance at court. Long ago Bachaumont tells us:

" The balls of Versailles are to begin again the 4th of next January. They will be held at Madame de Lamballe's, which fact will make them less formal. The queen will dance and sup with whomsoever she pleases."

The same writer tells us also that the Duc de Chartres gave a superb ball, at which the queen caused a sensation on account of a plume so high that it had to be considerably lowered before she could step into her carriage.

Bachaumont, who writes somewhat wrongly and at random the reports in circulation, is incorrect in his premature announcement of the receptions of the Princesse de Lamballe, for we read of Mercy's complaining because the superintendent did not give balls to the queen and the royal family.

" The Princesse de Lamballe," he adds, " gave up this advantage in order to avoid a small matter of etiquette, in accordance with which the princesses of the blood do not issue written or verbal invitations to their homes. Their method is to announce that they may be seen at a certain time, and their ladies-in-waiting then invite those on their visiting-lists."

All these annoyances wearied the queen, who already had enough cause of discontent against the princess. At first it was her love of ceremony, to the observation of which she strictly adhered. This caused Mercy to say:

" If the Princesse de Lamballe does not calculate more exactly in future, it is probable that the favor she enjoys, which seems to be somewhat diminishing, will die away in the long run.

In fact, her blindness was such that, instead of lessening the number of her claims, she increased them, and she was so eager and so haughty in defending these, that a part of the royal household rebelled against her despotism. Then Marie Antoinette, wearied by all the complaints and the interminable dissensions which she was called on to settle, and which interfered with the duties of the superintendent, ended, according to the predictions of the ambassador of the empress, by becoming out of patience with her friend, and almost regretted having revived the position of superintendent; the more so, as the jealousy of the two favorites was a constant source of private quarrels, which caused the princess and Madame de Polignac to offer to the queen petty slights under cover of the tenderest possible feeling.

In spite of all this trouble, was not Mercy somewhat hard on the princess when he wrote that she had lost much of the favor to which, according to him, her abilities gave her no claim ?

" I think that she will always be treated well by the queen, but there is no longer any intimacy between them, and her Majesty realizes that the superintendent has not sufficient depth to share her thoughts.''

At first Mercy thought Madame de Lamballe more dangerous than Madame de Polignac; but afterwards he hesitated, and finally followed the wisest course—namely, he pitted against each other the two influences, thus maintaining equilibrium. Afterwards our clever diplomat returns to the question of the princess, finding the influence of Madame de Polignac not to be trusted. In this he was not deceived, for all the members of the latter family pushed themselves forward, one by one, and strove to find positions for one another, as is shown by the '' Gazette de France '' :

'' June 23d, Comte Jules de Polignac, camp master and lieutenant of the royal guards, has had the honor to be presented to the king by the Duc de Fleury, first gentleman-in-waiting of the chamber, and to acknowledge his thanks to his Majesty for the position of first equerry to the queen on the reversion of the office of the Comte de Tessé, of which the king wished greatly to give him the advantage.

'' The following day Comte Jules de Polignac had the honor of taking from the hands of the queen the oath of first equerry.

One day in the midst of his confidence in the waning of the favor of Madame de Lamballe, Mercy was greatly surprised to see how much the queen was affected on hearing that the former was ill at Plombières.

"This accident," said he, "awakened all the queen's affection for her superintendent." He ingenuously admits that he had not supposed their affection was so deep. He seems to retrace his steps, but not very far, for he at once begins to prognosticate "the waning of the influence of the Princesse de Lamballe, and although she has her disadvantages," he fears still more "Madame de Polignac, who is more dangerous on account of her appearance and her views."

In her reply to her impetuous ambassador, Marie Thérèse is of the opinion that the princess deserves "more attention because of the resources she finds in the Piedmontese party."

From afar the empress is a better judge of the situation. For the rest, Bachaumont tells us that Mercy has in mind many occupations which may well influence his judgment, among them "his connection with Mademoiselle Rosalie of the opera, for whom he has conceived a violent passion. Although she is ugly, she is rather lively, and gifted with a certain amount of talent, and he permits her henceforth to call herself the Baroness de ——, with a barony of from twenty thousand to twenty-five thousand income."

At this time Madame de Lamballe was in very poor health, which fact caused her "frequently to be absent from court." Her nerves were extremely irritable, and made her disposition uneven and often disagreeable. Moreover, her constant fainting spells continued, and were produced by the slightest cause. Every year the poor woman was obliged to go to watering-places for six weeks or two months in order to recuperate. Mercy announces her departure in May for Plombières or Vichy, but the journey did not actually take place until June 7th, when the Duchesse de Chartres was travelling in Italy under the name of the Comtesse de Joinville. It was during this sojourn at Plombières that the princess was attacked with the measles, whereupon the queen " became so extremely anxious and alarmed " that Mercy's eyes were opened.

In his " Memoirs," Lauzun confirms the anxiety of the queen at this time. Entrusted with a large package of letters addressed to the princess, he joined her at Plombières, where he found her sufficiently recovered to reply to the voluminous letters from her sovereign.

The stay of the princess at Plombières lasted until the end of August, according to the " Gazette de France," from which we borrow the following interesting details:

" They write from Nancy that the Princesse de Lamballe, who left for Plombières the 7th of last June, appeared in this city the 26th of August on her return from the watering-place. A detachment of the Company of La Rochefoucault Dragoons met her. As she entered the town the royal troops formed a double line from the Porte Saint Nicolas to the government buildings, where she stepped from her carriage. The princess received the compliments of Parliament, of the Chamber of Deputies, of the Primatical Chapter of the University, and of the city troops. After dinner she walked through a part of the town, and about six o'clock left to spend the night at Toul. She expects to reach Versailles the 28th.''

On the 13th, the same paper tells us that in passing through a hamlet near Saint Dizier, the chaplain of Prince Charles de Lorraine paid his respects to the princess by presenting her with a copy of '' L'Histoire de Lorraine,'' which she deigned to accept with thanks.

After an absence of almost three months, Madame de Lamballe expected to find some change at court. So she was not greatly surprised at the progress of the favor won by Madame de Polignac. The husband of this latter lady had just obtained the reversion of Comte de Tessé, a signal favor to which Mercy had been opposed. Full of anger at the failure of his opposition, he was not afraid to draw a far from flattering picture of Monsieur de Polignac, finding that his one grade of colonel, his twenty-eight years, and his lack of wit were not sufficient claims for the position. The more so as, according to custom, it was usual for the incumbent to present his reversioner, a formality which in the present case had been wholly neglected. The Noailles ' were on the verge of becoming dazzled, for Monsieur de Tessé was the son-in-law of the marshal.

As always, the remonstrances of the ambassador were without effect. The queen had gone too far to draw back. The real object of her thoughts was else-where. What, in short, would Madame de Lamballe say? Resolved not to dispense with her entirely, Marie Antoinette received, without great difficulty, and even supported, the demand of this princess in favor of the Duc de Chartres for the government of Poitou, left vacant by the death of the Prince de Bour-bon-Conti.⁵ "This request," adds Mercy, "was made by letter, the Princesse de Lamballe still being at Plombières." The constant care of the queen to divide the favors equally might, up to a certain point, make one suppose that there was at least a temporary truce between the two favorites. But such was not the case, for the jealousy of Madame de Lamballe showed itself immediately on her return. Mercy, who really took no side in the matter, profited by the occa-sion to malign Madame de Polignac, and describes her as " a young woman who has no position at court, a rather dubious reputation, and not much sense." Finally, reviewing the expense necessitated by these two ladies, he says that Madame de Polignac costs less than the other.

If the princess was jealous, the Comtesse de Polignac strove to " destroy her rival," and to bring this about by little respectful and tender complaints, demonstra-tions of anxiety and grief, and by dwelling on the petty acts of ridicule attributed to Madame de Lamballe. She almost succeeded in her attempts, and the queen was on the point of becoming angry with the superintendent, as the result of a "slightly annoying incident." However, during the sojourn at Fontainebleau, the queen preferred the soirées of the Princesse de Lamballe to all other amusement, and Mercy complains bitterly of this because of the intriguers who curried favor there and the card-playing for which the queen seemed to have too great a predilection.

In the month of December the balls began again, but they were less frequent. However, the general complaint was about the small number of hospitable houses. If we believe our guide, who constantly fills in gaps, the real reason for the lack of eagerness with which the court attended these receptions was that "the superintendent, because of her punctiliousness, and still more because of her slight knowledge of the world, attracts few people to her." It seems even, according to Mercy, that, on account of improvements which were being made in her apartments, Madame de Lamballe thought it best not to receive; but, on very just representations made to the queen, the latter desired her to "give suppers on the few days on which there were balls."

The conclusion drawn by Mercy from all these private troubles is not to the advantage of the princess, who, according to him, "will end by becoming unnecessary, perhaps even wearisome, to the queen."

CHAPTER VI

In order to follow each step of the private life of the court, let us turn from Mercy for a moment, leaving him to engage at will in his investigations, which we will take up later, and let us occupy ourselves with the events of the year 1777.

In January, the Duc and the Duchesse des Deux Ponts arrived in Paris under the name of the Comte and Comtesse de Sponheim. They were received without ceremony, although the duchess, born Princesse de Saxe, was first cousin to the king. They went to the apartments of the princes and princesses, after having informed them by note of their arrival. Following are the two letters written by their chamberlains, regarding a proposed visit to Madame de Lamballe:

" Madame la Comtesse de Sponheim arrived, with Madame la Comtesse d'Esbach, at the Hôtel d'Yorck, Rue Jacob, and had the honor of seeing Madame de Lascaze, and asking her what day she might pay her respects to Madame la Princesse de Lamballe.

" Monsieur le Comte de Sponheim arrived, as well as the Baron de Geiting, Chamberlain of Monsieur le Duc des Deux Ponts, begged the honor of seeing Madame la Marquise de Lascaze, and asked her to be

good enough to set a day when he could be presented
to Madame la Princesse de Lamballe.''

On the 30th of January, the Duc de Chartres gave
a magnificent fête, at which the queen was present,
and whence she could watch the masked ball of the
Opera.   This prince was so pleased with the attention
of the queen that the following day the ''Journal de
Paris'' inserted this notice:

''At twelve o'clock last night, his highness Monseigneur le Duc de Chartres gave a ball at the Palais
Royal to which the queen and the royal family were
invited.''

A few days later, Bachaumont tells us the queen took
supper with the superintendent, and he describes to
us the ennui she felt there:

'' Last Thursday, the queen took supper with the
Princesse de Lamballe, where there were present twelve
ladies, but not a single man.   Apparently this greatly
wearied her Majesty, who hastened to don her ball
gown (that of a sultana), and set out for the Palais
Royal.''

Thus the queen, no doubt somewhat disillusioned,
ceased to attend the fêtes of her intimate friend, who
no longer had the faculty of entertaining her.   It is
true, according to Mercy, that the princess took advantage of every opportunity to obtain from Marie
Antoinette some fresh mark of favor, and this, in the

long run, wearied the queen, and not only dispelled her illusions, but spoiled her pleasure as well.

" The princess," he writes, " having given herself needless troubles and anxiety, is beginning to look more calmly at the advantage gained by her rival. This superintendent tries to gain compensation by obtaining for herself and her relatives small favors which are often a strain on the kindness and the protection of the queen."

We next see the princess, in company with her Majesty, taking part in the religious ceremonies of Easter. But the principal event of that time, which has to do more especially with Marie Antoinette, was the arrival of her brother, Joseph II.,[1] in Paris, under the name of the Comte de Falkenstein. Marie Antoinette wished this prince to be received with all possible honor. So in order to have an excuse to go to meet Joseph II. she induced the king to arrange a hunting party for the 18th of April, in the Forest of Bondi. " The queen," says Bachaumont, " drove through Paris with fourteen carriages." Unfortunately, the weather was frightful. The rain and the wind were incessant, and, as the carriages were open, " all the hats, in the style of Henry IV., and the plumes were soaked, blown topsy-turvy, and completely ruined." " This confusion," he continues, " made the queen laugh, and greatly amused her."

Marie Antoinette's brother arrived on Friday, the 18th of April, and did not leave until the 21st of May.

Wishing to preserve the strictest incognito, Joseph II. had refused to stay in the Château. " Be kind enough," he wrote Mercy a few days previous to his departure from Vienna, " to secure a couple of rooms for me in Versailles."

Realizing the interest attached to the prince's trip to France, Mercy was careful to keep a detailed account of the engagements, visits, and plans made by Joseph, of the general impression produced by him, and of the probable results. All these points are contained in his letter to Marie Thérèse, dated June 15th.

On the 22d of April, it seems, the prince dined at the Trianon. He had a long talk with the queen, and did not hide from her the fact that Madame de Lamballe had greatly displeased him. " The queen admitted that, through her infatuation, she had been deceived in her favorite, and that she was beginning to repent having placed her in such a position."

The confidant of Marie Thérèse maintained that Joseph II. received no one in Paris, and that people came to him " all day long " to beg an interview and ask for an audience. More fortunate than he, or rather disposed to hide nothing, we can easily rectify his account, for the National Archives possess a few documents relative to the journey of Joseph II., from which we quote the following passages, appertaining to our subject:

" Monday, 12th of May, the Princesse de Conti, Madame de Lamballe, and the Duc de Penthièvre called on His Majesty.

"The Duc de Chartres went there before leaving for Holland."

So, while Mercy says simply in the aforesaid letter: "On the afternoon of May 22d the emperor went to see the house of the Duc de Penthièvre at Sceaux; he retired early," we find some new documents which show that the reception of the Duc de Penthièvre had not the essentially simple character which Mercy would have liked to attribute to it.

"The Comte de Falkenstein went to Sceaux Thursday, the 22d of May, and walked through the gardens.
"Madame la Duchesse de Chartres, Madame la Princesse de Conti, and Madame de Lamballe were at Sceaux, but, instead of walking, they played the game of cavagnole."

Fortaire tells us, in regard to this visit, that "Joseph II. arrived after dinner, because he had not accepted an invitation to dine." The afternoon was spent by all in "visiting and sight-seeing."

The emperor took leave of his sister the 30th of May. Both were deeply affected. The queen even had a nervous attack, and spent the following day at the Petit-Trianon with a small suite, consisting only of Madame de Lamballe, the Comtesse de Polignac, and one lady from the palace.

As she had done the previous year, the princess went to Plombières, and did not return before the end of August. The queen received her with great demonstration of kindness, which, however, did not deceive Mercy, who saw in it only a "matter of courtesy." During her sojourn at the court at Fontainebleau, Madame de Lamballe accompanied the queen " regularly " to the theatre. " On rare occasions " she still received Marie Antoinette, " who almost always spent the day with Madame de Polignac " in the fortress near the apartments of the queen.

Gambling was indulged in to excess, " from fear of growing bored," and the queen consecrated a part of the night of November 3d to it in the apartments of the princess.

Mercy, who constantly made entries in his diary in regard to the queen, and who, when necessary, incited the gossip of people more or less informed, was able to appreciate the exact degree of whatever favor or disfavor was shown to Madame de Lamballe ; while the public, posted as to court affairs only by the official bulletins, continued to bow before her high position, and daily addressed lines or dedicated some new work to her. One day it was the Chevalier de Prunay, captain of the Grenadiers, who sought her protection for the "Grammaire des Dames," a work designed, in the words of the author, "to render easy for young persons the knowledge of the principles of the French language," etc. ; later, it was Monsieur de Fabre, " a young poet, who has as yet published nothing," says Métra, " but who has just made his début on Parnassus by an erotic poem, in four stanzas, entitled: 'Les

Quatre Heures de la Toilette des Dames ' ''—'' a magnificent work,'' he continues, '' embellished with every ornament of pen and typography.'' They gambled three times a week in the queen's apartments, and '' occasionally at the Princesse de Lamballe's,'' writes Mercy. Seeming always to take pleasure in telling the empress of the petty scenes of jealousy on the part of the princess, he continues:

'' The queen often feels some embarrassment in maintaining an appearance of harmony between the Princesse de Lamballe and the Comtesse de Polignac. As the favor of the latter increases, that of the former decreases, so that, finally, she is becoming distasteful and wearisome to the queen. However, as it is best not to show this change of feeling too openly, the queen submits to being bored, and now and then spends with the Princesse de Lamballe hours which are very painful to her Majesty.''

Let us not leave the month of January without referring to an incident in which Paris and the entire court was interested.

'' The queen,'' says Métra, '' with the Princesse de Lamballe and Madame, went incognito to the late ball at the Opera in Paris, dressed like an Amazon. Eight other ladies were in dominoes. Her Majesty having noticed a very lively mask, accosted it, and said : ' Who are you, handsome mask ? ' ' Your subject, beautiful Amazon,' replied the latter, removing his mask. It was the Comte d'Artois,[2] who had changed his disguise.''

The queen was eager for amusement, for Mercy wrote that some friends, whose names, however, he could not give, advised the princess to give balls, and not to leave to the other ladies of the court this means of pleasing the queen. This was one of the duties of the superintendent, but Madame de Lamballe did nothing about it, on account of the trouble, and especially because of the expense it would entail. This is not the first time Mercy accuses her of avarice, but he attributes the fact of her disgrace to other causes, such as "the wearisome importunities caused by her jealousy."

Not content with this severe judgment, he becomes, in our opinion, still more unjust when he ventures to maintain that it was especially because the queen perceived the lack of affection her favorite had for her. This is a false imputation, which elsewhere he strives to palliate by saying: "The natural goodness of the queen causes her still to hide somewhat her lack of affection; but her Majesty cannot prevent herself from secretly being thoroughly disgusted with the superintendent, and from regretting having put her in a position for which she is so little fitted."

It could no longer be doubted that Madame de Polignac was the favorite. If Mercy rejoices at this, he lets Marie Thérèse puzzle over it. She confides to Mercy her anxiety as to the great intimacy with Madame de Polignac, who she knows is pledged to the Choiseul party.

The first news of the queen's delicate condition occupied Mercy sufficiently to permit him to lay aside for a time his tirades against the superintendent; but he was not yet wholly disarmed, and we find him writing:

" The Princesse de Lamballe continues to lose more and more of the queen's favor, and it is fortunate that her Majesty's eyes are finally opened as to her superintendent, who joins to a lack of wit several more serious faults, which until now the queen has not suspected."

Disheartened by what she saw, and by all the plots against her, the princess made up her mind to go away. In company with the Duchesse de Chartres, she went to Holland, a trip which Madame de Genlis, usually accurate, places in 1775. Very naturally, Mercy does not approve of this departure. He even criticises it, and goes so far as to blame the conduct of the unfortunate princess, which he qualifies as "unbecoming," considering the condition of the queen. He pretends to be scandalized by a resolution which he claims is the result of her "disguised ill-humor." But as for us, who have not the same reasons for hatred as Mercy, we frankly declare that, in our eyes, Madame de Lamballe, unable to face the storm, showed herself, under the circumstances, wise and tactful. Only absence for a certain length of time could disarm her numerous enemies and bring back the calm which her health required.

The rumor of an unexpected conflict between the superintendent and the Abbé de Vermond had, in the meanwhile, gained enough strength to reach the ears of the empress, who begged Mercy to keep her informed as to this new incident. The ambassador hastened to reply that the rumor, which one might have called " a report as absurd as false," had, indeed, been accredited; but that, in reality, there was no truth in it, since the queen still received her reader, and continued to show him as much confidence as deference; and that, in short, only the Abbé's care of " private affairs " kept him away from court for the time being. He added that the " so-called quarrel " was an " absurd report," which greatly amused the queen when she heard of it. However, he was careful not to omit his usual little note, full of spite about the princess, who " is only tolerated, and almost always with weariness. "

Mercy, who until now has accustomed us to the smallest details, had, no doubt, important reasons this time for hiding a part of the truth from Marie Thérèse; but we who, not being influenced by any special motives, have not the same scruples, shall simply turn to Métra, sufficiently well informed on general subjects. Thanks to him, we know that the princess in some way offered to give up her position and hand in her resignation to the queen if the Abbé de Vermond did not go away; and that this step on the part of Madame de Lamballe had for a pretext the lack of deference to the established customs on the part of the queen's reader, who allowed himself to give up some memoirs before they had passed through the hands of the superintendent. That which, after all, might well have vexed Mercy was the necessity of admitting that Madame de Lamballe was justified by precedent, and that she would not see her rights trampled on. At the close of August, Madame de Polignac returned to her family and was taken ill there. Madame de Lamballe endeavored to take advantage of this to return to the good graces of the queen. It seems even, according to the statement of Mercy, that, with her "usual lack of tact," she merely bored the queen by asking impossible favors of her, such as "a part of the estate of Lorraine," with an "annual income of sixty thousand livres." Mercy found that it would be very embarrassing for Marie Antoinette to consent, and succeeded in completely turning her from any such attempt.

Nowhere else have we found the confirmation of this incident, and we should be inclined to believe that the untimely request of the princess was due to the inventive imagination of the grave diplomat, if we did not know that at another time Madame de Lamballe sent a petition to the king, asking the concession of the savannas of Léogane at Saint Domingo.

Two great misfortunes happened, one after another, to Madame de Lamballe.

To the loss of her mother, who had succumbed to a long illness, was added that of her father, who had been inconsolable.

We quote from the " Gazette de France " :

" TURIN, September 2d.

" Tuesday, the 31st of last month, Princesse Christine Henriette de Hesse Rheinfels, wife of Louis Victor Amédée de Savoie, Prince de Carignan, died in this city, after a lingering and painful illness. She was born the 24th of November, 1717. '

At this terrible affliction, Madame de Lamballe, in her grief, had, at least, the consolation of receiving from her friend the following tender letters, which the king himself had signed with his own hand :

" I have learned, with deep grief, my dear Lamballe, of the death of your mother. The king has come in, and wishes to add a few words :—One word, just one, madame and dear cousin, but it is from the depths of my heart. You know how much we love you. May God be with you."

Not content with this mark of friendship to the princess, the king and the queen ordered the Court to wear mourning for eleven days.

" TURIN, December 9th.

" His Serene Highness, Prince Victor de Carignan, died in this city last Sunday (December 6th), in the fifty-seventh year of his age."

The court again wore mourning for eleven days. Mercy, who is not lenient to the princess, writes, however, that, in spite of the news, received just as the queen was about to be confined, the superintendent did her duty, and " even fulfilled it promptly."

He adds that Madame de Lamballe returned shortly after to Paris, to her father-in-law, where she remained "in retirement during the first days of her mourning." At the Hôtel de Toulouse she received the visit of the king, who noted the fact in his diary:

"December 22, '78, visited Madame de Lamballe on the death of her father."

This is short and uninteresting, but, fortunately, we have the "Gazette de France," which gives us fuller details.

"On the 22d, after the mass of the king, his Majesty went to call on the Princesse de Lamballe, upon the death of her father, the Prince de Carignan. The Duc d'Orléans, the Duc de Chartres, the Duchesse de Chartres, the Prince de Condé, the Duc de Bourbon, the Duchesse de Bourbon, the Prince de Conti, the Princesse de Conti, Mademoiselle de Condé, and the Duc de Penthièvre were in the apartments of the princess and received his Majesty in the usual manner. Monsieur, Madame, Monseigneur le Comte d'Artois, Madame Elisabeth de France, Madame Adélaide, Madame Victoire, and Madame Sophie de France came in later, and were received in the same way by the princes and princesses of the blood.

"The same day, the Princesse de Lamballe returned to pay her respects to the king and the royal family."

During the confinement of the queen, verses of every description poured in constantly. We will cite only that of a poetic lemonade-maker:

79

MADAME DE LAMBALLE

> Without consulting the Sibyl,
>   Of merest chance a thing,
>   To the mother of our King,
> I told without much skill
>   That a prince she was to see ;
>   And so it chanced to be.
> Now, happy at seeing aright
> The same for you in sight,
>   A son I dare predict,
> And before the dawn, the light ;
>   But if my mind is tricked,
>   And if I do mistake,
> The dawn I shall see break
> Before the morning bright.

This muse was right in supposing that she was not infallible; for, December 20th, the queen gave birth to a princess, who was christened Marie Thérèse Charlotte.[3]

By January, the queen had recovered, and on the 8th of February the royal family set out with great pomp for Notre Dame. Marie Antoinette was attacked with measles, the end of March. Louis XVI., always so exact, gives us the date of the appearance of the disease.

" March 31, '79, the queen has measles."

If we believe Bachaumont, she caught it from Madame de Polignac. What is certain is that the latter was also confined to her bed, for we find the queen, during her illness, greatly pained by the absence of the countess.

Mercy wrote that Marie Antoinette " bore with great displeasure the absence of one of whom she was so especially fond.'' We must state that, in spite of the absence of her favorite, the queen was no less well cared for by Madame, the Comte d'Artois, and the Princesse de Lamballe.

Separated from her husband, for whom they feared contagion, Marie Antoinette had the society of four of her intimate friends, the Duc de Coigny, the Duc de Guines, the Comte Esterhazy, and the Baron de Besenval,' who took their places by her side as if they were nurses.

As soon as she recovered, she wished to see her favorite, and went to Paris, Rue de Bourbon, to dine alone with the Comtesse de Polignac.

Entirely well again, the queen, whose illness, according to Mercy, had prevented her from attending to her religious duties, received communion. Madame de Lamballe held the napkin for her.

A short time after this, Marie Antoinette was alone. Madame de Polignac had gone for her health to Spa, where she was to remain two months. Madame de Lamballe was at Bourbon.

But the separation had not the same results for the two favorites. Mercy wrote, regarding the absence of the princess, that " her favor has not ceased to decline, more and more, and that now she is much more tolerated than desired by the queen;'' while he soon announced the return of the countess by saying that he " has brought back to the queen the resources of society, the absence of which had been greatly noticed by her."

As we know that he always kept the most offensive epithets for the princess, who, no doubt, showed him some disdain, we are not surprised that, when Madame de Lamballe returned from Bourbonne les Bains, he wrote:

" The Princesse de Lamballe, who has spent almost three months at the baths, has returned and must notice more than ever the total loss of her favor with the queen. The superintendent has become for her Majesty an object of weariness and displeasure and is now even distasteful to her. The result is that the Princesse de Lamballe complains to her intimate men and women friends, who repeat her words in public. So little interest, however, is taken in the superintendent that no one troubles about it or comments on the changed attitude of the queen towards her former favorite."

CHAPTER VII

"In the Year of Adoption, 1778, on the 5th day of the second month," we read in a manuscript of the times, "the Loge de la Candeur was regularly convoked and fraternally assembled. The business was opened in the Orient by the Venerable Brother ' Marquis de Saisseval, accompanied by the Comtesse de Brienne, Grand Mistress; in the Occident, by the Brother Marquis d'Arcambal, and the Sister Marquise d'Havrincourt, Grand Inspectress."

This 5th of February, 1778, the lodge presented unusual animation. All the Brothers and Sisters were there. They wished to be present at the visit of the Duc and the Duchesse de Chartres, the Duchesse de Bourbon, and the Princesse de Lamballe, who had promised to honor the meeting by their presence and to participate in the work of the Assembly. The Marquis de Lusignem, the Comtes de Bethisy and de Salles were charged by the Venerable to give their hands to the illustrious guests and to conduct them to the reception room. On their arrival a deputation of nine Brothers paid their respects, and introduced the visitors to the lodge, in the midst of general acclamation. Immediately after, the speeches began. First came that of the Brother Orator, the Comte de Gouy, addressed to the Grand Master, to the Grand Sister Mistress, and to their Highnesses the other Sisters.

After him the secretary, Tissot, and the Comte de Sesmaisons spoke in turn.

" The business," says the manuscript, " was suspended to celebrate the Banquet," at which they blew out several lamps of obligation (*souffle plusieurs lampes d'obligation*): the first toast in honor of Louis XVI., the second in honor of the Grand Master and Grand Mistress of the Loges d'Adoption; finally, the fifth, in honor of the Duchesse de Chartres and of the Princesse de Lamballe. The orchestra of the lodge was then heard, and each amateur recited verses or sang songs.

" The Marquis de Caumartin sang stanzas composed by the Brother Comte de Saisseval. This proof of the Masonic zeal of these two Brothers was received with well-deserved applause:

SONG.

To the air of ' The Vaudeville Epicure.'

Our eyes alone persuade the fair ;
  Beauty brings loves galore ;
But they are faithless, so beware.
  Come, brothers, swear that never more
We shall thus fickle be ;
  To virtue, as to every grace,
We'll pledge our fealty.

84

Of wisdom sought I then to speak,
  In sweetest terms to trace ;
And likewise simply did I speak
  Of intellect and grace.
They very much admired
  These blessings doubly dear ;
But I am still. Copy, adieu !
  The model fair is here.

" The Sister Comtesse Dessalles sang, with much grace, the following stanzas of the Brother Comte de Sesmaisons, which were received with applause:

SONG.

To the tune of ' Que ne suis-je la Fougère ?'

Oh, goddesses kind,
  To whom all joys are due,
Whose hearts our glad voices
  Must touch through and through,
We know the great lack
  Of our talents so weak ;
But when one has feeling,
  Must one always speak ?

In vain would we paint
  Every virtue and charm ;
The mind feels constraint,
  The heart knows alarm.
It offers you homage,
  And asks of you ruth,
And by simple language
  It honors the truth.

Dear Sisters, whose presence
  Enhances our land,
Accept as reward,
  Our joy, now at hand.

Let us strengthen the bond
    That binds us to-day,
And ever to love
    Let all things give way.

It is thus that these goddesses
    Lay aside royalty ;
Asking through love alone,
    Purest equality.
Some mortals dare tell
    Of the love each one feels ;
Comprehension of this
    Inspiration reveals.

" The Brother and the Sister Comtesse de Bethisy
then sang couplets in dialogue, upon the reception of
the Sister the Comtesse de Roche Chouart, composed
by the Brother de la Chevalerie.
" The efforts of these brothers and sisters were
heartily applauded.
" Dialogue between a M :—: and a Proselyte.'

SONG.

To the air of ' Viens, Aurore, je t'implore.'

THE M:—:

Come, Julie !
Oh, agree.
Come and join our union.
    Let us show
    What you must know :
The rites of our communion.

JULIE.

No ; the fear
I cannot bear
Fills my soul with awe ;
86

Such torture
To endure
Makes me dread your law.

THE M:—:

Our probation
Of short duration
Need not make you fear ;
Courage
Is the gage
We ought all to bear.

JULIE.

Since the story
Of my glory
Lies in danger meeting.
I, sensitive !
You, imperative !
How my heart is beating !

THE M:—:

Thy confidence,
Thy confidence
Adds one delight the more.
By its charms
Your alarms
Will change to joys galore.

JULIE.

Modesty,
Sagacity,
Let them only meet
Without knowing
Or bestowing
A thought on how they'll greet.

MADAME DE LAMBALLE

THE M:—:

Our retreat
Is gentle, sweet,
A shrine of peace alway ;
The happy age
Of the true sage
Rules our hearts to-day.

Our life,
Without strife
Flows onward fair and free.
Our language,
Our usage,
Tell of liberty.

Glad
Or sad,
This weak humanity
Claims all ;
And at its call
We yield tranquillity.

The love we pay
Of good, to-day,
Is our sure guarantee.
Used for our pleasure,
Each mystic measure
Shows but humanity.

JULIE.

Ah ! Julie !
Will agree
To join you in your union ;
For I would know
What you must show :
The rites of your communion.

" Immediately after followed the toasts of all the Masons, men and women scattered over both hemispheres. This was preceded by a song of the Order of Adoption, rendered by the Brother the Vicomte de Gand and the Comte Maxime de Puiségur.

" When the Most Serene Grand Master, the Most Serene Grand Mistress, and the August Sisters, the Duchesse de Chartres and the Princesse de Lamballe, as well as the Brother and Sister Visitors who had accompanied them, had signed the platform, all the business of that day, so memorable and flattering for the Loge de la Candeur and interesting for the Order, was happily terminated in the midst of peace and joy and to the sounds of harmony, the fifth day of the month of February, in the Year of Adoption one thousand seven hundred and seventy-eight.

" To the regular business succeeded several forms of amusement, arranged for the *Most Serene Grand Master and Grand Mistress and the illustrious visitors*. Among others, the Brothers and the Sisters of the lodge gave a representation of the *Ami de la Maison*, a comic opera, the rôles of which were filled, in a manner very unusual even among society actors, by the dear Sisters the Comtesse de Brienne, the Comtesse Dessales, and by the Brothers the Vicomte de Gand, the Marquis de Caumartin, and the Comte Maxime de Puiségur. We give below the couplets of the vaudeville, composed by the Brother Comte de Gouy. They were enthusiastically applauded and were repeated at the request of the Most Serene Grand Master and of the august Sisters.

" Couplets composed by the Brother Comte de Gouy, Orator.

" To the air of the 'Vaudeville de la Laitière : J'étais gisant à cette place,' etc.

" Madame la Comtesse Dessalles played the part of Agathe, Monsieur le Vicomte de Gand that of Célicour.

> As a reward of love so true
> Hymen prepares my joy,
> Wife and mother I shall be—
> Sweetness without alloy.

TO MONSIEUR LE DUC AND TO MADAME
LA DUCHESSE DE CHARTRES.

> Because of my mother-love,
> From my love of a lord,
> Brothers, I choose from you,
> A happy couple for a model,
> A happy couple for a model.

" Monsieur le Vicomte de Gand playing Célicour to Madame la Comtesse Dessalles playing Agathe :

> I win a rank and you, my queen,
> Twice happy in a day ;
> Behold me captain under Mars
> And under Love, alway.

TO THE PRINCES.

> O, you of the ceremony
> Both the witnesses and ornament,
> If I win your consent
> I will renounce my company,
> I will renounce my company.

" Monsieur le Comte Maxime de Puiségur playing

MADAME DE LAMBALLE

Oronte to Madame la Comtesse de Brienne playing
Orphise:

> To my friends, to my prudence,
>   Our children's joy is due.
> As to friends, my vigilance
>   Shall guard my sister, too.
>   Many seem so,
>   Without being so.
>   I refer, Cliton, to you.

To Monsieur le Duc de Chartres.

> The true friends of the house
> Are the Brothers of the Grand Master,
> Are the Brothers of the Grand Master.

" Monsieur le Marquis de Caumartin playing Cliton
in the foreground and somewhat hiding the other
actors:

> Without imposition,
> I have passed many an examination
> In words of love ;
> And, in history
> I paint only lovers as heroes.

To the Princes.

> But history offers other charms
> To one who knows your home ;
> Princes, there lies true heraldry,
> Where Vict'ry has painted your arms,
> Where Vict'ry has painted your arms.

"This illustrious Chief, as well as the Most Serene
Grand Mistress and the august princesses, deigned to

amuse themselves at the ball which was then given and with which the Most Serene Grand Master wished to close the exercises.

" These Most Serene Brothers were accompanied by all the Brothers and Sisters of the lodge, whose hearts, long after their eyes had ceased to see them, followed these leaders so beloved and so worthy of being beloved. Let us now study the Loge de la Candeur in its usual routine. The secretary, Tissot, undertook this task in the discourse he pronounced before the twenty-first meeting, May 3, 1777. He began by saying that, thanks to the zeal of the Sisters, the Marquise de Courtebonne de Polignac, the Comtesse de Choiseul, and the Vicomtesse de Foudoas, the organization of the lodge had taken place the 21st of March, 1775. He went on to state that the ' Sister Marquise de Genlis was the first to admire the virtues of our Masons.' "

The interesting manuscript quoted by us contains, in its written minutes, which number sixty-five, curious details which we must not omit. Thus at the fifth meeting we find, among other things:

"The Marquise de Genlis having accused the Brother, Prince Salpieha, of having broken the rules of the lodge by leaving the temple without permission (although it was in order to satisfy the demands of nature), there had been a discussion as to whether he should be punished for this fault, and as to the kind of punishment. The Brother Salpieha was brought to the door of the temple; he was led in with his face turned towards the West; the Venerable then ordered the Brother Master of the Ceremonies to conduct him to a side room, in which he was to be locked during the entire session.''

This same report tells us that the princess was twice present at the meetings, or, at least, that she signed the minutes of two of the meetings.

At the twenty-sixth meeting, the 5th of February, 1778, which we have described, the princess signed herself *Sœur Princesse de Lamballe;* at the forty-third, which was held February 24, 1780, and at which she, as well as the Duchesse de Chartres, was cheered, she resumed her usual signature: *M. T. L. de Savoie.*

She did not affix her signature every time, for the minutes of the meeting at which she received the compliment paid her for having honored the meeting of the 8th of May, 1778, with her presence do not have it. This is the compliment:

"The Loge d'Adoption, under the name of la Candeur, the 8th of May, in the year 1778, to the Most Serene Sister, Princesse de Lamballe:

S:—: and T:—:   C:—: S:—:

"You have deigned to visit our climate, and your presence has awakened in the hearts of all our brothers and sisters that lively and pure sentiment which for many reasons your appearance inspires.

"To offer you the homage of our meeting is an act of gratitude; it will be one of kindness on your part if you will deign to accept it.

"We are, with the most respectful and fraternal sentiments,

S:—: and T:—: C:—: S:—:

"Your very humble subjects and servants, and very affectionate brothers :—: and sisters :—: of the Loge de la Candeur."

Our illustrious princesses were in good company there, for the list of the Brothers and Sisters composing the Loge de la Candeur shows us the names of almost all the court ladies, as well as those of the illustrious military officers of the time.[3] The majority of readers know but little of the ancient French Order of Masons, and will be surprised to see us refer to the subject in a study of the Princesse de Lamballe. Let us, therefore, assure them, without delay, that we shall touch upon the question only just enough to disclose the part taken by this princess in the mysterious ceremonies toward which her lively imagination impelled her. In acting thus, she merely followed the example given by almost every one around her.

It will be enough, therefore, for us to say that it was towards the middle of the eighteenth century that the Lodges of Adoption were founded.[4] By the Lodges of Adoption is meant those which admitted women. "The more perfect half of the human race," we read in the '*Esquisse*' of the works on Adoption, "could not always be banished from the places she sought to embellish. Is goodness perfect without grace? We, therefore, have admitted sisters to those of our rites in which they could and should participate; we have recalled to their minds our principle by making them adopt our aims.''

'' One doubts,'' says Bachaumont, '' if it is to the French that this happy innovation is due, and whether, in the land of gallantry, there could have existed for so long a time, in all its glory, a society from which the fair sex was totally excluded.''

For its part, from the 10th of June, 1771, the Grand Orient took under its protection the Masonry of Adoption, but with the expressed condition that a Venerable of the Lodge should be its president or, in his absence, should be replaced by the head Inspector, and that, furthermore, no meeting could be held without the presence of a certain number of regular Masons.

There were even general rules, in which we notice:

"Art. VI.—No woman in a delicate condition or at a critical period can be admitted to the reception.

"Art. VII.—No one can be admitted before the age of eighteen, unless the whole lodge unanimously gives permission.

"Art. XXIV.—Propriety is especially requested.

"Art. XXVI.—When a sister does not feel in a condition to preserve propriety during her reception she shall ask to retire.''

The sisters wore a robe of white stuff, an apron of white kid lined and bordered with blue silk, and white gloves.

Each wore about her waist a blue-watered belt, passing from the right to the left, at the end of which hung a flaming heart containing an apple. The dignitaries wore the same style of belt crosswise; but the flaming heart was replaced by a golden trowel.

Furthermore, all, whether men or women, wore on their left arms the badge of their Order, in white satin lined with blue, with these words embroidered in silk of the same color: *Silence* and *Virtue.*

The Masonry of Adoption at first consisted of three degrees: Apprentice, Fellow Craft, and Mistress. Later, two new grades were established, those of Perfect Mistress and of Sublime Scottish Mistress Elect. But, adds Monsieur Ragon in his Ritual of Adoption, the last two were given but seldom. However, we have found at the end of the manuscript of the General Rules, a diploma of this degree, which is rather curious.

Model of the Certificate of the Sublime Scottish Mistress.[5]

The parchment, or that on which the diploma is written, must be in the form of a pentagon.

The first three letters signify lodge of Masons, and the year of grace.

L. D. M.

Signed in the Garden of Eden, towards the East, whence comes the first light of the lodge for women, under the distinctive title of ———, by the mysterious numbers known only to the Enlightened.

We, earthly leaders, directing the sublime and respectable lodge for women, have seen the zeal and

the energy shown by the Venerable Sister, aged ——
years, native of ——————, follower of the Christian
religion, in her desire to reach the highest degree of
Masonic light. We have judged her capacity, life,
and morals, with a careful examination of her conduct,
as much in the lodge as outside of it, and feeling that
she has answered every requirement in her quality of
Mason, we make known that we have admitted her
to the degree of Apprentice, Fellow Craft, Mistress
Mason, Perfect Mistress, and Sublime Scottish Mistress, and we recommend all our Bs:——: and Sister
Masons to recognize her as such, and to give credence
to the present certificate given her for use, in case of
need, which we have signed with our own hand, and to
which we have affixed the seal of our respectable lodge,
the whole to be countersigned by our own secretary.

Signed in the Garden of Eden, on the side of the
Orient, the —— day of the week of —— month of
the Masonic year, five thousand eight hundred ——,
and, in vulgar reckoning, the —— thousand, eight
hundred ——.

XX, Chief Inspector.

XX, Chief Inspectress.

S:——: Grand Mistress.

Sealed by us, Guardian of the ——, by order of
X

Seals and Archives . .

The Very Respectable Lodge,

Secretary."

If the business of these lodges did not seem to be serious, the poor at least profited by them. A meeting never broke up without a collection, the proceeds of which, given into the hands of the treasurer, were spent in keeping the unfortunate. "Preference was given to those who shunned the eyes of the public." To the proceeds of the collections were added the fines, and each infringement of the rules was subject to a penalty of from six to twelve cents. Probably the strict punishment for the slightest offence brought in rather large sums. We see, in fact, that, besides some debtors released from prison, acts of courage worthily rewarded, prizes accorded to virtue, there was on the 14th of September, 1777, at a meeting of a Lodge of Adoption at Waux Hall, presided over by the Princesse de Lamballe, to celebrate the convalescence of the Duc de Chartres, a magnificent fête, at which three poor girls were married and three children of unfortunate Masons admitted into apprenticeship. Again, on November 26, 1781, the Mother Lodge, on the occasion of the birth of Monseigneur le Dauphin, ordered sung in the Church of Saint Eustache a musical mass from a composition by Floquet, who directed the orchestra himself. Madame de Lamballe, as well as a large number of lords and ladies of the court, was present. The Mother Lodge held a meeting in its rooms immediately after, and voted that it would take charge of the education of all the poor male children born the same day as the dauphin, in the Parish of Saint Eustache.

All these fêtes, as we have shown in this chapter, ended with a banquet, at which the table was in the shape of a horseshoe. The room was lighted by five chandeliers or, in default of these, by candles in clusters of five.

Everything was arranged, in accordance with the Ritual of Adoption, on five lines traced in different colors. The stars were placed in the centre, the dishes on the next outer line, the bottles and decanters on a third line, the glasses on a fourth, and the plates on a fifth along the edge of the table.

During the repast the serving was done by women who were received into the first degree without having to pay any assessment, and who rarely reached the second degree. By a wise precaution these serving sisters had to be thirty years old, for fear that " their babble might cause scandal in the Order," and they were accepted only after a minute examination and on the proper recommendation of the Sister who presented them. These meetings, which were greatly in vogue for a few years, met with certain criticisms when they were first started as well as when they had become more successful. Did not Bachaumont cry : " French gallantry has caused the Institute of the French Masons to degenerate here to a great extent "? Another anonymous author claims that they ridiculed women by demanding certain tests in which, according to him, the candidates learned nothing serious.

On the 10th of January, 1781, the Princesse de

Lamballe was nominated Grand Mistress of all the regular Scottish Lodges of France.

The curious minutes of this meeting, in which the Comtesse d'Affry, the Vicomtesse de Narbonne, the Comtesse de Mailly, Marie de Durfort de Donissan, Victoire de Durfort de Chastellux, Madeleine d'Affry de Diesbach, and Louise de Broc were received as Mason Apprentices, were offered for sale a few years ago, as well as a catalogue of books containing the report of the R.·. M.·. L.·. Ec.·. of the Social Contract from June 24, 1781, to February 1, 1786. Unfortunately for us, in spite of our researches, we have been unable to procure it. We know merely that it contained the following curious minutes:

" The eighteenth day of the eleventh month of the year of Science 5780, the Reverend Mother-Lodge of the Scottish Rite of Adoption, . . . the Most Serene Sister Louise de Carignan, Princesse de Lamballe, and the Venerable Brother Abbé Bertolio . . . and brothers; Marie Constance de Lesbiac, aged ——(*sic*); Pauline, Vicomtesse de Narbonne, aged 37, Jeanne Félicité de Narbonne, Comtesse de Mailly, aged 18, Marie de Durfort de Donissan, aged 33, etc., etc., ..."

The Lodge of the Social Contract had undergone numerous changes since its foundation, which dates back to the 30th of March, 1766. First reorganized October 9, 1772, by the Grand Lodge, then by the Grand Orient, the 21st of January, 1773, under the name of Saint Lazare, it resumed its original title of Saint Jean d'Ecosse, of the Social Contract, May 21, 1776.

Its Venerable was at that time the T.·. C.·. F.·. de Brommer, Chevalier of the Royal and Military Order of the Merit; and its Director the T.·. C.·. F.·. Abbé Bertolio, advocate of the Parliament, Rue des Maçons, near the Sorbonne.

It was said that this lodge would have endless difficulties, for we find the following motion discussed in the meeting of the tenth day of the tenth month, 5779:

" The G.·. O.·. declares in the name of the G.·. M.·. that this most serene F.·. has refused to sign the constitution of the R.·. L.·. of the *Social Contract* (called Scottish Mother-L.·.), according to the observation made by him that this title was signed by none of the officers of the G.·. O.·. which appointed a committee to thank the most Serene G.·. M.·. for that distinguished proof of his love for regularity.

" The G.·. O.·. announces to all the regular LL.·. that the time accorded to the R.·. L.·. of the *Social Contract* (called Scottish Mother-Lodge) to put itself into due form, having expired, it is this day crossed out from the list of regular LL.·."

Finally, to conclude, we should have been glad to be able to give extracts from a very rare pamphlet which would have furnished us with an ample amount of curious information on the initiation of the princess as Grand Mistress, the 20th of February,

1781. Unfortunately, these special volumes, drawn from a limited number of copies, are, apart from their extreme rareness, to be found in certain libraries of the New World to which it is difficult to obtain access.

Some of our readers, more fortunate than we, may be sufficiently interested to gain admission to these books, and we are glad to tell them of the pamphlet we have mentioned, under the number 2,142 of the " Bibliographie der Freimaurerei," by Doctor Georg Kloss (Frankfort-on-the-Main, 1844). The title is "Hommage maçonnique de la Mère-Loge Ecossaise d'Adoption to the Most Serene Sister Marie Thérèse Louise de Carignan, Princesse de Lamballe, its Grand Mistress, and the Official Sisters, the day of their initiation, February 20th. By the F.·. Robineau de Beaunoir, secretary of the Mère-Loge Ecossaise. Hérédon, 1781, in-8, 24 pp."

We will say, in conclusion, that the last Grand Mistress of the Lodges of Adoption was the Empress Josephine.

CHAPTER VIII

The coldness of Marie Antoinette towards the princess might easily have been attributed to the lack of order in the accounts of the superintendent and to her continued demands in regard to her position. All these facts came to the knowledge of the queen and irritated her against poor Madame de Lamballe, whose want of care in her business affairs perhaps explains the frequent demands.

About 1778 we see that a certain Mizet, clerk of her secretary, dismissed, no doubt, by his intendant Charles Joseph Loques, had compiled a lengthy memoir to inform the princess of the calumnies brought forward by the aforesaid intendant, and furthermore had cited various instances of abuse.

At first the princess seemed to attach only a relative importance to this information, but Mizet, who wanted to make trouble, was not afraid to write to Madame de Guébriant:

" MADAME:
" As perhaps you may have some orders to give me in connection with the memoir I have had the honor of addressing to you, I beg you to be good enough to permit me to affix my address to the present note. The

truth of most of the facts mentioned in this memoir is in your hands, and I am ready to prove, even in the presence of the guilty, those facts of which you have no proof. You are too just, Madame, and you hold the interests of the princess too dear for you not to enlighten her highness promptly. My rival does me great injury by the atrocious libels he spreads abroad about me. I have fought in vain against these, but I cannot convince people that he is an impostor, for they think him an honest man.

"I await with confidence the decision of your justice. I am, with deep respect, Madame, for your illustrious self, your very humble, very obedient, and very submissive servant, MIZET.

"Rue de la Vielle Draperie, House of Monsieur Gaillard, Notary."

Not content with an account of the misdeeds of his chief, an account which does not possess great interest and which deals with trifles, he again appeals to the Marquise de Guébriant to obtain the attention of the princess.

"It would be interesting for the princess," he concludes, in one of his notes, "if they should search Monsieur Loques' apartments without informing him in advance. They would discover, I think, many mysteries, notably in his red portfolio and in a small case which lies on his coffer.

"I persist in what I have just stated, and I very humbly beg Madame la Marquise de Guébriant, in whom I have the most perfect confidence, to be kind enough to take prompt measures in regard to all the facts mentioned in the present account, and to permit me to offer proof of them.

"I rely on the wisdom and the justice of Madame de Guébriant. Signed Mizet, Clerk of the Secretary of her Highness. Rue Coquillière, Maison de fayancier."

This new demand from Mizet, who had not left the service of the princess, does not seem to have had any effect; but the disdain with which his information was received irritated that singular person, who, in order to avenge himself, spread abroad most extraordinary reports as to the private accounts of the superintendent. This made the public suppose that her general accounts were in no better condition.

Madame de Lamballe, whatever the order in which she kept her private business affairs, nevertheless energetically demanded absolute control of those of her mistress, using her office of superintendent for this purpose.

Monsieur de Paulmy did not intend to be a victim of what he considered an excess of zeal, and complained to the queen in the letter we give below:

"MADAME:

"The fear of importuning your Majesty prevents my asking for an audience; but I owe you an explanation of my conduct, and I will give it in a few words.

"Madame la Princesse de Lamballe wishes to disregard the advice of your Majesty and to settle the accounts of the treasurer-general. She told me of this intention some time ago. I answered nothing, being persuaded that those who told her she had this right were sure of it.

"And yet the contrary has practically been proven to me. In short, I realized that there had been no rule nor precedent, at least for a hundred years, which authorized the claim of Madame la Superintendent. I had the honor of writing to her. I enclose a copy of my letter and two notes, which prove that Mademoiselle de Clermont, princess of the blood, although she had the title of chief adviser to the queen, as has Madame de Lamballe, never advanced such a claim. If the king and your Majesty will make a new rule regarding this subject I will submit to it without a word, but since there is no precedent for the claim of Madame de Lamballe a new law will be necessary. After receiving my letter, Madame de Lamballe sent for Monsieur Amelot and begged him to carry out the king's orders in the affair; this is all I ask, and I am ready to conform to them in every way.

"I am, with the most perfect submission to your Majesty, Madame, your very humble and very obedient servant and your very faithful subject and chancellor,

"R. DE PAULMY.
"Versailles, January 9, 1779."

The princess, whose star was visibly growing dimmer and dimmer as that of Madame de Polignac brightened, was on the point of not accompanying the Court during its sojourn at Marly; but, yielding no doubt to the advice of her friends, and especially to that of the Duc de Penthièvre, she changed her mind. This year Marly was particularly dull. The weather was frightful; walks and hunting parties suffered. No plays, for economy's sake. The afternoons were terribly long, the evenings interminable. Mercy undertakes to tell us in detail of the occupations of the queen. Marie Antoinette spent several hours of the day with the Comtesse Jules, and Madame de Lamballe was seldom admitted to those " private interviews." Card-playing was indulged in more than ever. The princess sanctioned it to such an extent in her own apartments, it seems, that the Duc de Chartres in one evening lost eight hundred louis. The rumor of this reached the queen, who was greatly displeased at it.

Always very much affected by the coldness of Marie Antoinette, the poor princess sought by every means in her power to approach her friend, took advantage of every circumstance, and carried out her slightest wishes; but, alas! it was almost wholly in vain. The health of Madame de Polignac had been uncertain since her attack of measles; she attended to her duties only now and then. Suddenly she stopped them entirely, and then it was that the queen, completely heartbroken, determined to go once a week to Paris to see her favorite. During this period of enforced separation " the princess appeared more frequently at Versailles, but was no better received."

The poor woman had already suffered cruelly enough from the indifference of the queen, without need of further cause for grief; but a fresh calamity arose to overwhelm her. Her brother, who, thanks to his credit and to the protection of the queen, had been appointed colonel in 1775, married at Saint Malo, where his regiment was garrisoned, a common woman, or rather one belonging to a family so little known that the union was looked on as a *mésalliance*. We quote the following details from Bachaumont:

" A Prince de Carignan," he tells us, " brother to Madame de Lamballe, colonel in the service of France in a regiment of his name, fell in love at Saint Malo with a Mademoiselle Magon, niece of the Magons well known in commerce and finance. She is neither wealthy nor beautiful, but has intelligence and a spirit of intrigue. She induced this weak-minded prince to marry her. The bishop of Saint Malo, satisfied with a vague license from the King of Sardinia, which the prince showed, permitting him to be married in France, gave a dispensation and the ceremony took place before the court could oppose it. It is thought that this marriage, although morally valid, does not exist civilly, and although it has been consummated, steps are to be taken to dissolve it. It is said that, in consequence, the King of Sardinia has recalled the prince to Turin."

We find also in the " Nouvelle de Paris et de Versailles," dated December 21, 1779, a slight variation of this account. The prince must have received orders to leave the kingdom; and it was even considered doubtful whether the court of Turin would receive him. This marriage, the subject of so much discussion, was in fact annulled in 1780 by a vote of parliament, but was again celebrated in 1781, at Saint Malo, as we see by what followed:

"The Comtesse Jules has completely succeeded her rival in the affection of the queen. It is only at rare intervals that we see the princess making a short stay at court." The correspondence of Mercy, silent on this subject, refers constantly, on the other hand, to Madame de Polignac. The ascendency of the latter was great and finally frightened the empress, who often spoke to her daughter on the subject.

The queen went but seldom to the Princesse de Lamballe's, "where they continued to play for money," says Mercy. The king never went there. His only visits were for the friend of the moment, for Marie Antoinette seemed to fear for him the society at the superintendent's, which she found too numerous and generally too noisy.

But Madame de Polignac was about to be confined, and it was a question as to how she could be seen without trouble or fatigue.

This difficulty was solved by the arrival of the court, which came to La Muette,[1] whereupon Mercy wrote, April 17th:

"It is practically decided that during the confinement of the Comtesse de Polignac, that is, in May, the court will make a short trip of ten days to La Muette."

In the meantime the two friends were together as much as possible.

"There are few people at Marly, where one is greatly bored, although there are three plays each week; the drawing-room is charming. The queen does not sup, she takes a drink of milk with Madame la Comtesse Jules, who has undergone a wonderful change."

All these imprudent and inconsequential acts of the queen ended by wearying people, and the court began to gossip about this *absorbing friendship*.[2]

"The Paris public," Mercy tells us, "did not at all approve of it, and regarded it as a demonstration of exaggerated favor; but little cared Marie Antoinette, who reached the young mother at ten o'clock in the morning, dined with her, and spent the day there."

The queen did not always go alone. During her stay at La Muette the king paid visits to the countess. "This was the only private establishment in Paris," observes Mercy, "which the king had entered since his coronation,"[3] and it was a great mark of distinction. Once at Versailles Marie Antoinette made only two visits a week to her friend, until the latter again appeared at court. Then the two met daily in the Trianon. Comedy was given there; the women's rôles were played exclusively by the Comtesse de Polignac and the Comtesse de Châlons; those of the men by the Comte Jules, the Comte d'Adhémar, and the Comte Esterhazy. It was decided that the sole spectators should be the king and the royal princes and princesses.

" Not even the ladies of the palace nor the ladies-in-waiting to the queen were to be made exceptions to this rule." Mercy adds: "If this plan is strictly adhered to it will no doubt keep out many of those who would be in the way."

Unfortunately, these plays and amusements caused jealousy, and the refusal to make exceptions, which was a source of such pleasure to the ambassador, was a mistake, and gave rise to numerous complaints. They became even wearisome—so Mercy says—and the queen put an end to them.

The Princesse de Lamballe had the mortification of being refused admission to the Trianon, an act for which public opinion blamed the queen, while in our eyes Madame de Polignac alone was responsible, having evidently asked it of her friend.

" The Princesse de Lamballe," wrote Mercy, " by right of her position as superintendent, thought an exception to the rule would be made in her favor; but this was not done."

What proves that this action in regard to the princess did not originate with the queen, who at heart was very kind, is the remembrance of her former friendship, of which she was soon to give proof in regard to the death of Monsieur de Carignan. For the rest, there was no possible doubt about this in the mind of the shrewd observer to whom we have so frequently and profitably had recourse. He says:

"The seclusion of the queen in the Trianon until to-day was suggested by the Comtesse de Polignac. The latter wished all the chief ladies to be excluded; the ladies of the palace and the courtiers. . . ."

Why this exclusion? Simply because the Comtesse Jules had a favor to beg, because she feared the influence of the princess, and because she wished to surround the queen with her own friends, that she might use them at need to carry out her secret wishes.

The truth is soon revealed to us. The Comte de Polignac was appointed hereditary duke, and his wife "prit le tabouret à la cour."

The excessive friendship of the queen blinded her. In spite of all the requests with which she was overwhelmed by the Polignacs she was not able to do without this not wholly disinterested friend.

"The trip to Fontainebleau is postponed from the 7th to the 11th. The queen and the king leave early in the morning. During the absence of the king the queen goes daily to dine and spend the day at Claye with Madame la Duchesse de Polignac."

But, as we have just said, Marie Antoinette could not on learning of the death of Prince Victor Amédée de Carignan recall her ancient friendship for the princess without being moved. She went to Paris to see her and spent "some time." We should prefer to think that she strove, by every possible means, to console her unhappy friend, rather than that she limited the visit to simply an ordinary call of condolence, as is the opinion of the faithful servant of the Empire, whose valuable researches come to a stop on the sudden death of Marie Thérèse, November 29th.

The king was so affected by this terrible news that he could not announce it to Marie Antoinette. To the Abbé de Vermond was entrusted this task, and only then could Louis XVI. appear before his wife. "I thank you, Monsieur l'Abbé, for the service you have just rendered me," were the first words, according to Madame Campan, that the king addressed to the abbé.

The queen's grief was violent. She shut herself up in her apartments and did not come out for several days, and then merely to attend mass. The only two friends she consented to see were Mesdames de Lamballe and de Polignac.

Mercy-Argenteau tells us that in 1778 Madame de Lamballe begged the queen to give her a considerable income from Lorraine; but his subsequent silence on the subject makes us think that this request, like many another, was not granted. The princess, who intended to return to the charge at the first opportune moment, was very careful not to forget a promise of the queen, vague though it was; for we see that she obtained an annuity of forty thousand livres from the department of foreign affairs, by order dated January 4, 1781. And yet Madame de Lamballe, whose need of money was great, had already some time before

obtained quite a considerable increase of salary, according to the statement of cash accounts.

" To the Princesse de Lamballe: The sum of forty-
two thousand five hundred livres for the first six months
of 1779 of the eighty-five thousand livres given her
annually in addition to her salary as superintendent
of the royal household, order of September 5, 1779."

A very small sum for that matter for the ex-favorite,
and one which could not be compared to the liberal
amounts of which the Polignacs had recently been the
recipients.   This family, extremely and unsurpass-
ingly avaricious, did not cease to plot to obtain favors
and privileges; their relatives, or even their allies,
equally unscrupulous, acted in the same way.

For a long time Madame de Gramont' had cherished
the hope of having Mademoiselle de Polignac as wife
for her son.   As soon as she thought of the possibility of this union, a result of her intrigues, she hoped
in spite of his youth to obtain for him the succession
to the Duc de Villeroy, as Captain of the Guards.
On the eve of the marriage, thanks to the kindness of
Maurepas, but to the great displeasure of the ambassador to Vienna, the Duc de Durfort-Civrac, who sought
the position for his son, the Duc de Lorges, she succeeded in bringing about the nomination.

" Yesterday, at Saint Sulpice," we read in the
' Journal de Paris,' " was celebrated the marriage of
the very high and very powerful Lord Monseigneur
Antoine Louis Marie de Gramont, Duc de Guiche,

with the very high and very powerful Mademoiselle Louise Gabrielle Aglaé de Polignac."

The Comtesse Jules, better informed, more practical and " more settled," according to the strange expression of Marie Thérèse, obtained as her share on the occasion of the great family event quite a sum, although just enough to pay her debts, and eight hundred thousand livres as dowry for her daughter.

At the confinement of the queen we again see the Princesse de Lamballe. As superintendent it was upon her that devolved the duty of informing the princes and the princesses of the royal family of the queen's condition.

In his journal, written from day to day, Louis XVI. traced briefly, even dryly, the smallest acts of his private life. For him, no details; facts and dates only; statistics were evidently his dominating passion. This once, to our great surprise, he enters into detail, for his delight at having at last an heir makes him loquacious. On account of this effort, which is only a passing one, it would be bad grace on our part not to let him speak:

" The queen passed a very comfortable night the 21st of October. She felt some slight pain on awakening, but this did not prevent her from bathing; the pain continued, but to no great extent. Until noon I gave no order for the shooting I was to do at Saclé. Between twelve and half-past the pain became greater; the queen went to bed, and just one hour and a quarter later, by my watch, she gave birth to a boy. There were present only Madame de Lamballe, the Comte d'Artois, my aunts, Madame de Chimay, Madame de Mailly, Madame d'Ossun, Madame de Tavannes, and Madame de Guémenée, who went alternately into the Salon de la Paix, which had been left empty. In the large cabinet was my household, that of the queen and the grand entries, and the under-governesses, who entered at the critical moment and who remained at the rear of the chamber so as not to cut off the air.

" Of all the princes to whom Madame de Lamballe sent at noon to announce the news, Monsieur le Duc d'Orléans alone arrived before the critical moment (he was hunting at Fausse Repose). He remained in the chamber or in the Salon de la Paix. Monsieur de Condé, Monsieur de Penthièvre, Monsieur le Duc de Chartres, Madame la Duchesse de Chartres, Madame la Princesse de Conty, and Mademoiselle de Condé arrived also; Monsieur le Duc de Bourbon in the evening, and Monsieur le Prince de Conty the next day. The following day the queen saw all these in turn.

" My son was carried into the large cabinet, where I went to see him dressed, and I laid him in the hands of Madame de Guémenée, the governess.⁶ After the queen had been delivered I told her that it was a boy, and he was brought to her bedside. . . ."

The birth of the dauphin filled the people with joy. Happiness was universal.⁶ From everywhere the king and the queen received congratulations on the happy event. We will quote, in passing, that of the women of La Halle:

" *Congratulations of the fishmongers of Paris on the birth of Monseigneur le Dauphin, pronounced by Dame Houdon, November* 4, 1781.

" To the King.

" *Sire :* Heaven owes a son to a king who looks upon his people as his family; in our wishes and our prayers we have long asked for him. These are at last answered. We are sure that our grandsons will be as happy as we are, for this cherished child must resemble you. You will teach him to be good like yourself; we will undertake to instruct our sons how they should love and respect their king.

" To the Queen

" *Madame :* All France has already proved to your Majesty its true and lively joy at the birth of Monseigneur le Dauphin. We have shown our delight with all the love we have for you; it is permitted us to-day to lay at the feet of your Majesty the expression of our hearts; this privilege is dearer to us than life. We have loved you, Madame, so long without daring to say so, that it requires all our respect not to abuse the permission to tell you of it.

" To Monseigneur le Dauphin :

" Our hearts have long waited for you; they were yours before your birth. You cannot yet hear the vows we make around your cradle, but some day they shall be explained to you; they all amount to seeing in you the image of those to whom you owe life.

" Read and approved, this 6th of November, 1781.
" De Sauvigny.

" Permission to have printed this 6th November, 1781. Lenoir."

CHAPTER IX

In the early part of this year Madame de Lamballe was sponsor to the daughter of the Marquis de Mordant de Massiac, with the Duc de Penthièvre.

" His serene Highness, Monseigneur le Duc de Penthièvre, and Madame la Princesse de Lamballe," we read in the ' Journal de Paris,' " the day before yesterday were sponsors at the baptism of the daughter of Monsieur le Marquis de Mordant de Massiac; the ceremony was performed by the curate of Saint Eustache in the chapel of the Hôtel de Toulouse."

A few days later the princess gave a ball to the royal family. The king informs us of the fact in the following terms:

" First ball at Madame de Lamballe's, January 12, '82."

On the 16th occurred the marriage of her maid of honor, Mademoiselle Etienne d'Amblimont, to the Comte de Lâge de Volude, ensign in the Royal Navy. The contract had been signed on the 13th by the king and the queen. On the 20th the princess herself presented the young countess at court. During the fêtes given by the City of Paris in honor of the birth of the dauphin, the princess accompanied the queen to every ceremony.

In its supplement of Tuesday, January 29, 1782, the "Gazette de France" tells us that Marie Antoinette left La Muette, the morning of the 21st, in her "state carriage," accompanied by Madame Elisabeth, Madame Adélaïde, the Princesse de Bourbon-Condé, the Princesse de Lamballe, and the Princesse de Chimay. The procession went first to Nôtre Dame and Sainte Geneviève, and then to the Hôtel de Ville, where, later, the king himself arrived. After a magnificent banquet of seventy-eight covers the royal family with the same ceremony and in the midst of illuminations returned to the Château de la Muette.

Two days later, having had a very gay supper given them at the Temple, the king and the queen attended the ball at the Hôtel de Ville, where unfortunately the crowd was so great that the queen cried out, "I am suffocating!" and the king was obliged to "elbow his way through the masses." This fact the "Gazette," with admirable ingenuousness, undertakes to prove to us.

"The astonishing crowding together of the masqueraders," it says, "that unconscious pressing forward which impels subjects to draw as near as possible to their sovereigns, made it impossible for their majesties to remain at the ball longer than an hour."

The Bodyguard also decided to celebrate the birth of the dauphin, and towards the close of December they planned to offer their sovereigns a ball. Unfortunately postponed on account of the health of the Comtesse d'Artois, the magnificent fête given in the grand hall of the Opera at Versailles could not take place before January 30th.

The Princesse de Lamballe was the only one of the family present at that time. The Duchesse de Chartres had measles, from which disease her four-year-old daughter, Mademoiselle d'Orléans, died a few days afterwards.

Let us speak now of the connection of Madame de Lamballe with the Grand Duke and the Grand Duchess of Russia, who were travelling incognito, under the title of the Comte and Comtesse du Nord, and who were long remembered for their affability and their knowledge and love of the arts.[1]

Delighted with their reception at court the Comte and Comtesse du Nord, during their stay in Paris, eagerly accepted the various invitations extended them by the members of the royal family, as well as by the princes of the blood, and went successively to Trianon, Chantilly, and Choisy.

The last of May the Duc de Penthièvre had the honor of receiving them on his beautiful estates at Sceaux. The Baronne d'Oberkirch left early in the morning with the Comtesse du Nord and, in her interesting memoirs, speaks enthusiastically of the splendid fête, in every detail worthy of its princely hosts, and the brilliancy of which, in the words of Fortaire, was enhanced by the beautiful spring weather and cloudless sky.

Arrived at Sceaux, the Comte and the Comtesse du Nord were received by the Duc de Penthièvre, aided by the Duchesse de Chartres and the Princesse de Lamballe, who rivalled each other in grace and amiability. Escorted by a numerous suite of highly distinguished guests they strolled through the park among gardens which were perfect wonders of order and beauty, filled with rare and lovely flowers. Later a collation of " exquisite magnificence " was served.

On leaving the table elegant carriages took the guests for a drive. The Comtesse du Nord, the Princesse de Conti, and the Duchesse de Chartres stepped into the first carriage, which was driven by the Duc de Penthièvre. The second, in which were some foreign ladies with Madame de Lamballe, had for driver the Comte du Nord himself. During the drive our tourists constantly admired the beautiful estate, on which everything had been wisely arranged to please the eye. A number of carriages filled with lords and ladies in beautiful attire drawn thither out of curiosity added to the interest of the scene.

That day the Comte and Comtesse du Nord must indeed have appreciated the reputed courtesy of the Duc de Penthièvre, and retained a delightful impression of the charming drive. On Saturday, June 8th, Madame de Lamballe also had the honor of receiving the foreign princes after the ball at Versailles. This fête, if we are to believe Bachaumont, was because of the illumination "*still more superb than that of the* Bodyguard's, and was no less well conducted."

In spite of all the splendors described by her, Madame d'Oberkirch could not refrain from admitting that "these formal gatherings are not amusing; when one has seen them he wants to retire." Young, fond of laughter and amusement, the baroness naturally preferred the supper of the superintendent, which she describes to us at length. The circle, composed of all the members of the royal family, was, it seems, small but select. According to his habit, the king left at the close of supper. The gayety was then freer, since "formality did not check their enjoyment." After a game of lotto, at which considerable money was lost, the queen herself gave the signal for the ball by dancing a quadrille, and the entertainment did not end until about four o'clock.

Endeavoring to trace faithfully the daily life of the Princesse de Lamballe and her relatives, we are obliged to pass suddenly from one subject to another, and to relate at random the joys and the sorrows of her life.

Thus the Hôtel de Toulouse was again in mourning, on account of the death of Messire Louis Samuel de Tascher, priest, doctor of the Sorbonne, chief prior of Sainte-Gauburge, and chaplain of his serene Highness Monseigneur the Duc de Penthièvre, Hôtel de Toulouse, Rue de la Vrillière.

Fortunately, it was not a member of the family; nevertheless the loss affected the Duc de Penthièvre, who felt himself robbed of an old confidant and of a friend of many years' standing.

In the meanwhile a piece of news, impatiently waited for, brought a happy diversion to the grief of the prince. A young gentleman, from infancy a page in the duke's household and lately appointed captain in his regiment of dragoons, had just "carried off the prize of poetry by a dialogue between Voltaire and a serf of Mont Jura." The duke professed the greatest friendship for this young man, who was essential to his court, but whose first dramatic attempts, in spite of his devotion, he had encouraged because of their absolute morality.

All of the host's guests congratulated him on the success of Florian, whose pleasant, cheerful ways and frank gayety were appreciated by every one. On August 25th, the day set for crowning the author, the appearance of the Academy was particularly interesting; the audience was, to a great extent, composed of the friends of the Duc de Penthièvre. The latter had promised to come to the gathering with the Duchesse de Chartres and several other personages of the court. Each one had said he would applaud the triumph of the young laureate; moreover (and this was not the smallest attraction, but a real literary treat), Dalembert was to have charge of the reading of the prize poem, and the company counted on his talent and his skill to show off the most striking passages, and so assure success to Florian.

Why was not Madame de Lamballe, who was a friend of Florian's, present at this family gathering? We have been unable to discover the real motive for her absence. Perhaps she had gone to the baths, as she usually did at that time of the year. However, we do not see her until a month later at Passy, where she had herself vaccinated; and afterwards, on the 8th of December, at the presentation of her maid-of-honor, the Marquise de Las Cases; and then, towards the end of the month, under the following circumstances:

Gaerat, that "astonishing genius" even among the "most clever musicians," was beginning to make a name, and the princess, who knew how to give the queen pleasure by speaking to her of a *débutant* for whose talent she could personally vouch, had readily consented to go to hear him at the Abbé d'Espagnac's.

Proud of this honor, and anxious to offer the princess a fête worthy of her, the abbé, finding his canonical quarters too limited, had obtained from his father, who was at that time governor of the Invalides, the reception-rooms of that hôtel.

So far all had gone well, and to his reputation as a wit and courtier D'Espagnac would have added that of being an accomplished host, had not an unlucky banterer, shocked at seeing the honors done by one of the De Giliberts, a cousin of the D'Espagnacs and a charming woman no doubt, but of a family greatly inferior in rank to that of the guests, given vent to his ill-humor in the following lines:

> " 'Neath porticoes with laurel twined,
> Whom do I see ?   Am I now blind ?
> Near Lamballe, in the warrior's place,
> At fête, and concert, with bold grace,
> Doing the honors there,
> Whom see I ?   Gilibert?
> Oh, social outrage !   You, the niece,
> Daughter and sister of police !"

On the 7th of January, 1783, there was a fête in the Hôtel de Toulouse, on the occasion of the baptism of the daughter of the Comtesse de Lâge de Volude. The child was held over the baptismal font by the Duc de Penthièvre and by Madame de Lamballe, surrounded by several friends whom the chapel of the hôtel could scarcely contain, so great was the desire to congratulate the happy mother, that gentle and amiable Etienne d'Amblimont, loved like a daughter by the princess.

A few days later Louis XVI., in his diary, tells us that she gave a ball and, as usual, states the date.

The chief event of that time was the purchase of the house at Passy, which the princess concluded with the Duc de Luynes for the price of one hundred and ten thousand livres, on the 1st of February.

What could have been the motive of Madame de Lamballe in making this purchase ?   We do not exactly see.   Probably the poor princess, feeling that she was kept at a distance by the marked coldness of her sovereign, did not wish, though yielding ground, to cut herself off entirely from the court, lest she might be reproached for neglecting her duties. In spite of all the injustice and the mortification she had to endure it never entered her head to resign her position.

On the other hand two reasons convincing to our mind prevented her from continuing to live in the Hôtel de Toulouse. Her father-in-law rarely came to stay in Paris, and, by its deserted appearance, this palace augmented the grief of the unfortunate woman, who needed light and sunshine.

With its park, its beautiful flower gardens, and its delightful terraces whence one obtained a fine view, Passy would give her the calm and the repose her whole being craved. And the fresh park with its sunny and artistically laid out parterres brought back in part the smile to her face, already faded and overshadowed by the clouds of a real grief. Besides, she felt herself more than ever drawn to her father-in-law. Extremely sensitive and of an impulsive temperament she had to love and be loved. Repulsed in the great friendship she had given to Marie Antoinette it was on the good duke that she turned the overflow of her soul. Thus it was this venerable prince who profited by all the devotion of which she was capable. And with what touching care, what delicate attention she surrounded the excellent man, who consoled her for the most cruel of misfortunes! If she could escape for a few days, if she needed to open her heart on the bosom of some friend who understood her, she at once went to him whom she ingenuously called her "dear papa," were he at Eu, at Aumale, at Châteauvillain, Amboise, or elsewhere. She knew beforehand that she would find in that peaceful home the precious joys of a well-filled life; for the Duc de Penthièvre used his immense fortune, which had caused enough umbrage at court at the time of the death of the Comte d'Eu to arouse the report that in high life they wanted to see the heir of so large a property marry again, in the most lavish charity, and people vied with one another in praising his inexhaustible generosity.

The duke's kindness of heart was proverbial. To give only one instance of it, a servant never left his employ save by his own free will, and that in his household positions were held from father to son. This is proved by the following:

"Philippe Lelong," we read in the 'Gazette de France,' "the pensioned concierge of the Duc de Penthièvre, died at the Hôtel de Toulouse, Versailles, the 30th of last month, in the eighty-first year of his age; he was the son of Jean Louis Lelong, the prince's concierge, who died in the same hôtel in November, 1765, in the one hundred and second year of his age."

Bachaumont traced for us, some years later, in the list of well-known men who met at the assembly of January 29, 1787, a not very flattering portrait of the venerable prince. But we know well enough how this writer allowed himself to be carried away both by the tendency of the times and by an unreasonable bitterness and rancor.

"A weak prince," he says, "honest and reserved, who took nothing upon himself, but who did good if the necessity for it were brought forcibly to his notice, and if he did not fear to displease the king."

Though few people knew the prince well, he was much talked of. Some thought his mode of life singular, and blamed him for the even tenor of his days. Others thought that his home life must be monotonous and tiresome, and wondered how the princess could find pleasure in it; others went so far as to reproach the good man for his great piety.

We will not pause to consider these various opinions, but will give preference to that of the Comtesse de Lâge, because she had talked with him, had known him, and had seen for herself what took place around him. We rely on her the much more readily as she was endowed with penetration and was a profound observer.

"Although unusually pious," she writes, "he [the duke] was lively in his own home, and not at all exacting. A thousand times he left his daughter-in-law and myself in his house reading novels together while he went to church. As he passed us he would say: 'I leave you because you are butterflies. Youth must have its day. Some time you will read other things.'"

If the amusements of the princess were not numer-

ous, at least that placid life exempt from care, confusion, and display was not displeasing to her, and the
absolute liberty she enjoyed, joined to the affectionate
regard of the duke, was sufficiently attractive to induce
her to prolong her visits.

And if there were need of further proof in favor of
the Duc de Penthièvre, we could cite this testimony
of Madame de Lamballe herself.

" I tried my best, my dear little one," she wrote,
" to read the letter from your sister. I could not
reach the end, for her handwriting is not at all like
her pretty fingers. . . . I should grow very tired
here were I not with Monsieur de Penthièvre, who
treats me with ever-increasing kindness. . . . I de-
vour letters and books. I have gone through the whole
of the little library. The stories of Marmontel seem
to me to be very dull."

Reading, we see, formed their chief distraction.
The duke himself, in spite of the austerity with which
he was credited and the reproaches so unjustly flung at
him, did not scorn it, and willingly commissioned
Florian to procure some books for him which he
thought he could read.

There was offered for sale a charming letter of Florian's, addressed to Monsieur Girod, at the Marais,
September 13, 1790, in which the writer gives him
several commissions, among others to buy, *at any price*,
for the Duc de Penthièvre the " Chansons " of Cou-
langes, in a small and well-bound volume. " They

are rare," said he, " but Monsieur de Bure knows what that means."

The Duc de Penthièvre adored his grandchildren and went several times every year to Belle Chasse, says their governess, and overwhelmed them with gifts.

In his correspondence Grimm tells us in regard to these presents a pleasing story, which must greatly have embarrassed the grandfather, always so punctilious as to the choice he made.

" There were no New Year's gifts this year," says he, " about which more has been said than about those which Monsieur le Duc de Penthièvre sent to Mademoiselle d'Orléans, his granddaughter. This is the story: Having deigned himself to visit all our great toy-shops, his Highness decided finally on a beautiful little palace, which in every respect seemed worthy of his preference. The idea was a novel one, and its workmanship was as elegant as ingenious; thanks to the play of a spring, easy to handle, all the windows of the palace opened one after another and there were seen innumerable numbers of the sweetest dolls in the world. This gift, carried to the little princess at the convent of Belle Chasse, soon became an object of admiration to all the nuns, who gathered around to see it. One of the youngest nuns in particular could not keep from looking at it. After examining it in detail and trying all its springs she finally perceived a small secret button which had not yet been touched; her finger quickly pressed it. Great heavens, what a strange surprise! All the dolls, which until then had appeared, were at once replaced by piquant figures of the Arétin. The scandal throughout the entire community was great, no doubt, but it is said that even the piety of the Mother Superior could not prevent her from smiling when she saw what hands the devil had dared to use in order to play such a trick. The toy merchant was deservedly censured, but he protested his innocence, and, impertinent as the whole conception was, it was easily proved that chance alone was to blame.''

CHAPTER X

For some time the king, to whom the chase was the most agreeable if not the only pastime, had been anxious to obtain Rambouillet, which was near, and included a forest reputed to be full of game. Until then, however, he had not dared to make known his desires openly, either from reasons of economy (for the cost of such an estate was great), or because he feared a refusal on the part of the duke, whom he knew to be but little inclined to give up his property. More than anything else, he had in mind the mortifying reply which Turgot, empowered to purchase Sceaux for his aunts, brought on himself.

" Monsieur le Contrôleur Général," the duke answered him, " I well knew that you preached liberty, but I did not suppose you were a man to take such a liberty."

Moreover, Louis XVI. well knew that there was an obstacle to his project very difficult to overcome. Rambouillet contained the treasures of the family of the Duc de Penthièvre, and it seemed improbable that the son of the Comte de Toulouse would consent to give up those precious heirlooms.

But such was the kindness of the venerable prince, such was his constant desire to be agreeable to the king, that as soon as he heard of the latter's wish he consented to everything, and the price was fixed, by common consent, at eighteen millions.

The removal of the regiments for Dreux took place with great pomp, Tuesday, November 25th.

Thus, for Madame de Lamballe the whole of the year 1783 slipped by gently and quietly. She kept away from the intrigues of the court; but, in spite of everything, backbiting concerning her went on just the same. Bachaumont would have failed in the task he had evidently imposed on himself of exposing the smallest details if he had not made some allusion to the pamphlets on the degeneration of the morals at court, " which spare," he adds, " neither the Polignacs, nor the Polastrons, nor Madame de Lamballe."

Base calumny was hurled against the royal family and all those who had any connection with the court were greatly abused. Bachaumont, always vigilant, takes care to inform us both of the date of the appearance of the libel and its title, " Bibliothèque des Dames de la Cour, avec de nouvelles Observations. Décembre, 1783," as well as of the title of the article which especially concerns our princess, " La Matière préférable à l'Esprit," dedicated to Madame la Princesse de Lamballe by the Marquis de Clermont, and reviewed by La Vaupallière.

The princess returned to court at the approach of

Easter, as at that time the duties of her position called
her back to the queen.

" On the 5th the queen went with ceremony to the
church in the parish of Nôtre Dame, where she received communion from the hands of the bishop, the
Duc de Laon, her grand chaplain; the Princesse de
Lamballe, superintendent of the royal household, held
the napkin, which was also held by the parish chaplain.

" The afternoon of the 8th, Holy Thursday, the
queen heard the sermon preached by the Abbé Duvan-
cel, canon of Meaux. The bishop of Saint Papoul
gave absolution, after which the queen washed the
hands of a dozen poor girls and waited on them at
table. The Marquis de Talaru, head-master of the
hôtel of her Majesty, set the table, the plates of which
were brought in by Madame Elisabeth of France, the
Princesse de Lamballe, superintendent of her Majesty,
and by the ladies of the palace, and the ladies-in-waiting of the princesses.''

The Baronne d'Oberkirch tells us that she went
twice to Madame de Lamballe's house in the month
of June, first on the 13th, after her presentation at
court, then on the 27th.

" Madame de Lamballe,'' she says, " invited me to
supper by order of the queen.''

The baroness insists on the " order.'' Was it to
make herself important, and to show, by the insistence
of the queen in inviting her, the esteem which Marie
Antoinette felt for her ?

Two foreign princes again came to visit Paris in 1784, the King of Sweden, travelling incognito under the title of the Comte de Haga, and Prince Henry, brother of the King of Prussia, also incognito, under the title of the Comte d'Œls. Both claim our attention, for both were received by the Duc de Penthièvre.

The first of these noble visitors arrived in Paris on Monday, June 7th, and did not leave until July 19th. During his six weeks' sojourn he paid several visits to the Duc de Penthièvre and to his daughter-in-law. Historians do not agree as to the date of the prince's visit to the Hôtel de Toulouse.

While Fortaire places it on June 27th, Métra assigns it to the 8th. But both are mistaken; we prefer a third version, that of the Duc de Penthièvre himself.

"The day after his arrival in Paris," Métra tells us, " he was with the Princesse de Lamballe, and was announced only from the ante-chamber. The princess was greatly surprised, but she had to receive a friend from his court, charged to give her a family kiss. The count asked for the Duc de Penthièvre, to whom the princess sent word, and the visit took place. '

Another contradiction, for according to Métra it was Madame de Lamballe who received the prince first; and according to Fortaire, it was the contrary which occurred. He makes the Comte de Haga say, on taking leave of the Duc de Penthièvre: " I am going to pay my respects to Madame la Princesse de Lamballe." To establish the truth, we will give the diary of the Duc de Penthièvre himself, only a few pages of which are in the national archives.

" On June 9th," we read, " the King of Sweden arrived at the Hôtel de Toulouse and asked for Monsieur de Penthièvre and Madame de Lamballe, who were at home. His Swedish Majesty first ascended to Madame de Lamballe's rooms (the King of Sweden did not salute Madame de Lamballe, nor did the latter salute the Comte de Haga), Monsieur de Penthièvre going there as soon as he was sent for. Madame de Lamballe had chairs brought and the King of Sweden seated himself before the arrival of Monsieur de Penthièvre. When the latter entered the room the visit took place, the guest and the hosts standing. Monsieur de Penthièvre asked the King of Sweden if he wished an arm-chair and his Swedish Majesty replied that etiquette did not give one to the Comte de Haga. Had he accepted, Monsieur de Penthièvre would have had one brought for himself and one for Madame de Lamballe. The King of Sweden told Monsieur de Penthièvre that he expected to go to the home of the latter; he introduced to him Monsieur de Fersheim, who accompanied him; and Monsieur de Penthièvre, in turn, presented to him Monsieur le Chevalier du Authiers, captain of his guards, and Monsieur de Las Cases, who was with him. The Duke said that the latter did not belong to his household, but that he was there a great deal as his wife was lady-in-waiting to Madame de Lamballe.

" They opened the two folding-doors for the King of Sweden, who wished to be conducted neither by Monsieur de Penthièvre nor by Madame de Lamballe, both of whom, nevertheless, did go with him as far as the door of Madame de Lamballe's sleeping-room, in which the visit had taken place. He sent back Monsieur le Chevalier du Authiers, who had followed him half-way to the stairs, still saying that he was only the Comte de Haga. Monsieur de Penthièvre and Madame de Lamballe addressed the King of Sweden as ' Monsieur le Comte.' The valet who announced Monsieur le Comte de Haga, while opening the two folding-doors, announced Monsieur de Penthièvre in the same way.''

This document, sufficiently curious in itself, proves how punctilious the duke was, how much he observed matters of ceremony, and what care he took to note, from day to day, all that he and his daughter-in-law did. He does not stop at this point, and we return to his diary:

'' On the 10th Madame la Princesse de Conti, Madame la Duchesse de Chartres, and Madame la Princesse de Lamballe, who was not with the Comte de Haga on his ' arrival,' went to see the King of Sweden, but did not find him. On the 12th the Duc de Penthièvre did the same with no better results. On the 13th a gentleman came to the Hôtel de Toulouse, on the part of the king, to invite the duke to a ball to be given in honor of the Comte de Haga on the following Friday. On the 14th there was the opera and the king occupied his box. The Duchesse de Bourbon and Madame de Lamballe occupied the two first boxes on the right and left sides of the house, according to their rank.

'' 18th.—Court ball.

'' 23d.—The king sent up a balloon at Versailles in the courtyard of the ministers of state.

'' 30th.—The Duc de Penthièvre left for Château-villain.''

Balloons were the rage at that time. Every one talked of them; they were the fad of the day, so we are not surprised to see the novelty of the Duc de Chartres mentioned; but we doubt if the princess was of the party, as is stated in the " Nouvelles de Paris et de Versailles ":

" The balloon from Saint Cloud, constructed by the Robert brothers, which was to have started this week, has been postponed because of some accident which happened to it during the bad weather of the past few days. It is torn in several places. There is a report that Monsieur le Duc de Chartres and Madame de Lamballe will ascend in it with the Robert brothers, and will dine at Villers-Cotterets."

After the few documents from which we have quoted, we should be glad to give a bit of verse, composed this time in honor of the princess. To hear her praises sounded at this late day is a matter of such rare occurrence that we cannot afford to omit these lines.

" The ' Six Nouvelles ' of Monsieur de Florian," we read in the " Journal de Paris," " have just appeared in Paris, from Didot, Senior, Rue Pavée-Saint-André, and Debure, Senior, Quai des Augustins, in-18. 222 pages."

Monsieur de Florian has chosen for his epigraph this beautiful verse of La Motte's :

L'ennui naquit un jour de l'uniformité.
(Ennui was one day born of monotony.)

The epistle, dedicated to her Serene Highness Madame la Princesse de Lamballe, contains a delicate eulogy

> Your pardon, Princess, if you trace
> In reading this, by my hand penned,
> The charming features of your face—
> My volume's fate I thus defend.
> My heroines I would enhance :
> One has your frankness without guile,
> Another has your charming smile—
> Graces that everywhere entrance.
> Thus, all your charms I've portioned out
> To Céleste, Félice, Elvire.
> A single charm, without a doubt,
> Had made each lady doubly fair.

We will close the year with an event which caused great excitement at the Hôtel de Toulouse. A fire broke out in the night above the rooms of Madame de Lamballe.

" The princess," says Fortaire, " who had just retired, at once arose and joined her father, whom she did not leave until the fire was entirely extinguished."

According to the same authority it seems that " all Paris came or sent to inquire after Monsieur le Duc de Penthièvre and Madame de Lamballe." Moreover, the king and the queen, at the first news of the fire, despatched pages and equerries to find out about it and to show the duke and his daughter-in-law the interest they took in the circumstance.

In order to prove the anxiety that followed we

cannot do better than to quote the lines the prince inserted in the "Journal de Paris," under the signature of his secretary:

"CHÂTEAU OF SCEAUX.

"December 28, 1784.

"To the Editors of the 'Journal.'

"GENTLEMEN: Several persons having written me concerning the accident which happened four days ago in the hôtel, I beg you to be kind enough to insert the following announcement in your next edition.

"I have the honor to be, etc.,

"(Signed) DE MUTRÉCY,

"*Secretary in ordinary to his Serene Highness Monseigneur le Duc de Penthièvre.*"

"The Hôtel de Toulouse caught fire on the night of the 23d of this month, about one hour after midnight. Flames were first seen in the roof above the ante-chamber of her Serene Highness Madame de Lamballe, in a corner of the building facing the Rue Baillif. By about half-past three in the morning the fire was under control and at seven only a few pieces of wood were smoking. A portion of the roof and a part of the storeroom were destroyed. No one perished in the accident. Monsieur le Lieutenant-Général de Police, Monsieur le Prévôt des Marchands, and Monsieur le Procureur du Roi au Châtelet went to the Hôtel de Toulouse as soon as they learned that it was on fire and offered their services. The energy of Monsieur Morat and the zeal of the firemen cannot be sufficiently praised.

"Members of the Regiment of the French Guards and of the Regiment of the Swiss Guards distinguished themselves as usual on this occasion.

" The Augustine monks from the Place des Victoires and the reverend Capuchin fathers from the Rue Saint-Honoré came to the Hôtel de Toulouse and gave active help."

The following notice appeared three days after the article we have just quoted, and shows that already in the eighteenth century officers did not consider it unpleasant to state publicly the services they had been able to render:

"We omitted to say in the notice referring to the fire in the Hôtel de Toulouse that Monsieur le Chevalier Dubois rendered great assistance."

The fire was generally attributed to malice, and Métra tells us that suspicion pointed to a certain Poulailler. This man, a famous brigand of the day, had already three times set fire to the forests of the duke in order to avenge himself because, after the murder of one of his guards, the prince had promised the reward of one hundred louis to any one who should arrest Poulailler. Other crimes led the man to the gallows and he was hanged at the Porte Saint-Antoine.

In February, 1785, the princess purchased for the sum of one hundred thousand livres the Hôtel Louvois, in the Rue de Richelieu, opposite the Arcade Colbert, in which she had her horses and coaches stabled.

On the 26th of March, Marie Antoinette gave birth to the Duc de Normandie. According to Bachaumont, there was no change in the formalities which had been adopted at the birth of the dauphin. The "Journal de Paris" stated that, contrary to custom, the Princesse de Chimay was summoned by the queen. We think this is a mistake and that its bulletins on the condition of the sovereign are at fault, especially as Lassonne, the court physician, makes this complaint.

Everything leads us to suppose that Madame de Lamballe went to the queen, and this is confirmed by the "Gazette de France," which usually derived its information from a reliable source. Moreover, the same paper tells us that the princess was present at mass in the chapel of the château on Easter. We know that it was not her custom to remain at court when her duties to the queen did not detain her.

The health of Madame de Lamballe demanded the greatest care. For a long time she had had to go to the baths to seek rest from the terrible nervous affection which still troubled her. Discouraged by the results the princess, like every one attacked by a similar malady, tried a little of everything, listened to every one, and hoped to find in the remedies of quacks a cure for her trouble.

The previous year Dr. Deslon, a celebrated disciple of Mesmer, came to Paris, and was not slow in winning an unprecedented reputation as much on account of the widespread though unfounded reports of his marvellous cures, as because of the constantly increasing number of his patients, who were almost all women.

His success had not failed to provoke jealousy and

to arouse the interest of even the royal circle. Thus Bachaumont tells us that the king finally appointed a committee consisting of four commissioners from the Faculty, four from the Academy of Sciences, and as many from the Royal Society, and that he had charged it to examine the doctor's methods and his treatment and to give him an account of both.

Naturally, Madame de Lamballe wished to try the famous remedy, and the same author tells us, in these terms, of the visit she made to the doctor for this purpose:

" Finally, Madame de Lamballe, with a lady of her suite, went to Dr. Deslon while he was mesmerizing. It was impossible to refuse a princess, and in spite of the word given by this physician to his patients, her Highness saw them surrounding the mysterious tub, surrendering themselves wholly to the influence of Deslon. The women, especially, were greatly outraged by such curiosity, for it was they who underwent most singular convulsions, experiencing intense ecstasies of pleasure."

This remedy was no more successful than the others in effecting a permanent cure of the aggravated condition of the princess. We find her a few months later under the care of Dr. Saiffert, consulting physician of the Comte d'Artois, a man of great reputation, who, moreover, left some enjoyable works on his science, especially on the kind of malady that according to his diagnosis afflicted Madame de Lamballe. Bachaumont tells us, in short, when Madame de Lamballe went to the " great pill doctor of France," and how the queen avenged herself by a bitter speech for the grudge she claimed to have against Beaumarchais. Doctor Seiffer (*sic*)—a German physician attached to Monsieur le Comte d'Artois in the capacity of consulting physician —says that, while attending Madame la Princesse de Lamballe, the queen came there and asked him if he was, as people said, the physician of the Sire de Beau-marchais. Whereupon the doctor answered her Majesty that he really had charge of the health of that celebrated man, that he had been to Saint-Lazare to see him, and that he was treating him at that time. " You will purge him in vain," cried the queen; " you cannot remove all his evil habits."

In the month of May, Paris, as usual, celebrated the birth of the Duc de Normandie with fêtes which lasted several days. Madame de Lamballe received the queen at Nôtre Dame the morning of the 23d and accompanied her as far as the Tuileries. On the 25th Marie Antoinette left La Muette, to take supper with the superintendent and to attend the play at the Comédie Italienne.

The queen returned to Paris shortly after to sup with the princess again, and to condole with her on the death of her brother, the Comte de Villefranche, colonel of the regiment of Savoie-Carignan; he had succumbed to an attack of quinsy at the château of Dommart, near Amiens.

The prince had been ill for some time, but, at the

instigation of the queen, his condition had been hidden from Madame de Lamballe.

Here is an autograph letter from Marie Antoinette to the Comtesse de Lâge de Volude regarding this, dated June 28, 1785—that is, two days before the death of the prince:

" I think that you are right, madame, to hide from Madame de Lamballe her brother's condition. Since you have sent to the Château de Domar it is just as well to wait for news before saying anything to her. I shall be delighted to see her this evening and shall tell her nothing. I was at table when I received your courier, but I will not detain him longer. Rest assured, madame, of all my friendship."

10

CHAPTER XI

Madame de Lamballe had scarcely had time to shed more than a few tears for her brother, who had died far away from her in disgrace because of his marriage with Mademoiselle Magon, when a report of the most serious nature concerning the queen suddenly arose. It was early in the month of August when that scandalous Affair of the Necklace [1] came to light, involving in the most compromising fashion the name of Marie Antoinette.

On the 15th the Cardinal de Rohan [2] was arrested at the palace of Versailles, still wearing his priestly robes. Three days later, on her return from a trip to Châteauvillain, where Monsieur de Penthièvre had just given a splendid fête, Madame de Lamotte, [3] the accomplice, was also imprisoned in the Bastille. The court was absolutely panic-stricken and, in addition to all the difficulties by which the throne was endangered, the most complete confusion reigned. The impression was so deep that passion ran away with every one. The police were powerless to prevent the circulation of libellous pamphlets, filled with stories more or less calumniating, which the populace eagerly devoured.

Every attack was naturally directed against the queen.

146

She became an object of hatred.[4] From day to day, as the law took its course, her enemies became more numerous. To these were joined the friends of Madame de Lamballe. Then the torrent reached its height and every moment a new pamphlet appeared, containing attacks which, although not always well founded, were none the less cruel. Meanwhile, what was going on at court ?

The king and the queen were holding the Duc d'Angoulême over the baptismal font.

The absence of the Princesse de Lamballe at that time, wholly unlikely as it may seem, is justified by the conduct of Marie Antoinette towards her, and by the mortification from which she had never ceased to suffer since the ascendency of the Duchesse de Polignac. Now the queen showed her almost indifference, as is proved by this letter that Marie Antoinette addressed to the princess, under the date of May 14, 1783:

"I answer you merely to show you how much I love you, for I am besieged with audiences and business."

Formerly when the princess was in favor there had been neither audience nor business to interfere when the amiable and good Lamballe came, or when the queen desired and sought her society. However, appearances were always guarded, as is proved by the formal visit referred to in the following lines:

" The queen left Trianon the 3d of this month, and the same day her Majesty reached Paris. She supped with the Princesse de Lamballe and condoled with her on the death of her brother, the Prince de Carignan."

If the queen was affected by the gossip caused by the scandalous Affair of the Necklace, she did not forget—and that very thing was perhaps the cause of the estrangement of the princess—to make sure of the emoluments to the Polignacs, always greedy for honors and especially for money.

Métra tells us that the Duc de Polignac, feeling that, because of his age (forty years), he deserved a higher position than that of colonel, had offered his resignation; but he was not the man to give up thus easily something for nothing, and must surely have had the formal promise of a compensation—if not more honorable, at least more remunerative—which tallied exactly with his ideas.

In fact the king, by vote of the State Council on October 30th, had granted to the retiring colonel the position of director-general of relays and messenger service, a position created and established solely for the need of the case.

According to the " Gazette de France," it was not until the 2d of the following August that he was sworn into office by the king.

In 1786 Madame de Lamballe did not appear at any of the court fêtes or ceremonies. Marie Antoinette received communion at Nôtre Dame, the napkin being held this time by the Duchesses de Luxembourg and de Luynes. At the birth of the Princesse Hélène Béatrix Sophie the queen sent for the Princesse de Chimay.

Certainly one would be led to suppose that the estrangement of Marie Antoinette in regard to her superintendent was the only cause for that absence, and yet we must state that the health of the princess was poor, and that it was all she could do to attend to the honors of the house of her father-in-law during the visit of the Archiduc Ferdinand, as is shown by the following detailed account, taken from the diary of the Duc de Penthièvre:

" The Archiduc Ferdinand and his wife, Marie Béatrix d'Este, arrived at Paris May 11th, under the titles of the Comte and Comtesse de Nettembourg, and left the 17th of June."

They were present at a grand dinner of more than eighty covers, given at Sceaux on Wednesday, May 24th: " My daughter-in-law dined at a small table because she was indisposed," wrote the duke.

On Thursday, May 18th, the Princesse de Conti gave a supper to the archduke and the archduchess. Monsieur de Penthièvre and Madame de Lamballe were present; " the latter, being indisposed, did not appear at table."

On Sunday, May 28th, Madame de Lamballe gave

a supper to the archduke and the archduchess in the large hall of the Hôtel de Toulouse. It seems that *Monsieur* deigned to be present.

The Duc de Penthièvre, very punctilious as to matters of form, thanked *Monsieur* on June 3d for the honor he had done the princess by his presence, and a few days after Madame de Lamballe visited them, and thanked the archduke and the archduchess for their kindness in having come to supper with her.

However this may be, to whatever causes one wishes to attribute the absence of the princess from the court ceremonies, not a paper nor a journal of that time refers to her as present, and we do not see her again at Versailles until the 24th of December, when she presented the Comtesse de Faucigny. We can merely say that, as usual, she had spent some time at her father-in-law's in company with her sister-in-law, and that all three made a visit on October 16th to Monsieur de Belleval, whose Château of Bois-Robin was in the neighborhood of Aumale. This Belleval wrote an account of the visit.

"The friendship which Monsieur le Duc de Penthièvre deigns to show me," he wrote on October 17, 1786, "is very dear to me and he never loses an opportunity to give proof of it. Every time he comes to Aumale, of which he is very fond and where he is venerated and loved beyond description, he makes a point of paying me a visit at Bois-Robin, and as I always know in advance when to expect him I am

careful not to be out of the country, and come from
Abbeville to meet him.

" His Serene Highness travels as a simple gentleman,
in a coach and four preceded by an outrider. Madame
la Duchesse d'Orléans, his daughter, often accom-
panies him and sometimes, too, Madame la Princesse
de Lamballe. It is a fête day for my children; they
always appear, and in spite of my warning want to embrace the august subjects, who shower a thousand
favors on them, as they do on all the other ordinary
visitors. His Serene Highness and the two princesses,
who arrived at Aumale the day before yesterday, did
me the honor of coming yesterday."

In August, thanks to Bachaumont, still on the watch,
we know that Madame de Lamballe went to see the
Comtesse de La Motte. We cannot say from what
motive she acted, whether by order of the queen, or
from pure curiosity. Note in what terms our precious
novelist tells us of the singular visit and the reply,
quite as extraordinary, which the princess received
from the Mother Superior.

" During the last few days Madame de Lamballe
went to visit the general hospital, with which she was
unfamiliar. Having examined it in detail she asked to
see Madame de La Motte. Sister Victoire, the Mother
Superior, made excuses and evaded the request. The
princess insisted, taking advantage of being a princess
of the blood, which fact gave her the privilege of going
everywhere. Sister Victoire, unmoved, continued to
state that it was impossible. ' But why can I not see
Madame de La Motte ? ' asked her Highness impa-

tiently.—' Madame, because to that she has not been condemned.' ''

We thought, and still think, this reply of Sister Victoire extraordinary and we try to believe that it is one of the many shafts of wit let fly from time to time by Bachaumont.

The Assembly of Notables was the chief event of 1787. Originally called together for January 29th, Parliament did not meet again until Thursday, the 22d February. This delay, unfortunate in every respect, aggravated the situation by prolonging the mental anxiety and throwing the country into great trouble.

The princess appeared but seldom at court. Her duties even to the queen suffered by her absence, which seems to have been voluntary, either from indifference or because of her health, or perhaps from some other motive of which we are ignorant.

This year, as during the preceding one, the Duchesses de Luynes and de Luxembourg again held the napkin when the queen took communion.

Bachaumont tells us of the departure of the princess for England, whither Madame de Polignac had already gone. She was charged, according to him, with an important mission to Monsieur de Calonne.

" About a fortnight ago the queen came to Versailles and before nine o'clock in the morning went to the Princesse de Lamballe's; it was supposed that there was business of great importance between her

Majesty and the superintendent.   Shortly after, it was
learned that Madame de Lamballe had started for Eng-
land.⁶ Innumerable conjectures arose as to this journey.   The general opinion at court was that the princess was going to negotiate with Monsieur de Calonne
in order to prevent him from publishing in his ' Mémoire ' articles written for private reading only, such as
the mention of loans of money sent the emperor by his
august sister, etc., etc.   Somewhat of an obstacle to this
theory was the fact that Monsieur de Calonne was in
Holland, unless it might be that the superintendent
first went into that country or for less formality had
planned with the ex-comptroller-general a meeting in
Great Britain.''

The opinion of Bachaumont, unfortunately, is not
always to be trusted ; it is far from infallible and his
accounts are very often invented.   Thus, in the present case why does he wish to make the princess undertake missions more or less agreeable, more or less delicate ?   It is so simple and so much more probable
to suppose that the journey was necessitated wholly by
the wretched state of health of the poor woman, who
was soon to be placed under treatment, according to a
letter written by her to her " dear little one "—Madame
de Lâge Volude, no doubt.   In this letter she says that
she is taking baths and staying in various country houses.
She had heard Madame Obart, who had been acting in
Paris.   This celebrated actress was playing the rôle of
Nina, but in a manner ridiculous enough to make one
die of laughter.   She took so much trouble in the

declamation that she was all in a perspiration. " Adieu, my little one; I am going to bed, in order to get up early in the morning for the baths."

Madame de Polignac also was at this time in England for her health. It was no secret that several months before she had offered her resignation to the queen:

" The resignation of Madame la Duchesse de Polignac is now a settled fact; her poor health obliges her to take the water cure in England; what epigrams and jokes on this retirement!"

The queen, with Madame Elisabeth, went to Trianon for a month.

We have no doubt that the princess went to England on account of her health, but Bachaumont, who clings to his first idea, tells us that Madame de Lamballe returned with two copies of the " Mémoires " of Monsieur de Calonne, one of which was for the queen.

Madame de Lamballe arrived in France in time to be present at the exile of the princes of the blood, whom Louis XVI., more and more dissatisfied at their conduct, more and more annoyed by their ceaseless opposition, relegated, each to his own estate.

On Tuesday, November 20th, at six o'clock in the evening the Duc d'Orléans received, through the Baron de Breteuil,[6] a letter from the king ordering him to leave for his estate of Villers-Cotterets before the meeting broke up. The prince was expressly forbidden by his sovereign to see any member of his family or his household, and the instructions of Monsieur de Breteuil in this respect were so precise that he had orders not to leave his royal prisoner. At the moment of departure, as anxious about his duty as about the orders received, Breteuil looked as if he were about to step into the carriage of the prince, which proceeding drew from the latter, already in a bad humor, the following sharp remark: " Well, get up behind!"

As always in such a case, royal severity made a victim of the Duc d'Orléans, of whom every one thought proper to complain; complaints, for that matter, which were not of long duration and which, by witty sayings and jokes, promptly became ridiculous. "They say," cried Bachaumont, "that, contrary to the rules of optics, the duke becomes larger the farther away he goes."

At the first news of the exile of her brother-in-law, Madame de Lamballe had gone to the queen to beg her to intercede with the king in his behalf, but it seems that she found her friend inflexible.

Disappointed with her cold reception the princess resolved to betake herself to Villers-Cotterets, where she found the Duchesse d'Orléans and her children. She took to heart the interests of the duke, her brother-in-law.

But let us leave politics for an instant and turn our attention to an episode in the world of letters.

On Friday, February 29th, the Théâtre Français

gave the first representation of a metrical tragedy in five acts.

The hero was a young, insignificant author.   It was known merely that his father was in the service of the Duc de Penthièvre, and that his early efforts had been furthered by some powerful aid.   Let us now explain the help received by Népomucène Lemercier, and let him tell how Florian encouraged his first literary steps.

" I never forget," said he, " that our amiable Florian was the one to give me the first encouragement in my literary vocation.   He did not scorn to mount to the third floor of the lodging of a timid scholar, whom he flattered with his praise.   He returned later to compliment me enthusiastically on my tragic essay, in the name of the Princesse de Lamballe, of whom I was the favorite godson.   Moreover, he prevailed on me to read him the tragedy of ' Méléagre,' which my fifteen and a half years excused, and which the princess hastened to have put on the stage by an order obtained from Queen Marie Antoinette."

In his reception address at the French Academy, Victor Hugo spoke of his predecessor in these eloquent terms:

" A devoted subject and almost personal servant of Louis XVI., he saw the coach pass by on the 21st of January; godson of Madame de Lamballe, he watched the pike pass on September 2d; the friend of André Chénier, he beheld the cart of the Seventh Thermidor. Thus at the age of twenty he had already seen be-

headed, in the three beings most sacred to him after his
father, royalty, beauty, and genius—deity excepted,
the three most beautiful attributes of the universe.''

At the close of the play the public demanded the
author, and the princess, after she had pressed a
motherly kiss on his brow, presented him in the hall.
But let the ancient minister of public instruction
of the monarchy of July speak. He is much better
fitted than are we to describe the early attempts of the
future Academician.

"You have spoken of 'Méléagre.' At the age of
fifteen you were writing odes, Lemercier, and trag-
edies. The queen wanted 'Méléagre' to be played.
The queen wanted to be present at the performance.
The queen wished to have the boy-poet in her box, the
better to enjoy a success of which she had no doubt,
and which, in short, answered her expectations. The
queen, finally, when the audience shouted for the
author, had him presented by Madame de Lamballe,
his godmother, to the delighted public, which, in turn,
wished the princess to embrace the young laureate.
This she did with much grace in the midst of the
applause of the audience.''

In spite of the ceremony, in spite even of his illustrious helpers, this first attempt, although it denoted a
wonderful gift on the part of the author, did not have
the desired success.

"The play," according to the "Correspondance
littéraire," "was heard to the end with attention and

good will, but it was not hard to see the feeling which inspired the listeners. The young author and his friends had the good sense to withdraw the piece after the first representation.''

Perhaps this occasion served as a step towards a reconciliation between Marie Antoinette and the princess, or perhaps the health of the latter allowed her to return to her service. We know only that she accompanied the queen to her devotions.

'' On March 29th the queen formally went to the church of the parish of Nôtre Dame, where she received communion from the bishop, the Duc de Laon, her grand chaplain; the Princesse de Lamballe, superintendent of the royal household, held the napkin.''

Six weeks later we find the princess at the baptism of her nephews, aged respectively fifteen and thirteen. And it is the '' Gazette de France '' again, always accurate in such matters, which gives us the most exact details as to the ceremony:

'' On the afternoon of Monday the 12th, the king and the queen held over the baptismal font, in the chapel of the château, the Duc de Chartres and the Duc de Montpensier. Their Majesties were accompanied by Madame, daughter of the king, Monsieur, Madame, Monseigneur the Comte d'Artois, Madame Elisabeth de France, their Royal Highnesses Monseigneur le Duc d'Angoulême and Monseigneur le Duc de Berri, the Duc and the Duchesse d'Orléans, the Prince de Condé, the Duc and the Duchesse de

Bourbon, the Duc d'Enghien, the Prince de Conti, the Duc de Penthièvre, and the Princesse de Lamballe.

" The Duc de Chartres was christened Louis Philippe, and the Duc de Montpensier Antoine Philippe.

" The baptismal service was performed by the Bishop of Melun, grand chaplain of France, in the presence of the Sire Jacob, curate of the parish of Nôtre Dame.

Two days later a reception was given to Florian in the Academy, of which he had been the laureate. For some time the Duc de Penthièvre had warmly supported this candidate. In 1785 the Duchesse de Chartres and Madame de Lamballe had solicited the position left vacant by the Abbé Millot for the friend and the guest of their house, the faithful confidant of the joys and the sorrows of their father. The princesses had been on the point of succeeding, but the Academy, resisting in the end the pressing solicitations of the two amiable women, gave the preference to the Abbé Morellet, who, because of his age and his works, seemed more worthy in their eyes to replace the preceptor of the Duc d'Enghien.

Florian was, indeed, very young to aspire to such an honor, but his patience and the ardent zeal of his patrons were not long tried, for the death of the Cardinal de Luynes permitted him, at the age of thirty-three, to realize his ambition. He held at that time the chair of the archbishop of Sens,[7] who, twenty years before, had blessed the unfortunate union of the Prince de Lamballe.

It was, without doubt, the result of chance, but the coincidence was none the less curious.

The gathering was magnificent and the presence of the Duc de Penthièvre, whose joy was boundless, of the Duchesse d'Orléans, surrounded by her children, and of Madame de Lamballe, added great brilliancy. Having paid a just tribute to the memory of his predecessor, Florian spoke in most praiseworthy terms of his illustrious patron, to whom he was modest enough to attribute his triumph.

Let us mention, in passing, an event cruel for the Duc de Penthièvre and his relatives. The Marquise de Lur-Saluces, who for some time had been attached to the house of Penthièvre, first as lady-in-waiting to the duchess, and later as governess of Mademoiselle de Penthièvre, afterwards Duchesse d'Orléans, died on the 15th of June at the Hôtel de Toulouse.

It is probable that the princess passed the close of the year 1788 in travelling with her father-in-law, still busy visiting his estates. Fortaire tells us that the Duc de Penthièvre made these journeys between 1787 and 1789.

In any case, here is one of the pretty episodes of an excursion to Tours, made by the princess and her charming companion.

" This year (1788) the princess and her young friend made a journey to the west of France.[8] They stopped, among other places, at Fontevrault, as guests of the Abbess, Madame de Pardoillau d'Antin. I record a little incident of their trip. The princess, who was travelling incognito and who desired to return promptly to the queen, had left early in the morning and had given orders to pass through Tours as quickly as possible; but the secret of her going had been so poorly kept that on arriving in front of the city she found the whole populace in holiday attire, barring the way, shouting to her ' Long live!' and compelling her to stop. The princess was affected, no doubt, by these demonstrations of affection and yet a cloud veiled the joy which she felt at such a welcome. This cloud Madame de Lâge took care to note. It was, she said, the shame of wearing short percale skirts and straw hats in the midst of the beautiful ladies covered with diamonds and plumes.

" During the journey we quickly put on rouge, and tried to improve our appearance. We made a mirror out of the coach windows, back and front, when we saw all those regiments approaching, the city troops, which in the hubbub led us as far as the archbishop's, where we had to remain to dinner."

11

CHAPTER XII.

It was during the absence of the princess that Mademoiselle Charlotte la Chassaigne made her début at the Comédie Française. She was said to be the daughter of Mademoiselle la Chassaigne and the Prince de Lamballe. Regarding her début, we quote an article from the "Journal de Paris," but we will state that on this subject the paper was in error, or at least that it was mistaken as to the age of the actress. Granted that she was really the child of the wretched prince, who died in May, 1768, she was at least twenty. But even at that time it was customary to take off a few years from débutantes, no doubt in order to make them more interesting.

"Yesterday a young and new actress, who had been neither announced nor expected, appeared in the rôle of ' Sophie ' in the ' Bienfait Anonyme.' We refer to Mademoiselle Charlotte la Chassaigne, daughter of an actress who for many years was prominent in this theatre on account of her talent and her energy. For this reason alone the débutante is interesting. Her age (she is only fifteen) and the modesty of an unannounced début entitled her to indulgence, and in the course of her acting this was justified. She received well-merited applause. The public saw her with pleasure and

eagerly encouraged her. In an age in which no one
shows more than a leaning towards talent or asks more
from a débutante, it must be admitted that intelligence,
modesty, and truth are very happy auguries. We
urge her to perfect them by work and study."

The first two months of the year 1789 we again
lose sight of the princess. Was she at Vernon with
her father-in-law ? This is probable. The poor duke
was ill and his condition prevented him from attending the court festivities. His correspondence proves
his poor health:

"VERNON, December 29, 1788.

" We were told that you were to preside over the
Order of the Church at the States-General. I would
that this news were true; although I have been troubled
the whole year with dizzy spells. For this trouble I
wear on my left arm an inconvenient blister, which
obliges me to keep out of a crowd. I shall nevertheless have the pleasure of seeing you for a few moments.
I have asked permission not to go to Versailles next
New Year's Day."

We do not again see Madame de Lamballe at court
until Holy Thursday, April 9th, when she went there
in order to accompany the queen to service.

Three days after, a new religious ceremony took
place, which concerned her more especially as it had
to do with the baptism of her niece.

" On the afternoon of the 17th, Mademoiselle, who
had been presented to the king, the queen, and the

royal family, was held over the baptismal font in the chapel of the château by their Majesties, accompanied by Monsieur, Monseigneur Comte d'Artois, Madame Elisabeth de France, their Royal Highnesses Monseigneur le Duc d'Angoulême and Monseigneur le Duc de Berry, the Duc and the Duchesse d'Orléans, the Duc de Chartres, the Duc de Montpensier, the Duchesse de Bourbon, the Duc d'Enghien, the Prince de Conti, and the Princesse de Lamballe. Mademoiselle was christened Eugénie Adélaïde Louise. The baptismal service was performed by the Cardinal de Montmorency, grand chaplain of France, in the presence of the Sire Jacob, curate of the parish of Nôtre Dame.''

The times were growing more and more troubled. No one escaped the shafts of the pamphleteers, who aimed particularly at the most prominent. Two ribald notices, specially directed against those who are of interest to us, appeared:

'' New Books.—' Traité de l'usure et de la lésine ' ('Treatise on Usury and Stinginess'), dedicated to Monsieur le Duc de C. by the Duc de P., to be had from the curate of Saint Eustache.''

Then this villainous and wicked calumny directed against our unhappy princess, who had no one to defend her:

'' Un petit Morceau de la Chemise de la Chaste Suzanne '' ('' A Small Fragment of the Chemise of the Chaste Suzanne '').
'' This was offered in vain to all the court ladies.

The Princesse de Lamballe took a part of it; it is suitable for no one but a simple bourgeoise.''

We are as yet only at the beginning of the Revolution, but there was interest in popular questions. Madame de Lamballe acted like others and went to the Petits Carmes to attend an exposition of some new theories which were advanced.

" On the 21st," we read in the " Souvenirs d'Émigration," " Madame de Lâge went with Madame de Lamballe to a meeting of the Third Estate at the Petits Carmes. A box had been arranged for Prince George de Hesse, then in Paris, and the prince hastened to make room there for the ladies. These inquisitive dames brought away from the meeting a painful impression akin to fright. On her return the countess wrote to her mother:

" Did·not we two, on foot, the princess and I, attend the meeting of the Third Estate, at the Petits Carmes, in the box of the prince, without saying a word to any one ? We drew the curtains, for those *wretches* were wholly capable of driving us away. They show very evil tendencies. We remained there three hours, but left because they were making a frightful uproar. We saw a poor gentleman arrive who had been raised to the peerage four days before. He had presented himself yesterday at the Assembly of the Nobility, where he had not been received; he came to-day to that of the Third Estate, but was sent away. I was troubled about him. In the same way Barthès was refused in both the Assembly of the Nobility and the Third Estate, but he withdrew before he was put to the vote. Monsieur de Vémerange likewise;

nowhere would they receive him, and when Monsieur de Simon wished to present himself they cried out, ' No de Simon! No de Simon!' ' ''

A few days later the States-General opened. All the princesses attended, taking seats in the galleries, which were saved for them. The attitude of the queen was so noticeable that it drew this exclamation from the Comtesse de Lâge:

" How beautiful the queen was that day! Her melancholy air added still more to her noble and dignified bearing."

In addition to this event—the prelude of many others which for more than one reason wise heads feared—the queen had good cause for melancholy. She was taking account of the situation and she saw how day by day the prestige of royalty was lessening. But, before all else, as mother, loving and passionate, the mother of a family that was dying out, had she not already the presentiment that her son, the dauphin of France, alas! was to be taken from her, that God was soon to reclaim him ?

Let us leave to the adorable Comtesse de Lâge, our invaluable chronicler, the task of showing the progress made by the dread maladv of which the poor child was to die:

" April 8th.

" This afternoon we went to see the little dauphin," she wrote. " It is heart-breaking. Such endurance, such consideration and patience go straight to the heart.

When we arrived some one was reading to him. He had had a fancy for lying on his billiard table where they had placed his mattress. My princess and I looked at it, and it occurred to us both that it resembled the mournful state bed after death. Madame de Lamballe asked him what he was reading. ‘ A very interesting period of our history, Madame: the reign of Charles VII.; there were many heroes then.’ I took the liberty of asking if Monseigneur read connectedly or merely the most striking episodes. ‘ Connectedly, Madame. I have not known them long enough to choose; besides, it all interests me.’ These were his very words. His beautiful dying eyes turned towards me as he spoke. He recognized me; he said in a low tone to the Duc d’Harcourt that they had been told of the arrival of the princess, and that she had just come. ‘ It is, I think, the lady who so greatly likes my map of the world.’ Then turning to me, ‘ This will perhaps amuse you for a moment.’ He ordered a valet to turn it around, but I will confess to you that although when I saw it on New Year’s Day I had been delighted with the perfection of the immense machine, to-day I was much more interested in listening to that dear and unfortunate child whom we saw hourly growing weaker.’

Finally, here is another very touching visit, in which Madame de Lâge gives an account of the gentleness of the child and the mother-love of Marie Antoinette.

“ The poor child,” wrote the countess, “ is so ill. . . . Everything the little one says is beyond belief; he breaks the queen’s heart; he is wonderfully tender to her. The other day he begged her to dine

with him in his room. Alas! she swallowed more
tears than bread."

The doctors had long before given their opinion
about this frail, sickly child. Every possible care
could not win against fate, and the 4th of the following June he, who one day would have worn the crown,
passed away at Meudon. The fatal news spread
rapidly. Some sincere tears were shed, but in silence,
almost in secret. Although they dared not pity the
queen openly, great and small, noble and plebeian,
with common accord wept at the grief of the mother.

The princess was among the first to reach Meudon,
in company with the countess, who, some days after,
described to her mother the sad visit:

" The coffin of Monsieur le Dauphin was open. I
was at Meudon with the princess, to sprinkle him with
holy water. Everything was white and silver and in
the room in which he lay the light was brighter than
anything I had ever seen. His crown, his sword, and
his orders lay on the small coffin covered with silver
cloth, and two rows of monks on each side prayed
continually, day and night."

The Duc de Normandie was at once declared dauphin
by the king and the court went into mourning for two
months and a half. But terrible events were not slow
in obliterating the memory of this domestic sorrow.
The populace took possession of the Bastille.[1] Three
days later this same populace danced on the still smoking ruins of the State prison.

Information concerning the Princesse de Lamballe during these events is lacking. She was not in Paris and was probably with the Duc de Penthièvre, whom ill health still kept away from court.

"Paris, July 4, 1789.

"I am only passing through here, whence I send this letter. My health, which is still poor, compels me to keep away from a crowd. My Æsculapius wanted to send me to Italy, thinking that a warmer climate might help me."

This letter, written a few days before July 14th, evidently proves the absence of the duke. Furthermore, we know that in the month of August the princess was travelling in Switzerland with her faithful companion, but without her father-in-law, who wrote on February 26, 1790:

"My intended journey to Rome is of the same nature as my reported journey to Switzerland last autumn. . . ."

Fortunately, Fortaire, who kept a diary of the facts and engagements of his master, and who, on the whole, is exact, tells us that Madame de Lamballe came to her father-in-law at Aumale, the 2d of September, to go again to Eu, where she spent a month.

At this time, as dangers began to increase on all sides, examples of devotion became more and more rare. A sort of madness seized many, and turned from the throne those who were its natural support, and who should never have deserted the royal family.

The Comte d'Artois, giving the first example of desertion, thought he ought to go away, and left the court to face dangers of every kind.

Some time after, the Comtesse d'Artois also left. Her departure was variously interpreted.

" To-day," we read in the " Journal de Versailles," " Madame la Comtesse d'Artois with a suite of about thirty has left to join her husband at Turin. She announces her return for next spring, but it is not supposed that it will take place so soon. All the silver-ware, the horses, and the carriages of the prince have been sold and converted into money. He wishes also to dispose of the superb library which he bought from Monsieur de Paulmy for six hundred thousand livres. We do not know how France will regard this prince who converts into money and carries into a strange country, not only his revenues, which are, in part, the sweat of the people, but the stocks he possesses in the kingdom.

" It is reported that Bagatelle is for sale. They add that the officers of the prince were merely thanked, and received no kind of remuneration. This is not the way to preserve people's good opinion or to repair mistakes. ' ’

A departure still more to be censured was that of Madame de Polignac. This woman, whom the queen had overwhelmed with most signal favors, who had lived on absolutely intimate terms with her, did not hesitate to desert her friend the moment she felt her own safety at stake. Appointed governess of the children of France in 1782, she had been sworn in November 3d, but some time previous, under the pretext of the constant care demanded by her failing health, she had, merely to gain her liberty up to a certain point, offered her resignation, which she knew would be refused. In her generosity or her blindness, and to keep for a friend, whose pressing need of money she well knew, the salary of her position, Marie Antoinette, they said, had declared herself willing to undertake the education of the princes. This *modus vivendi* had been readily accepted and the duchess would certainly not have thought of changing it had it not been for circumstances. The day after the taking of the Bastille she again offered her resignation, which, formally expressed this time, was finally accepted, the 16th of July.

Times had greatly changed. Formerly if a position became vacant, either from a resignation or death, at once every one sought it, exerted himself to obtain it, intrigued, and put forward his claims to it. But now it was not so. The competitors could be counted, and yet the king had the rare good fortune to place over his children a woman of great merit, full of noble sentiments. The Marquise de Tourzel, although ignorant of none of its dangers, accepted, without fear, the position of governess, and held it to the end, giving the royal family marks of a disinterestedness, a courage, and a devotion without limit. Presented to the queen soon after her appointment, Madame de Tourzel was sworn in August 2d.

During the whole of September, which she spent at Eu with her brother-in-law, sad memories of the past must have haunted the mind of Madame de Lamballe. Already singularly distressed and broken-hearted at the waning popularity of Versailles, the news from court, which she did not fail to receive, could not but augment her scorn for the mob of courtiers. How fortunate, then, she must have thought herself to have lived for so long apart from that class which in happier times was deterred neither by acts of baseness nor by the most degrading humiliations. In our opinion, there is no need to seek for other causes for her temporary estrangement. The princess rose in so great indignation at the flight of Madame de Polignac, who had left without any intention of returning, and so bitterly criticised the conduct of certain other persons, that not for one instant can a similar accusation be brought against her. Her promptness in coming to the humiliated royal family is sufficient proof of this.

A courier arrived at the Château d'Eu on October 7th, at nine o'clock in the evening, and brought to the Duc de Penthièvre and to Madame de Lamballe the news of what had happened at Versailles, October 5th and 6th, and of the return of the king and his family to the Tuileries.

The first moment of stupefaction over, the princess, whose one idea was to leave, said, still according to Fortaire: "Oh, papa, what a horrible thing! I must start at once."

Such feelings were too strongly shared by the duke for him not to encourage them in her. His health alone prevented him from leaving at once, and his departure did not take place until the following day.

About two hours after the arrival of the news, in a frightful storm and on the darkest of nights, accompanied by a single maid and by one of the duke's gentlemen, Madame de Lamballe was rolling along towards Paris.

Many a woman would have been overcome by fear. The princess, on the contrary, had long before planned her line of action, which was suggested by the feelings of her heart, and hastened to the queen, of whose peril only she now thought. It seems that, by a very natural sentiment, her affection increased as her friend became more and more deserted and as she saw her abandoned. What a contrast! In the midst of all these desertions the frivolous woman, considered until then as weak, the woman of pleasure parties, the life and the soul of balls and sleighing parties—in short, the companion of Trianon—through her unselfishness became heroic. In spite of all possible haste, the princess was unable to reach Paris before late in the evening of October 8th.

Those two October days, so fatal to royalty, showed the people how far insolence could lead them. Nevertheless, those men and women who had come to Versailles to protest against the scarcity of bread acted without premeditation. The court was so ill informed as to their coming that Marie Antoinette was at Trianon, absolutely ignorant of what was taking place, while Louis XVI. was quietly hunting in the suburbs. Thus there had been no warning of the event, near as it was.

As further proof of this, there is a joint letter which was addressed to the princess by the king, the queen, and Madame Elisabeth. The first seven lines are in the king's handwriting, the seventeen following in the queen's, and those remaining in that of Madame Elisabeth.

Louis XVI. was sending to Madame de Lamballe some papers for which the Duc de Penthièvre had asked. Marie Antoinette was begging that she would go at once with Madame Elisabeth to the gardens at Trianon, which Monsieur de Jussieu had come to visit, and where she was making new and extensive plantations. "We are quiet enough here for the present," she continued; "the bourgeois and the good people are kindly disposed towards us."

CHAPTER XIII

The royal family had now for good or bad been installed two days in the Tuileries. The " Gazette de France,"[1] mute as to the 5th and 6th of October, deigns to come out of its enforced silence and tells us this fact:

" Last Tuesday " (October 6th), it says, " the king arrived in Paris with the queen, the dauphin, Madame, Madame Elisabeth, Monsieur and Madame."

The journal carefully refrains from making the smallest comment.

On her arrival at the Tuileries Madame de Lamballe was struck by the consternation depicted on every face, and by the universal confusion. In a short time she learned of the terrible events which had just taken place, and heard with surprise, mingled with indignation and anger, through what a humiliating ordeal the royal family had passed. The queen threw herself weeping into her arms, told her how she had been insulted, and what fears she had for the future.

In order that she might the more readily attend to the duties of her service and devote herself wholly to the queen and the royal family, Madame de Lamballe at once settled in the Pavillon de Flore, which she did not leave, except for short visits to her estates at Passy or to her father-in-law, who, Fortaire tells us, was established until the beginning of 1790 on his property of Châteauneuf-sur-Loire.

It was no doubt during one of these absences, necessitated by the precarious condition of the Duc de Penthièvre, that Marie Antoinette addressed to the amiable and devoted princess the following letter, tenderly reproaching her about her health, of which, so great was her desire to please and to be loved, she did not take enough care:

"To-day, November 9th.

"You will not take care of your health, and this troubles me. See, my dear Lamballe, I shall be angry with you in earnest. My health is tolerably good, that of my children excellent; they are almost continually with me, and occupy me much of the time; the dauphin is easier to manage; he no longer has those attacks of anger. My daughter is very sweet. The poor little thing wants to see you. . . . I am sad and greatly worried at the condition of affairs, although the outlook seems to be somewhat better; but one cannot trust anything, for I see even in our friends only a weakness which cannot hold out against the slightest violence of the wicked."

Meanwhile a report was spread abroad that the reserve of the treasury was completely exhausted. This fatal error, due partly to foolish extravagance combined with a deplorable management of the finances, although long foreseen by the wisest heads, did not fail to cause serious alarm. On account of the lack of credit, it was necessary to resort to subterfuges to meet the daily needs.

In September, Parliament stated that, for the time being at least, it was able to continue payments.

It was a question of coming to the aid of the country by "patriotic gifts."

Always animated by the highest sentiments, always eager to set a good example, the Duc de Penthièvre was one of the first to conform to the suggestion, and, on October 3d, sent to the mint his silver plate, amounting to eighteen hundred and forty-eight marks, sixteen deniers, and twelve grains.

The princess did not send hers until a month later (November 3d), and her gift, although more modest, was, nevertheless, quite important, since it amounted to six hundred and twenty-five marks, three ounces, sixteen deniers, and twelve grains. At this point we must state that Madame de Lamballe was somewhat reluctant and decided to offer her plate only after having held with Monsieur Toscan, her treasurer, an important correspondence in which she recommended him to find out, before giving up anything, what her brother-in-law the Duc d'Orléans was going to do. This letter, no doubt written in September, bears a seal of red wax, on which is a tree with these words: "*Plutôt mourir que changer*" (die rather than change).

"To-day, the 25th.

"My brother-in-law, after the edict of the council, is sending a courier to give orders to take his silver plate to the mint. You must say to Emy to collect all I own, which you will have valued by Auguste and taken to the mint, of course under the conditions stated in the decree of the council. You will first find out from Monsieur Villot, to whom my brother-in-law gives his orders, what Monsieur le Duc d'Orléans intends to do about this. You will give only as much of my plate as my papa gave of his. Meanwhile you will have it put away, so that it may not appear again in my rooms. It goes without saying that none of the plates or spoons, nor the two or three silver pans which I ordered for the kitchen when I was poisoned, shall be included in the plate taken to the mint. I know all that you can write about my making away with my property, but enough has been said about the matter; it is not necessary to add anything further. The poorer I am, the more necessary it is to show what my position is under the present circumstances; moreover, this sacrifice will not be the most painful of all those which I shall have to make, if my fortune lessens, as I expect it will. When I go to Paris I shall see about getting myself a service of English earthenware. You will let me know what Monsieur Villot says to you and the estimate of my plate."

A few days later, she again wrote (dated October 1st) for an exact inventory of the contents of her house.

" I cannot," said she, " at present explain my questions about the inventory of my house, for it would be too long for Émile. Besides, as it is necessary for Monsieur d'Yanville to have his package, it will be better to wait. I need, also, the old inventories of Monsieur Loques's time, which I have not with me.

So, until my return, patience, although you have none too much. . . .''

The wretched woman, becoming frightened, countermanded the order for her plate and ended by saying that she was going to practise economy and to reform the management of her house; '' unfortunately for my servants,'' she adds.

Here are further details which show her state of mind. She sacrificed Passy, which she rented furnished. Then she recommended to Toscan the greatest secrecy concerning her plans.

Her treasurer sent her his accounts and, after examining them, the princess tells him of some errors.

'' To-day, the 23d.

'' You have made a mistake in the salary of the surgeon. You give it as twelve hundred and it is only one hundred. Monsieur Saiffert ought to know about the pensions since he has the brevet. . . .

'' Have you given Monsieur Loques ten louis for the pension of my nurse at Turin, which I told you to pay and which I mentioned to my sister ?

'' Tell Mademoiselle Mertins that she had me subscribe for Monsieur Gorsas and not for the ' Courier Français.' ''

'' To-day, the 21st.

'' . . . If the wall had not fallen,'' she writes again to Monsieur Toscan, '' nothing would have been further from my intention than to have you repair Passy, especially as I knew beforehand that it would be expensive.

" However, I hope the cost will be reasonable when all is finished. I want nothing paid until all the accounts have been collected and examined by me. I also wish —— —— to make an estimate as to the cost of my drawing-room. I shall decide nothing as yet in regard to the livery of my servants; for the present those whose duties bring them near me are in uniform, and this must suffice for a time; as there are no longer liveries, neither vests nor trousers need be furnished. There will be a wholly different order of things in future.

" I am charmed that the house at Passy is destroyed, but you must have seen from the letter I sent you that I never gave permission, and that I never want it given without my consent. Send me the estimate of my drawing-room, and that which Monsieur L—— made of my flower garden."

In spite of the words of Fortaire, in which now and then we find some slight errors, the Duc de Penthièvre was at Amboise early in the year 1790. The poor prince was still ill with asthma and required great care and attention. And yet, weak as he was, so great was his wish to do his duty that he strove in spite of his invalidism to carry out his obligations. In spite of his suffering, in spite of the difficulty he had in walking, he wished to pay his respects to the king and the royal family. This is what he says on this subject.

"AMBOISE, January 19, 1790.

" No one could be more sensitive than I," he writes to the Cardinal de Bernis, " of the new proofs of interest which your Eminence is kind enough to show me on the new year. . . . My health has obliged me to ask the king to allow me to spend the winter on the estates I have bought on the banks of the Loire. I have very troublesome attacks of dizziness, which my physicians say are not dangerous, but which prevent my going into society. I have not come to the place whence I am writing this letter without having paid my respects to their Majesties at the Tuileries."

Were we not right in saying that the excellent prince, although living in retirement, nevertheless fulfilled all the duties of his position—namely, those demanded by his birth—as well as all those of a French citizen?

"To-morrow," he wrote from Amboise the 26th of February, 1790, to his friend and confidant the Cardinal de Bernis, " I shall take the civic oath, before the municipality of the town of Amboise, the castle of which I am occupying. This house is very poorly decorated in comparison with Chanteloup, but the view from it is superb. I will send at once the report of my taking the oath in the district of Saint Honoré, within the limits of which is the Hôtel de Toulouse. The Commune of Paris seems to set some value on this step of mine. I think I ought to do it, as the king has accepted the new constitution, and as Monsieur has taken the oath they desire of me. I have given an account to his Majesty, as he prescribed, of the course I am following."

The enforced absence of the Princesse de Lamballe,

at this time with the Duc de Penthièvre, weighed heavily on her. She was anxious about the position of the queen, but Marie Antoinette, without wholly hiding the truth from her, reassured her as much as possible.

"Dear heart," she wrote the 4th of March, "present circumstances occupy my thoughts so constantly that I have not seemed very appreciative of your letter and your sweet friendship. You are of those whose hearts never change and whom misfortune renders still more affectionate." Then she continues: "You know everything that is taking place here. It is impossible to go out without being insulted a dozen times in an hour, so I walk no more and sometimes I stay in my room for days without thinking of a change."

Once settled in the Tuileries, even suitably, as Madame Campan says, each member of the royal family, in so far as was possible, resumed his ordinary habits.

The king continued to hunt and to make almost daily entries in his diary, with a calmness and serenity in which it would be hard to believe if one did not read the facts written in his own handwriting. One example will suffice to show us how indifferently he speaks of the events of October and of the return of himself and his family to Paris. His mild temperament must have prevented him from realizing the gravity of his position.

"Oct. 5th, went shooting near the gate of Châtillon; killed eighty-one head; interrupted by events;

went and came on horseback.—6th, left for Paris at half-past twelve, visited the Hôtel de Ville, supped and slept at the Tuileries.—7th, nothing; my aunts come to dine.—8th, nothing. . . .''

The queen, on the contrary, kept in touch with affairs and was so preoccupied that she could not read, and spent all her time working on tapestry. On her return to Paris Madame de Lamballe, who probably received orders to that effect, for she had no such inclination, gave some brilliant fêtes in her private apartments. At first the queen assiduously attended them, but soon ceased going, '' evidently convinced,'' says Madame Campan, '' that her position did not permit her to appear at large gatherings.''

The chief lady-in-waiting might also have said that the news of the death of the queen's brother had just reached Paris and that the court was going into mourning for two months.

'' To-day, Friday, March 19th,'' we read in the '' Journal de Paris,'' '' the court will assume mourning for two months on account of the death of Joseph II., Emperor of Germany, King of Hungary and Bohemia, Sovereign of the Austrian States, born March 13, 1741, died at Vienna, the 20th of last February, in the forty-ninth year of his age. His Majesty will wear violet.

'' First period, from March 19th to April 18th inclusive, men will wear complete black cloth suits with buttons, sleeves with single fringe, bronze buckles and swords.

" Women will wear woollen gowns trimmed with bunting or black crape, crape bonnet (the *coëffe* for nine days only), gloves, black fans and hose, and bronze buckles. ''

Although the queen felt neither great grief nor intense regret, nevertheless it was good taste for her not to appear at the fêtes, which, for that matter, were not official, even after the expiration of the term of mourning adopted by the court. This, to our mind, was probably the reason, and no doubt the only one, which caused Marie Antoinette to give up the gatherings at the superintendent's.

Events hastened on. Every day a new pamphlet appeared, the more willingly received by the public as it attacked more prominent personages, and as its violence was tuned to the passions of the moment.

Madame de Lamballe was too easy a prey to escape their attacks.

We shall be satisfied to quote two of the best known:

" ' La Galerie des Dames françaises. London, 1790,' and the ' Imitateurs de Charles IX., ou Les Conspirateurs foudroyés. A prose play in five acts, with five characters, by the editor of the Vêpres Siciliennes and of the Massacre of Saint Bartholomew. Paris. From the Press of the Clergy and the Nobility. 1790.' "

The first of these libels, which had for epigraph this passage from Virgil:

Nullo discrimine habebo, Tros Ratulusve fuat,"

was, they said, written by the Marquis de Luchet. It was a violent diatribe against the best-known women. Madame Necker appeared in it under the name of " Statira," her daughter under that of " Marthésie "; the Comtesse de Beauharnais became " Corylla "; Madame Lebrun, " Charites "; the Comtesse Diane de Polignac, " Tenesis "; the Marquise de Sillery, " Polixène "; Madame Denis, " Fulvia "; Madame de Montesson, " Olympe "; Madame du Barry, " Elmire." The pseudonym of the princess was " Balzais."

The second, attributed to Gabriel Brizard, was no less violent than the first. The same allusions, often the same errors. One of the figures goes so far as to represent the princess on the knees of Marie Antoinette.

Madame de Lamballe left early in August to join the Duc de Penthièvre, and returned to Paris the end of November. But fortunately for us, thanks to the information of Fortaire, we can follow her, step by step, during this long absence. She spent a month at Amboise; then, in October, while her father-in-law was at Fontevrault with his cousin Madame de Pardaillan, she went to Maine to visit the Marquis de Clermont-Gallerande, a friend of long standing and of sure judgment, whom she liked to consult in times of doubt and whom later she appointed one of the executors of her will.

Fortaire, who is sometimes tedious because of his

attention to details, tells us of the brilliant reception which the Tourangeaux gave her, and the words of gratitude she addressed on this subject to her father-in-law. It is most important to know that she found the Duchesse d'Orléans at Amboise, that later the two princesses accompanied the Duc to Châteauneuf, and that they did not return to Paris before November 28th. The Duc de Penthièvre remained there only a few days, leaving December 4th for Eu, where according to the same author the Duchesse d'Orléans joined him, February 10, 1791, to leave him no more.

We must explain why and how the Duchesse d'Orléans went to live with her father-in-law. Many seeing that she thus failed in her duties as wife and mother, think themselves authorized to throw out insinuations against her, and, although recognizing her noble devotion to her father, seem to blame her for being away from her family at such a time.

What was there left for the unfortunate mother to do at the Palais Royal? To watch over her children, to surround them with maternal care, to guide their education. But had they not been placed in charge of a governess who intended neither to give up her position nor to have her duties shared by any one—that Madame de Genlis, who was said, rightly or wrongly, to have dominated completely the Duc d'Orléans, and to have the most pernicious influence over him? Could she reasonably continue to occupy the Palais

Royal and to be daily exposed to insults even in her own family ?

Assuredly not. The private life of the one who some time after added to his name that of " Égalité," must have hurt her as much as his political conduct.

If their separation was arranged privately the division of money matters was done officially.

" Monsieur and Madame d'Orléans," we read in the " Journal de Paris," " wishing to keep their accounts in order, inform all the merchants and salesmen that from the 6th of the present month of January, 1791, they will buy only for cash; that, consequently, no one can claim the price of merchandise furnished to the credit of Monsieur and Madame d'Orléans."

Already, a year before, the report of a separation had attained sufficient publicity to arouse the interested parties, or rather the interested party, to make a correction in the newspapers.

Here is a curious letter, taken from the " Journal de Paris " dated December 13, 1789:

" PALAIS ROYAL, December 12, 1789.

" *To the Editors of the ' Journal' :*

" It is with confidence, gentlemen, that I have the honor of addressing you to beg you, in rendering homage to truth, to aid me in refuting a statement as false as it is calumnious, which was boldly published by the ' Gazetier de Leyde ' in the supplement No. 97, concerning the assumed separation of the property of her Serene Highness Madame la Duchesse d'Orléans from that of his Serene Highness Monsieur le Duc d'Orléans. This was recently granted, it said, as a result of the disorder of the business affairs of this prince. I am authorized, gentlemen, by the princess to refute formally this fresh calumny and to beg you to make known, through the medium of your paper, that the alleged cause for a separation is as groundless as the reported result, and that her Serene Highness signed the day before yesterday an authentic act, in presence of Messieurs Rouen and Brichard, notaries at Paris, whose papers were left with the latter; by which act Madame la Duchesse d'Orléans, to speak the absolute truth, declared that she and the prince, her husband, held their property in common, and that she had filed no petition for a division of said property.

(Signed) " THE COMTE DE LA TOUCHE, " *Chancellor of his Serene Highness Monseigneur le Duc d'Orléans.*"

The publicity given the affair by this paper was not found sufficient, since, two days later, the " Journal Général de la Cour et de la Ville," in No. 88, dated Tuesday, December 15, 1789, published a similar article under the heading " Important News."

The fact this time is undeniable and the memoirs of the times confirm it by adding some comments very little in sympathy with the one guilty party.

" The conduct of Monsieur le Duc d'Orléans," said Madame de Tourzel, " opened the eyes of Madame la Duchesse. She demanded and justly obtained a division of property, and then went to stay with Monsieur le Duc de Penthièvre, her father."

And the good Madame de Tourzel even adds a reflection to which we should not have dared to give expression, it seems to us so serious.

"Madame de Lamballe," she continues, "whom he accused of having urged the separation, was from this time the object of his hatred. This fact, they say, was one of the causes of the unfortunate end of the unhappy princess."

Father Lenfant also refers to this separation in his letter of April 16, 1791. We have voluntarily insisted on this point, as we have proved that only the constant presence of Madame de Genlis with her children determined the Duchesse d'Orléans to abandon them. And it should be made known that even under the circumstances the poor victim of such shameful treatment did not cease for a single instant, in spite of her absence, to love her family. This is shown by the following letter, written on the day after the Massacre of September:

"Your attention touches me deeply. You share, I am sure, my own indignation and my father's, and you may imagine the affliction in which we are plunged. All the circumstances of this death tear my soul. We are heartbroken over it. To my grief is added my *maternal anxiety.*"

A few days before the return of Madame de Lamballe the "Journal Général de la Cour et de la Ville," in its edition of Thursday, November 8, 1790, pub-

lished a letter addressed to its editors, relating to the recent duel of Charles Lameth and the Duc de Castries.

The writer, concealing his identity under the initials
F. B., said:

"That Mesdames de B——, la Ch——, Saint
Ch——, Des——, Lamba——, the heroines of the
democracy, who, they say, find that the Revolution
has cost very little blood, have been in despair, does
not surprise me, . . ." etc.

The friends of the princess were annoyed at such
unfortunate and imprudent remarks, and in order that
such an allegation should be at once refuted, took
steps against the paper.

This refutation, as complete as the most particular
could desire, appeared the following day.

"We hasten to explain to the public," we read in
the edition of Friday, November 19th, "that the person referred to in yesterday's paper by the letters *Lamba*
is not Madame la Princesse de Lamballe, who takes no
part in public affairs beyond desiring the happiness of
the king and the tranquillity of the public."

CHAPTER XIV

It is difficult, not to say impossible, to follow Madame de Lamballe, step by step, during the first months of 1791. Doubtless she was with the royal family, giving them the greater part of her time, whenever the health of her father-in-law did not require her with him; but we have consulted the " Gazette de France " in vain in regard to this year, as in regard to the preceding one. We have been unable to find mention of the princess. Apart from the religious ceremonies in which the court shared and about which this paper continues to inform us, never was her reserve, no doubt out of devotion to the royal family, more apparent; never was her silence regarding the private life of the château more absolute. Determined as we are not to trust to mere conjectures, let us now give a summary of the events which probably took place under the eyes of Madame de Lamballe. We shall hasten, we take pains to state, to bring back the princess as soon as possible upon the scene. For this, important documents or authentic historians will furnish us the means. The Tuileries had assumed a lugubrious aspect. No more coming and going of visitors anxious to pay court; no more fêtes; everywhere reigned an abnormal calm. It seemed as if a resolution had been taken to bring the smallest word and act of the king and his family to the attention of the people. The populace were filled with restlessness and agitation, waiting almost continually at a certain distance from the royal residence, as if forming a sort of sanitary cordon around a plague-stricken community.

In the château not a day passed that some new danger was not feared, some snare laid by ever-increasing hatred, which the faithful and zealous friends hoped to escape. Everywhere they were on the alert, watching, planning. Every one foresaw the coming events.

In the midst of these agitations, which her nervous nature strongly resented, Madame de Lamballe had at least the consolation, in the early part of February, of hearing of the arrival of her sister-in-law at Eu. Feeling sure that the tenderest care would surround the Duc de Penthièvre, and that the Duchesse d'Orléans would devote her life to the vacillating health of this good prince, Madame de Lamballe could at last devote herself without reservation to the royal family, which was more than ever in need of attention. The aunts of the king, according to the captious words of Delessart to his colleague Duportail, had for some time '' formed a plan to travel in Italy.'' The date for the departure of the daughters of Louis XV. was changed from the 15th to the 25th, in order that they might perhaps profit by the first favorable opportunity to baffle the surveillance of which they may have been the object, and thus avoid being detained at the last moment on some trifling pretence.

" February 19th, departure of my aunts at ten o'clock in the evening." This is all that Louis XVI. wrote in his diary. These constant announcements of " journeys " troubled the Parisians, who realized the effect they might produce and wished to put a stop to them. To-day they would go to Bellevue, to-morrow to the Luxembourg, to make sure that Monsieur was among them; afterwards the Tuileries would receive a visit from them, and this time they would not leave until they were sure that the dauphin had not been sent away secretly, as report said. Finally—and this was more serious—they went to Vincennes, with the fixed intention of destroying the donjon, in which it was rumored means of defence had been accumulated.

This restlessness did not seem to affect the king, who merely referred to it in these terms:

" February 22d, nothing; populace rushed to the Luxembourg.—24th, nothing; populace rushed to the Tuileries.—28th, nothing; populace rushed to Vincennes and the Tuileries."

Nevertheless, during almost the whole of March he was ill, and on the 18th there was a celebration of a *Te Deum* for his convalescence. The report of the section of the Gravilliers on this date mentions the deputation which was present.

On the 2d of April Mirabeau died. It was a public loss. The queen herself could not fail to regret

this ardent champion, whom Madame Campan desig-
nates as a " mercenary democrat " and a " venal royalist."

His sudden death, after only two days of illness
they said, gave rise to the most unfortunate stories
and the blackest hypotheses. The term " poison " was
uttered and was, unfortunately, at once accepted by the
public. This report, which the hesitation and evasive
replies of Vicq d'Azyr had helped not a little to
strengthen, was openly and energetically contested by
Cabanis, the confidant and the friend, much more
than the physician, of Mirabeau. Nevertheless, in
spite of the efforts and the formal denials of the doctor,
the most sensational version spread abroad.

As soon as the civil constitution of the clergy was
voted on, the king, in order to be more master of his
actions, Madame de Tourzel tells us, decided to spend
the two weeks of Easter at Saint Cloud.

At the close of mass the royal family stepped into
the carriages, but the national guard prevented them
from leaving. In vain the king protested, claiming for
himself the liberty he had given to the country; nothing could alter the determination of the militia. The
king had to give up his plan.

" April 18th.—We were prevented from leaving for
Saint Cloud at half-past one o'clock," wrote the unfortunate Louis XVI. in his diary.

It was, no doubt, from this time on that the idea

of leaving Paris came into the king's mind; but, as always when he had to decide anything important, he lost precious moments in hesitation and indecision. The whole of May and the first part of June were spent in combining plans and making arrangements which finally were found poor or, at all ·events, impracticable. The departure, originally fixed for Sunday evening, June 20th, was postponed until the evening of the 21st, on account of the mother of a serving woman whom because of her relations with La Fayette they dared not trust. The following day they started after a slight delay, augmented still more by various incidents on the road. Then an inconceivable blunder which well illustrates the madness, or rather the inexperience, of very devoted friends to whom the king had entrusted his safety and that of his family, occurred. They neglected to inform the troops stationed to protect the royal carriages, so that the regiments, having waited in vain without orders, believed the journey given up or deferred, and in order not to arouse needless suspicion, went back as quickly as possible to their cantonments.

We shall now return to the princess, whom we shall scarcely leave again during the whole of her stay abroad.

It is absolutely certain that Madame de Lamballe had in no way been informed of the events which were taking place at court about her. Up to the last moment nothing in the attitude of the queen had caused

her to suspect the preparations for flight, and the first
inkling she had was a farewell, perhaps more affectionate than usual, from Marie Antoinette, as they left
the card-table Sunday evening, June 20th.

The Marquis de Clermont-Gallerande gives us, on
this point, the most detailed information:

" The Sunday previous to the departure of the queen,
this princess on leaving her game told Madame de
Lamballe to go to the country during the week, and
taking her by the hand, said adieu. The farewell,
uttered in a more tender tone than usual, struck the
princess so that, on returning to her apartments, she
told me of it. As no one had spoken of the departure
of the king we did not pay much attention to the
matter."

In fact, the princess was so little informed of the
plans of the flight of the royal family that the queen's
courier surprised her at midnight in her house at Passy.
Careful to avoid showing the slightest emotion or
anxiety, without losing her head she hastened to make
her preparations and to give her final orders. At one
o'clock she stepped into a post-chaise, accompanied by
Mesdames de Ginestous and de Lâge, her ladies-in-
waiting, and drove to her father-in-law, having spread
among her household to divert suspicion the report that
the health of Monsieur de Penthièvre was the sole
cause of so sudden a decision.

The journey was made under the best possible conditions, for the same day at six o'clock in the evening

a carriage covered with dust stopped before the modest lodging in Aumale which the Duc de Penthièvre usually occupied. Fortaire, from whom we borrow these details, was the first to recognize Madame de Lamballe and hastened to inform the prince and prepare him for the unexpected visit.

The duke, followed by the Duchesse d'Orléans, came to meet his daughter-in-law. Madame de Lamballe at once made them understand that she must speak to them alone. " Soon after, they went into a private room, the door of which they locked," adds the faithful servant.

While the princess was informing her relatives of the flight of the king, and begging them to accompany her, the ladies of the suite descended to recruit their strength as quickly as possible. Finally the door opened and Fortaire perceived the duke writing and giving orders, while the Duchesse d'Orléans wept, and madame counted the moments, urging their flight and saying to him : " I beg you to double your orders if possible; in a quarter of an hour we must be on our way."

Fresh horses were harnessed, and when the ladies stepped into the carriages Madame de Lamballe said good-by as calmly as if it were merely a question of a few days' separation. So much so, that Fortaire admits ingenuously that he was deceived by it. But the good man, naturally inquisitive, was soon disabused, and is careful to tell us that his curiosity, a characteristic peculiar to him, made him find out at once the princess's change of route.

On leaving Aumale, the carriage took the road to Abbeville.

Scarcely recovered from the surprise which this news caused him and still trying to explain the reason for the short stay of Madame de Lamballe, her sudden arrival and her hasty departure, Fortaire received from the Duc de Penthièvre the order to prepare everything for a return to Eu the following day.

The carriage of the princess continued on its way and arrived at Boulogne in hot haste on the 22d. Madame de Lamballe at once set out in search of a ship about to sail. Her first step was successful, facilitated as it was by the lieutenant of the Admiralty, for whom, the previous evening, her father-in-law had given her a letter of introduction.

An English vessel bound for Dover was then in port. The princess made terms with the captain and embarked at once, having taken care, in order to hasten her departure, to have provisions brought and to encourage the work of the sailors by her presence.

The coast of France was already presenting to the eyes of our fugitives nothing but uncertain outlines when the sound of a cannon, fired from Boulogne, warned them of the danger in which they had placed themselves by delaying their departure.

The following day they landed at Dover and at once reëmbarked for Ostend, which they reached the 26th. From there they set out for Brussels, where the wretched travellers, worn out with fatigue, were finally able to enjoy a few days' rest. Monsieur de Fersen, one of the chief actors in the journey of Varennes, dined in that town with the princess and, in passing, notes the conversation he had with her.

" The 6th of July," he writes, " dined and spent the evening with Sullivan; talked nonsense and gossip with Madame de Lamballe."

Apparently he was not indulgent and seems to have attached no value to the words of the princess.

Finally, having made up her mind to stay at Aix-la-Chapelle, the princess left Brussels the 10th and reached the end of her journey July 11th. Having decided on the Rue Saint Jacques, Maison Schleiden, with Mesdames de Ginestous and de Lâge, the princess inscribed herself under the name of the Comtesse d'Amboise. But the apartment was probably neither sufficiently large nor comfortable, and a few days later she settled permanently in more commodious apartments on the Comphausbad, which Madame de Lâge has described for us.

The small circle, already enlarged by the Marquise de Las Cases and the Comte de Ginestous, was increased still more by the Marquise de Brunoy. The house was too small to accommodate the new arrivals, and Mesdames de Lâge and de Las Cases were obliged to go next door to Houpers *à la Botte*, also on the Comphausbad.

The 26th of June the royal family returned to Paris

and that same day the " Chronique de Paris " and the
next day the " Journal de la Ville et de la Cour "
published the following article:

" Madame de Lamballe has left for England.   It is
said she sailed from Montreuil."

To our mind, this note was inserted without any
evil intent or any definite object of harming the princess.   Insignificant as it may seem at first glance,
since the report of her trip to England, supposedly
on a secret mission, was public property, it did not
pass unnoticed and a new cause, perhaps the most
serious, was furnished for the accusations of which the
unfortunate woman was the target.   These were made
by the journalist Carra, who was in the pay of the ex-
Capuchin Chabot and his followers.

In going abroad, Madame de Lamballe had merely
obeyed the formal injunction of the queen.   Could
she have acted otherwise to Marie Antoinette, who
at the last hour had told her of her departure, and had
appointed a rendezvous at Montmédy ?   But no sooner
did she know of the arrest at Varennes and the return
of the royal family to the Tuileries, than her energy for-
sook her entirely and she knew not what course to
follow.   Should she return to Paris ?   Her friends advised her to do so, counting on her influence and her
kindness to help restore them to the favor of the king,
whom they had so prematurely abandoned.

Should she go to Turin to her family ?   This decision, by far the wisest, was strongly urged by her spoiled child, Madame de Lâge. There, in the midst of her relatives, surrounded by the affection of her sisters, she probably would never have returned to France.

However, the princess could not make up her mind to follow this last suggestion. Her hesitation, described with much animation by Madame de Lâge as greater than ever, kept her where she was, waiting for events.

Thanks to the correspondence of the countess, carefully preserved by her family, we are able to initiate the reader into the house on the Comphausbad occupied by Madame de Lamballe and her ladies. Without being luxurious, and leaving much to be desired in the way of comforts, the apartment was situated in the most elegant quarter of the city. Furthermore, the princess had the great advantage of being near her friends, the Marquis de Clermont-Gallerande and Monsieur de la Vaupalière, whose advice was invaluable to her.

"We are," writes the amiable young woman, "on the principal street, which is very beautiful, in a wide open space, a kind of square called the Comphausbad, near the Redoute. This makes it easy to go to play *rouge et noire;* it is very near to some beautiful baths and mineral waters, but this is the least interesting fact to me in Aix-la-Chapelle. We have a very large drawing-room, long and narrow. I occupy the sleeping-room which opens from this, because my sister (Madame de Lamballe) preferred the one at the rear, although it is unattractive and inaccessible except by way of a dirty corridor. It has closets however and her women can be lodged near her, while the rooms of the countess and myself have nothing adjoining them; but we do not need to have our women nearer than the end of the corridor. The room of the countess (Madame de Ginestous) opens into mine; each has a door into the antechamber. They gave us new beds with snowy white curtains and a good canopy in each room, and, now that we have taken possession of all the tables, we are very comfortable. The brunette occupies the rooms below, in which she settled two months before we arrived. The large lady (the Comtesse de Las Cases), with her husband and children, is above, as are many others. We have the entire first floor to ourselves. You know that the large lady came away several months before we did, leaving my sister rather informally; so the latter gave her to understand that she would be delighted to have her for a visitor, but that while she was at the watering-places their households would be separate; that she and her husband could come and dine as often as they wished, but that when my sister travelled she should not take her. Neddy and the husband of my companion are living in the same house. The Marquis de Clermont occupies the ground floor. ''

The description is complete, almost minute; but in order to satisfy our desire to know everything, in order that the picture may not be incomplete, we must be wholly informed as to the life of Madame de Lamballe during her emigration, we must know her habits, the society she frequented—must gain, in a word, a clear idea of her occupations in the midst of her preoccupations.

This is what the amiable countess seems to have understood, and unconsciously she made herself in her *naïve* account, which is accurate and without needless detail, the most faithful as well as the most authentic historian of this interesting period, about which we have scarcely anything more than general documents.

This almost daily correspondence gives a new point of view very different from that which we had thought correct. We believed that these *émigrés* who had gone abroad, fearing the persecutions of which they might be victims, must have broken with the past, and have given up that unhealthful frivolity, the fruit of their more or less prolonged sojourn in Versailles. We pictured them a prey to the most cruel uncertainty, deploring the fate of the king and his family, of many of their relatives or friends, and bemoaning their own misfortune; while we find, on the contrary, that they longed only for pleasures and distractions, gave themselves up to card-playing, and in spite of the difficulty they already had in procuring money, risked in this favorite pastime considerable sums.

Is there need to say that at the princess's they played in moderation ? ' She always disliked playing, except the game of *quinze*, with which she loved to pass away

the evening; for the rest you can judge for yourself
from the following, and if Madame de Lâge gave
herself up to her little passion, the fact was wholly
unknown to Madame de Lamballe.

"The drawing-room," wrote Madame de Lâge,
"is vacant at half-past eleven in the evening. Almost
every one rises early for the waters and the baths;
moreover, social life begins early. There is much
visiting during the day, and always in order to discuss
the same thing, which is very tiresome. We lead a rus-
tic life. The ground floor as well as the second story
of this great hotel, in which we occupy the first floor,
is tenanted by society people. I cannot satisfy you as
easily about the card-playing. At my sister's they do
not play for more than a crown, but the Redoute is
very near. We go there from time to time, during
hours when we hope to avoid meeting people who will
tell my sister of it. I do not go alone, but always
with the countess or with my large cousin and a few
men who, like ourselves, do not care to have the fact
that they go known."[1]

Madame de Lamballe might, perhaps, have accepted
this kind of life, succumbing to circumstances, had
it not been for her cruel anguish of mind, and her
constant thought for the miserable fate of the royal
family. Her heart continually turned towards the
Tuileries, and the poor woman rarely enjoyed real
rest. A prey to an indescribably excessive excitement, still more augmented by her nervous condition,
she imagined she heard the voice of the queen. Now

this voice seemed to call her back; then the next instant
to beg her to defer her return, in order to avoid the
perils which her presence might arouse.

During the few months of their separation the two
friends kept up a more or less regular correspondence.
The queen, giving free rein to her most intimate
thoughts, described with the greatest sincerity her
troubles and griefs. Frequently even she confided to
the princess her dearest hopes and her most secret plans.

One day weeping for her family, her friends, but
not for herself, she foretold in her letter the total dissolution of France.

" The good people," wrote the daughter of Marie
Thérèse, " do us justice; but they are silent, they
droop their heads, and do not know what to do.
The villains are strong in this weakness. Ah, if they
knew how we loved the people, they would blush
at the outrages which we are made to suffer. . . ."

Another day she would be more cheerful, or tried
to appear so, in order not to further sadden her
" dear Lamballe." But even then she did not forget
to speak of the wicked men and the scoundrels.

" . . . I showed your letter to the king," she
wrote, October 19, 1791, " as you desired; he asked
me to tell you that he would be delighted to do anything to please you; he is really quite angry with you
for not having spoken sooner. . . . We are so surrounded by wicked people, and so hampered, that we

cannot answer one day for the next, but the king will do what he can. . . . What is Monsieur de Penthièvre doing ? . . .'

It is rather interesting to note that the princess still dared to ask a favor of the king, who probably was at a loss to grant what she wanted. But Louis XVI. gave some sort of promise, at least, since he said he would do " his best."

The following article proves beyond a doubt that Marie Antoinette, answering the timidly expressed desire of the princess to return to France, forced herself to dissuade her from this idea, and admitted that Madame de Lamballe would be throwing herself into the *jaws of the tiger.*

" The trouble does not lessen," she said. " I see the boldness of our enemies increasing and the courage of honest men growing less. One can think only from day to day, fearing a frightful to-morrow." Then she speaks of her daughter, whose health was good. " You know," she continues, " how well this little one loves you, as does my darling who at this moment is on my lap and who wants to write to you." In fact, the unfortunate child signed the letter.

However, the dangers she might run mattered little to the princess if her presence could be useful to the royal family. No doubt it was in answer to the assurance she gave Marie Antoinette, to return as soon as the latter should show a desire for her to do so, that the queen wrote and acknowledged that her friend's generosity had made her weep.

"I well know," she continued, "that you love me, and I had no need of this new proof. What happiness to be loved for one's self! Your affection, with that of a few other friends, constitutes my entire strength. . . .'

Did our poor princess have a presentiment that her friend, fearing to frighten her, was voluntarily hiding a part of the truth? Did she think that La Vaupalière and Clermont-Gallerande, with whom she lived at Aix, wished, for the same reason, to give her only a partial idea of the actual situation? Be that as it may, we see her returning to Spa with the Marquise de Las Cases as sole lady-in-waiting, and we can find no more plausible reason for her sudden departure than this state of mind; unless she conferred, entirely in secret, with the King of Sweden, who was residing in that place.

CHAPTER XV

At Spa the princess went to the Hôtel du Lion Noir, on the Grand' Place, already occupied by the Comte de Haga, and the list of foreigners shows us that in this change of residence she still bore the title of Comtesse d'Amboise.

We have no account as to the sojourn of Madame de Lamballe, but we know from the same paper that Spa was filled with foreigners and that the society there was very select. Madame de Lâge, unfortunately, was not of the party and therefore could not give us, in her usual animated manner, the charming descriptions in which she excelled. However, that inquiring lady knew how to listen and, thanks to this characteristic, which we are now tempted to regard as an advantage, she draws, according to her information, a picture which cannot fail to be extremely attractive.

" Spa," she said, " has been more brilliant this year than ever. Seventeen princes or princesses, one might say all brothers and sisters, children or nephews of the king. As for the petty German princes, we do not count them; the streets are paved with them; and there is one king worth a thousand of them—namely,

the King of Sweden. . . . They claim that it is
the only spot in the world in which the Revolution
is forgotten.''

In the early days of September the princess returned
to Aix-la-Chapelle and lived the same life, surrounded
by the same friends. The King of Sweden paid his
respects the 7th of October and the following day a
great dinner was given in his honor; the last, no
doubt, for on the 13th there arrived at Aix a mysterious personage, charged with a mission from the queen
for Madame de Lamballe. It is again the Comtesse
de Lâge who tells us this important fact and who
describes in so true and lively a manner the make-
shifts of the unfortunate princess.

"... In all probability,'' she wrote, '' we will
return to Paris in a fortnight, on Friday morning,
October 14th. *Some one else* arrived yesterday; we
foresee that my sister will think herself obliged to join
my aunt, with whom it is said she is anxious to be,
while they tell her that my aunt wants her. They
say that my sister offers to go, and they imply to my
aunt that by refusing to have her she would offend her.
However, as my sister fears the journey as much as
we do, she is vacillating, which fact will do her an
injury. Ah, if she only had done as I wanted, and
accepted the offers of her relative in Italy; if she only
had not been detained here; if she only had gone at
once we should be settled there, and from such a
distance one could not easily return! Besides, there
would have been no one there to trouble her. If this

return to France would bring me at once to you, not only should I know what to do, but I should be happy. Instead, I shall have to stay in Paris and drain the cup of bitterness to the dregs. If you would only come here! Every one assures me that, in case anything happens, Paris will be the safest place in France. For the rest, so far as I am concerned, my course is clear: so long as there is danger and she is unhappy, I shall not leave her. Since yesterday my heart has ached for her. . . ."

Some parts of this letter, which we have quoted almost in its entirety, are of real value. In the first place they show us that the princess, urged on the one hand by some of those about her; influenced on the other by the wish to satisfy the desires of the queen, was incapable of reaching a decision. On the 13th the messenger arrived whom Madame de Lâge qualifies as *some one else*, thereby showing that he was not the first she had received, but that several times she had been already solicited in the same way.

At all events, the queen must have been eloquent, since Madame de Lamballe suddenly made up her mind to return to France.

The Comte de Las Cases, in a passage of the Mémorial de Sainte Hélène, dedicated to the sojourn of Madame de Lamballe at Aix-la-Chapelle, wrote:

" The emperor then passed on to speak of the Princesse de Lamballe, about whom he knew nothing. I could easily satisfy him, as I had known her well.

One of my relatives was her maid of honor. When I reached Aix-la-Chapelle, at the beginning of my journey, I was received by her as if I were one of her household, and was treated with great kindness.

"The Princesse de Lamballe, I said, gathered about her in this city much of the atmosphere of Versailles, in courtiers and gentlemen of the old school. Many illustrious strangers came also. I often saw the King of Sweden, Gustavus III., there under the title of Comte de Haga; Prince Ferdinand of Prussia, with his children, the eldest of whom, Prince Louis, was killed a few moments before the battle of Jéna; the Duchess of Cumberland, widow of a brother of the King of England, etc.

"When Louis XVI., accepting the Constitution, reorganized his household, the princess received a formal letter from the queen asking her to resume her duties as superintendent. The princess took the advice of her old councillors, all of whom thought that, considering the fact that the queen was not free, and that there was a possibility of great danger in Paris, the princess need not return there and might regard the letter from the queen as null and void. The princess having asked elsewhere what people thought, some one was ill-advised enough to reply: ' Madame, you have shared the prosperity of the queen, it would be generous to show her fidelity, especially now when you have ceased to be her favorite.' The princess was high-minded, deeply affectionate, and unconsciously romantic; the next day she announced that she would leave for Paris., So the unfortunate woman returned to the capital, fully realizing the danger; she fell an illustrious victim to her generosity and her feelings. My parents offered me to her; for an instant

I might have followed her. Because of my youth
and the short time I had been in Paris, I was almost
unknown and could have remained near her, and perhaps have been useful to her; but at the moment of
departure the princess found obstacles in the way and
urged me to give up the idea; however, I remained
her chronicler. Every other day I sent her, with the
best intention in the world, stories and all kinds of
ridiculous tales by which our illusions were flattered
and which we did not fail to accept with the greatest
faith. I sent them to her when we were in the
country; I sent them to her when she was no longer
there. . . . To the heartfelt grief I felt for her
pitiful lot was sometimes added the secret fear of
having, perhaps, augmented it by my bulletins. And
by chance, I added to the emperor, I happen to
have here a few lines she wrote some days before the
hideous catastrophe of which she has left a terrible
reminder. They are dated from the *top of my donjon*.
It was thus she designated the Pavillon de Flore, which
she occupied at that time in the Tuileries.'

Although in the words of Madame de Lâge and
according to the belief of certain fugitives, an opinion
spread by them no doubt to serve their purposes, Paris
was "the safest spot in France," the princess departed *with a deep realization of the dangers she must
run.* Her will, made at Aix-la-Chapelle and dated
October 15th, is proof of this.

The strong determination of the princess was nevertheless variously interpreted. If the greater number
attributed it to generosity and great-mindedness, others,

on the contrary, accused her of another motive, to which we must refer although we refute it with indignation.

Thus does not Madame de Tourzel, whose testimony, however, is usually credited, go so far as to say that the queen, fearing that after the acceptance of the Constitution she would be forced to take from Madame de Lamballe the position of superintendent of the royal household if she continued to remain away from France, induced her to return ?

In that case it would have been simply for the emoluments of the position that Madame de Lamballe exposed herself to the dangers which awaited her on her return.

This is scarcely probable, and the conduct of the princess, considering the gravity of the situation, seems to us to contradict the story of the governess of the children of France.[1] The dangers to be run were too great for one to attribute her action to motives of self-interest.

Fortaire, without any reservation, says that the return of the princess was due entirely to the " urgent solicitation " of the queen. He repeats this opinion later when he speaks of a " pressing invitation."

Did not the Comte d'Allonville attribute to the princess this lofty sentiment, made in response to the supplications of her friends, who were seeking to dissuade her: " The queen wants me; I must live and die near her " ?

Moreover, the same author returns to this point and again says:

"We saw this good and devoted Princesse de Lamballe leave an hospitable land, in spite of the prayers of her friends, in order to soften the grief and share the danger of a queen whom she loved as much as she was loved by her."

This is scarcely what Madame de Lâge tells us of the friends of the princess, who counted on her to bring them back to favor and urged her to shorten her stay away from France.

The departure of Madame de Lamballe, postponed from day to day, actually occurred, according to the Comte de Fersen, on Saturday, October 29th.

Although it must have cost her dear to be separated from her two ladies-in-waiting, of whom she was particularly fond, the princess, after mature consideration, decided to set out alone for France. In fact it was more prudent to travel without a suite and with a modest equipage. We will even add, in support of the delicacy of her feelings, that she did not wish to expose her ladies-in-waiting to the dangers she herself was braving without fear. Moreover, if the words attributed to her by the Comte d'Allonville are true, she did not deceive herself in regard to these dangers.

The separation was cruel. Only the Comtesse de Ginestous could legitimately cherish the hope of return-

ing to the princess, for, as a foreigner, she was insured
against certain dangers.

On the 4th of November the papers announced the
return of the princess to Paris:

" Madame de Lamballe has returned."
" Madame de Lamballe as well as several quondam
courtiers has returned to Paris," said the " Journal
de Paris," without further comment.

On her arrival the princess took rooms in " an
apartment, which was separated from that of the queen
only by the landing-place of the stairs, on the same
floor as that of the queen, at the Pavillon de Flore, '
says Madame Campan.

That which she most feared was to see again, after
so long and so cruel a separation, the queen whom,
a few months before, she had left young and full of
attractions. She was not ignorant, however, of the
fact that, since the arrest at Varennes, the hair of Marie
Antoinette had become almost white; her friend had not
hidden this from her in her letters, and had even sent
her a proof of it.

It was none the less a sad moment for her when she
saw the queen with entirely white hair, her features
worn and sharpened by loss of sleep.

The royal countenance reflected proud surprise,
haughty calm, and feverish courage. Later, to this
surprise, to this calm, to this courage was added scorn.

" Always imposing in her bearing, there was no

longer seen on her lips that kindly and charming smile which had added to her beauty. '

" Profoundly moved, she still preserved her quiet visage and a bearing full of dignity.'

The loneliness and desolation which the princess felt in the Tuileries affected her no less acutely. Feeling only shame and scorn for those who had not feared at the first danger to flee and irrevocably abandon the royal family,[2] she resolved to devote herself wholly to the king and queen, whose reception of her had been so touching. This was, then, her one thought, her one ambition; but there remained a duty to be fulfilled, a sacred duty, sweet to her since it was one of gratitude: to go to her father-in-law, whose health was precarious and whom she wished to see again.

So the princess left for Anet and remained there from November the 14th to the 18th. She could freely discuss her plans with the Duc de Penthièvre, by whom her course, in spite of the dangers it entailed, could not fail to be approved.

The poor duke was, in fact, very ill. The quarrels to which he had constantly been exposed had greatly affected his health, although he had preserved excellent spirits.

We know of no better way to depict his state of mind than to give here some passages from the correspondence between him and his faithful friend the Cardinal de Bernis, then in Rome.

" We have had," he wrote from Châteauneuf-sur-Loire, May 30, 1790, " some excitement at Amboise from a cause which in these times is unimportant: the people from one of the parishes of this town wished to reëstablish the third fête of Pentecost, which for several years has been given up. This excitement came to an end in a touching manner for me. The curate, towards whom they were beginning to use threats, said that the disturbances would end by forcing me to leave Amboise and every one retired without a word."

" CHÂTEAUNEUF-SUR-LOIRE, July 4, 1790.

" It is very kind in your Eminence (I believe that this title is always correct in Rome) to concern yourself with a poor servant on the eve of becoming royal shoeblack. I do not know, however, what I shall be in France, or how I shall exist under the new order of things; the decree of June 19th is being returned to the hands of the Committee of the Constitution, to undergo a new examination before being promulgated. Some of the gentlemen from Orléans actually have desired that the man who carries my letters to the post-office in their city, and the conveyance which is sent thither for my provisions, should be divested of my livery and my coat-of-arms. I have yielded. For that matter, I could not fail to be pleased with the friendship the people show for me. Why should they wish me harm ? I have always thought that the high position I occupy compels me to sacrifice myself for them.

" Preserve our country from schism. The Pope is a prudent man in whose wisdom I put great confidence; the form of apostolic instruction by the bishop, together with communion with the successor of Saint Peter, is not unknown.

"A thousand thanks to your Eminence for the interest you have been good enough to take in my health. I have been much better since I have been living on the banks of the Loire, although I am still weak. I was troubled by a summons to the act of federation of the 14th of this month, whither it would have been impossible for me to go. Fortunately, on the decree's being examined further, I found that I was not compelled to be present.

"My tender and sincere affection for your Eminence deserves that you keep a small place for me in your thoughts.

"L. J. M. DE BOURBON.

"There is no need for me to say how I hope this letter will find you argus-eyed."

"AMBOISE, August 13, 1790.

"Monsieur de Bourbon Penthièvre (such is the name I now bear) renders a thousand thanks to Monsieur le Cardinal de Bernis for the last letter he was kind enough to write him. He is about to try to make use of the means suggested to him concerning the affair of poor Father Denis. Monsieur de Bourbon Penthièvre still uses his own seal, and will continue to use it until the decree of June 19th shall be in force; only he countersigns admiral. His servants wear any color.

"I came to Amboise for my customary change of air; otherwise my health, which needs care, might have suffered. It has not been possible this year for me to look into my accounts as usual. My ignorance of the means I have left compelled me to begin by curtailing expenses; moreover, I am very glad to reserve enough for a journey to Rome if I cannot settle permanently in my own country.

" I am in the hands of Monsieur Barnave³ and Monsieur Charles de Lameth. One of my old farmers to whom my counsel has been refusing for ten years to pay an indemnity of ten thousand crowns at the lowest, has complained to these gentlemen and has been heard by them. Monsieur de Lameth, to whom, at my orders, a secretary had been speaking, said some very kind things about me, but did not cease to reiterate the fact that he was the friend of the people and the savior of the oppressed. I wrote that they should try to prevent my being decried in the National Assembly. I ask your Eminence not to refuse the continuation," etc.

Monsieur de Penthièvre was not at the end of his troubles. Every instant he feared that the schism would come, and after a time this fear was realized.

Villenave, in his " Vie du Duc de Penthièvre," tells us that " while the Princesse de Lamballe had her priedieu under a dais in the choir of Saint Eustache, the prince was on the bench of the church-wardens' pew, in company with the wardens."

The duke was very fond of his parish of Saint Eustache, near the Hôtel de Toulouse. He did much good there. What a cruel awakening, then, when he learned, early in December, that his coat-of-arms had been torn down from Saint Eustache! Foreseeing what would occur, he wrote, January 1, 1791:

" In case we are so unfortunate as to suffer from a

schism, could you procure me the means of holding service in my rooms, according to the Catholic ritual, without my being forced to expatriate myself?''

The prince thought of leaving, of exiling himself, in order to escape having to renounce his religious practices; but in the following letter he shows that he is reassured, and has changed his plans, for between times he speaks of the answer of the cardinal, an answer in which the latter tells him that he may continue to follow his own religious observances:

"Eu, February 6, 1791.

''Monsieur le Cardinal, there can rightly be no schism when the majority of bishops are united; but there can actually be one when the supreme power prevents the orthodox ministers from fulfilling their duties, and has them carried on by intruders. I shall have recourse to you if circumstances require it.

''It is said that your Eminence is about to receive mesdames. I congratulate you for extending your hospitality towards such personages. Perhaps I shall ask you to procure a cabin for me near Saint Paul *fori mura*, if I do not confine myself to paying a visit to Madame la Princesse de Conti in Savoy, in case my continued poor health obliges me to travel.

''I am still in the city of Eu. I do not know how long I shall remain. The four curates of this city have taken the oath; their vicars have joined the opposite faction. The curate of Choisy le Roy was appointed bishop of Rouen the beginning of this week. The town of Eu is in this diocese.

''My tender and sincere affection,'' etc.

"Eu, March 23, 1791.

" What I foresaw in regard to the schism has happened, Monsieur le Cardinal. The Church of France is very Catholic, the majority of bishops holding together; but schism does exist in this country, the administrative power binding the hands of the legitimate ministers and committing their duties to the hands of intruders. Your Eminence has told me that it would not be impossible to procure for myself the means of living at home as a Catholic in the midst of heterodoxy.

" I beg you to pay my respects to mesdames when you have time, and to remember me to Madame de Narbonne. You must always address my letters to the Hôtel de Toulouse in Paris, in order that they may surely reach me, because I may change my abode from time to time.

" I trust that your Eminence will never doubt," etc.

The health of the poor old man was very wretched. The following letter was written by his secretary. To his physical suffering was added mental pain; the good man had just lost a priest whom he had honored with his friendship.

"RADEPONT, September 17, 1791.

" . . . It is very interesting that the health of the Pope undergoes no change. My daughter and I beg you to offer our humble respects to mesdames. My daughter asks me to thank you for the interest you never cease to feel in what concerns her. The condition of suffering in which I live is somewhat augmented by the loss I have just sustained of the priest in whom I placed my confidence after the death of poor Monsieur d'Appolonie. This loss, which would have affected me at any time, is rendered more painful, if possible, by circumstances. Yesterday I resigned from the Order of the Saint Esprit; perhaps to-day I shall separate myself from the Order of the Golden Fleece, to which the king, according to his latest letters written from Paris, still belongs. I deserve from your Excellency,'' etc.

If only the poor duke had known how good a prophet he was in uttering the words Fortaire has handed down to us!

" I greatly admire the attachment of my daughter-in-law to the queen. She has made a very great sacrifice in returning to her. I tremble lest she be a victim to it.''

Even then the unfortunate woman was morally a victim. Her devotion was not slow in exciting the bitterness of the pamphleteers.

" A long, detailed account of the reception of Madame de Lamballe at court, Wednesday, the 12th of this month, and the pleasant welcome she received from the king and the queen.

" Also the superb discourse of their Majesties, as well as that of this *ci-devant* ' princess, concerning the *émigrés* and their intentions in regard to France.

" Madame de Lamballe, admitted to the king, addressed him in these terms:

" ' Sire, no one has shown more love than I for the sacred person of your Majesty. If I regret that I was separated from you, at least I have the consolation of not having lost the confidence with which you have deigned to honor me. Nothing is dearer to my heart. I shall always preserve the memory of it as well as the joy I now feel. To-day will be so much the more precious to me since I can tell your Majesty that the intention of the French princes is to follow my example. Kindly add to this expression of affection my boundless devotion to the Constitution, to your Majesty, to the queen, and to the royal family.'

"THE REPLY OF THE KING

" ' I, as well as the queen, am greatly pleased by your return to us. I was ignorant of the motives which kept you away, especially as we had told you that you had nothing to fear. Perfect tranquillity reigns here. The French, worthy of our love, have some affection for me, and for all of us. Deep in our hearts we carry this healthful balm, which makes us forget all the ills we have suffered, and all that were feared by those who left.

" ' I must tell you, my dear cousin, that this moment brings back life to me. What joy! I cannot forget it, and if ever I felt the sweetness of royalty, it is now when I see all souls united, all members at one with their leader, and all Frenchmen gathered about us.

" ' A large part of the inhabitants of this vast empire, in a burst of regeneration conceived, it is true, some alarm in regard to the purity of our sentiments; the ill-disposed profited by their anxiety, the flame of discord grew so warm that no power could have averted the incalculable evils of which France would have been the theatre. A great nation having been led away, wrongly interpreted our slightest actions; in a word, caused such anxiety in our soul that we thought we ought to make sure whether there existed a unanimous desire for a constitution, which I as well as the queen have adopted. I assured myself of this desire unconditionally; consequently, I repeat to you that no consideration can outweigh with me the general wish.

" ' We have obtained from a feeling and generous people the forgetfulness of personal enmity. Those whom you have looked on as your enemies come with open arms to receive you, to guarantee your person and your property. Can you regard such conduct with indifference ? I cannot make myself believe this, especially as we are allied with the blood of the Bourbons, and as we now form with all Frenchmen one and the same family.

" ' I flatter myself that you will adopt my plans. I beg you to overlook all mistakes. I ask you also to contemplate with us the lively pleasure of a people pleased with the laws they have dictated for themselves, and to feel that your return makes a part of their joy, of mine, and of the queen's.'

" REPLY OF THE QUEEN

" ' I share the sentiments of the king in regard to you. I will not recall the cruel remembrance of the motives which have kept you away from me. Resume your rank and the place you have always held in my heart.

" ' Finally, let us draw a veil across the past; let us turn our thoughts to everything which will contribute to a happier future and let us be forever friends.'

" At this point the queen embraced Madame de Lamballe with the liveliest affection.

" Copy of a letter addressed to the former editors of the ' Courrier des Frontières '

" ' GENTLEMEN : The arrival at court of Madame de Lamballe, announced in a very estimable paper (" Le Thermomètre du Jour," No. 65), is assuredly not falsely reported. This *ci-devant* princess, for whom for several days they have been preparing apartments in the Hôtel de Toulouse, arrived the night of the 10th. On Wednesday, the 12th, she was admitted first to the king and then to the queen. Two of my friends who were present at the ceremony customary under such circumstances told me the chief points. As they are very interesting, it is a real pleasure to me to send them to you, and you may, without doubt, give them the publicity they deserve.

" ' I have the honor of being your, etc.,

" ' DAVID,

" ' *Citizen of the District of the Tuileries, Paris, 14th October,* 1791.

" From the Press of Pellier, Rue des Prouvaires, No. 61."

15

CHAPTER XVI

On her return to Paris, the princess opened her salon to receive "many people," and succeeded in gathering about her all that the capital still contained of the royal suite.

On November 28th Monsieur d'Amblimont supped with her before going to Aix-la-Chapelle, where he was to join her daughter, the Comtesse de Lâge, to give her the final instructions from the princess, who urged patience, and forbade the countess to think of returning, unless she received formal orders to do so.

Several writers have told us of the efforts of the princess to hide from the eyes of the royal family the void caused by the migration.

She sought to gather together all those whom fear had not driven away, and solicited their presence at her receptions, even at her informal teas, hoping to find in all these evidences of devotion, neglected for some months, a last support for the tottering royalty.

Monsieur de Clermont-Gallerande has made of this desertion, which in her solicitude the princess desired to hide, a true and painful picture. We should like to pass it over in silence.

"The court of the queen was as little attended as
was that of the king. Those holding important offices
were either absent or had deserted her. Of the princesses only Madame Elisabeth and Madame de Lamballe remained; the Duchesse d'Orléans was with her
father; the Duchesse de Bourbon never came."

What a contrast ! How painful it must have been
for such a woman to see herself deserted, to find herself misjudged by those who ought to have known her
better, to see herself abandoned by her own household, by those who had received for their families, as
well as for themselves, the greatest favors from her
hands ! I must say in praise of their Majesties that,
although sensitive to this general desertion, they were
far from showing any displeasure at it. Never a
murmur escaped them, never a complaint, never a
single moment of ill-humor or reproach. There was
the same kindly welcome, the same graciousness, the
same indulgence for all who approached. No doubt
they favored those on whom they most could count.
They must have done so; but it was in no way embarrassing for the others, who could neither show
offence nor complain of it.

What patience ! What courage! What resignation
and virtue in these unfortunate sovereigns ! How con-
soling must it have been to have shown them devotion
in their trouble. Madame de Chimay, maid of honor,
unable to follow her own creed at court, had left on
account of religious reasons. Fear had led Madame

d'Ossun, lady of the bedchamber, to go abroad and join her mother, Madame de Grammont. The Duchesse de Luxembourg was at Lisbon with her husband. Mesdames de Luynes, de Duras, d'Hénin, de Bergues, and de Polastron had left. Of the court ladies, there remained only Mesdames de la Roche-Aimond, de Tarente, de Castellane, and de Maillé; and Madame de Lamballe, who filled every position, so to speak, held court every week, and gave several dinners and suppers, which the queen attended. This was the sole diversion Marie Antoinette allowed herself. The household of Madame Elisabeth was likewise scattered; she had with her only Madame de Sérent and a few other ladies. Monsieur d'Adhémar had just died, and the Comte de Coigni was in Italy. Of the queen's household, Monsieur de Tessé was in Switzerland, the Duc de Polignac at Vienna, and Monsieur de Saulx was dead.

Following is a letter from the queen, with a few autograph lines from Louis XVI., addressed toward the close of the year to the Duchesse de Polignac. It shows that Marie Antoinette fully realized the value of the devotion of the princess and did not hide it from herself, and that the king, in spite of his unfortunate position, continued to devote himself calmly to his favorite pastime.[1]

"Your last two letters," wrote the queen, "arrived together, dear heart, and it is impossible for me not to reply at once to tell you of my friendship for you. . . . The good L——, who seemed only waiting for danger to show what she was worth, is slightly ill at not being able to leave the house without overhearing the most atrocious remarks; for myself, I do not need to go out: I enjoy all that at home, as it suffices for me to go to the window. From time to time I find faithful men amongst those on whom I had not counted, but we have about us, and in our own service, others who betray us.'

" I am returning from hunting," continued the king, " where I met your friend, but we were surrounded by so many people whom we could not trust that we did not have a long conversation. The words exchanged, however, were sufficient for your purpose and mine. Know, Madame la Duchesse, that I fully realize the value of your affection.'

It was in the midst of these events and sorrows, which were nothing in comparison to what we are about to see, that the fatal year 1792 opened. Our princess, whose devotion was limitless, was never more careful to fufil her duties. Thanks to her unflagging zeal, she spared her friend the fatigue with which she was constantly threatened, and averted from her the coldness which was so painful to the queen. She was the first to express good wishes for the new year —" wishes which were as sincere," writes the poor woman, " as the hope I have of her continued kindness."

In spite of her cares and anxiety, Madame de Lamballe had perfect control over herself. She was even self-possessed enough to think of her own interests. It was no longer possible for her, at least for the present, to stay in Versailles.[2] So we find that she decided to rent an apartment in her hôtel in the city. Madame de Lamballe made every effort to induce her friends to remain near the Throne; at least, this is what Madame de la Rochejaquelein[3] says in her Mémoires. This authority tells us that when she was presented to the queen in February Madame de Lamballe prevailed on her, as well as on Monsieur de Lescure, not to go away. Later, similar overtures were made to Monsieur de Marigny by the princess, who still recommended the most absolute silence and the most impenetrable mystery. The court no longer presented its former aspect and the description given of it by Monsieur de Clermont is far from pleasant.

" The court," he says, " is sad, and painful to look upon. Surrounded by spies, it would be a crime for the royal family to favor any one; the moment one receives a welcome or any mark of preference, he is suspected and watched. The queen has given up the dinners and teas at Madame de Lamballe's, because they displeased Monsieur Pétion, and she goes there only in secret to spend a few moments of recreation or to summon the princess to her in private.'

Madame de Tourzel on this point is equally positive ; but she attributes the cause of it solely to the princess, saying that it was due to the latter's constant

fear of compromising herself personally, and, consequently, of compromising the queen. On the other
hand, Madame de la Rochejaquelein, whose relations
with Madame de Lamballe were very marked at this
time, does not give us the slightest hint of this, although
she might well have known and mentioned it, inas-
much as, even if not exactly in the intimate circle of
the superintendent, she remained near her until the
end, visiting the princess as late as the first part of
August. This enabled her to sound the truest note as
to the high character and cool head shown by our
wretched heroine.

" So far as I am concerned," says the Marquise,
" I withdrew from society, going scarcely anywhere
except to Madame de Lamballe's. I saw her every
anxiety, her every grief; never was any one more
bravely devoted to the queen. She sacrificed her life.
A short time before August 10th she said to me, ' As
the danger increases, the greater I feel is my strength.
I am ready to die; I fear nothing.' "

The court was again thrown into mourning in
March on the death of the brother of Marie Antoinette,
the Emperor Léopold.

" March 10, '92, nothing; news of the death of
the emperor," the king was satisfied to note.

But this was not all. In the meantime arrived the
order for the arrest of Delessart, an order which was
carried out during the night of the 10th. The affair, at
first considered but slightly important, soon assumed a

serious and grave aspect, and the accusation seemed so terrible that no further thought was given to the mourning of the previous night. The Comte de Fersen tells us, in regard to the trial of Delessart, that the princess wrote to Monsieur de Breteuil, to keep him informed of the denunciations of which the queen had been the victim, and to tell him that there had been a question of removing her from the king and of placing her in a convent. The unfortunate queen was accused of giving pernicious counsel to Louis XVI.

Fortunately, nothing came of this cruel plan, but Marie Antoinette long preserved the remembrance of the horrible idea, which, for the time being, had greatly startled those at court.

Let us speak now of the Austrian Committee, on which we will dwell in order to prove how great, even at this time, was the hatred against Madame de Lamballe.

This Committee, we think, never existed except in the feeble imagination of the orators of the Palais Royal and the Tuileries. Their audience, composed for the most part of idlers and of vagrants, had constant need of new food, and to meet the necessities of their cause our public speakers did not fear to organize this gathering of conspirators in the heart of Paris. So long as the accusation was confined to the public streets, none of the persons incriminated thought of protesting against the attacks made on their names. The Minister of Marine, Bertrand de Molleville, did not publish his denial refuting the actions concerning his friends and himself until the journalist Carra, at the meeting of the Friends of the Constitution, held at the Jacobins May 7th, allowed himself a violent sally, a real prosecutor's address, full of evil insinuations which he took care to reproduce in his "Annales politiques."

Bertrand de Molleville and Montmorin, at whom the attack was principally aimed, commissioned La Rivière, justice of the peace in the so-called Henry IV. district, to prosecute their calumniator. But Carra, far from being embarrassed, replied that he had confined himself to the facts advanced by Bazire, Merlin, and Chabot, all three members of the Vigilance Committee, and, furthermore, that these members had before them every proof of the legal existence of this Committee.

The National Assembly then summoned them to lay before it the evidence concerning the affair. La Rivière subpœnaed both Madame de Lamballe and Regnauld de Saint Jean d'Angely. The latter protested energetically against the allegation of an individual who had dared to testify against him (Regnauld) whom Madame de Lamballe had invited to her apartments. This passionate accusation made the session of Wednesday, May 23d, one of the most stormy they had ever had. Gensonné demanded the arraignment of Montmorin, and Brissot spoke to the same effect, demanding that of Bertrand also.

Neither orator, in spite of the talent and the passion he put into his speech, succeeded in moving the audience. Chabot was forced to come to the rescue and to take part in the discussion. Full of rage, with threatening words on his lips, he inveighed in turn against all and affirmed at the close of the argument that he had one hundred and eighty-two proofs at hand. "For the rest," he added, perfidiously, "the speeches of Gensonné and Brissot have already driven away Messieurs Montmorin, Caraman, and Madame de Lamballe. They have embarked at Boulogne-sur-Mer; and we have proof of this in a letter from the municipality of this city."

A newspaper immediately published the following paragraph: "Monsieur de Montmorin and Madame de Lamballe have left for England." But the following day it was compelled to contradict this statement, so carelessly accepted.

"We spoke of the departure of Monsieur Montmorin and Madame de Lamballe according to a letter from the municipality of Boulogne, which announced it to the National Assembly, and which was sent to the Committee on Research by the municipality of Paris. Monsieur Montmorin is in Paris, where he is awaiting the decision of the Assembly on matters which concern him."

Thereupon an energetic letter was needed from Montmorin to the Assembly to put an end to the calumniating reports brought forward with such grace by the ex-Capuchin Chabot, whose reputation and good faith were, moreover, strongly questioned in the following lines:

> Chabot, chaplain of the fair,
> Whose motives are beyond compare,
> Has, with the greatest tact, been thieving—
> So great his method of deceiving—
> Throughout his term of office quite,
> To carry out his schemes aright.
> The nation's deputy forsooth !
> Unprinoipled, unlearned, uncouth!
> One day this sarcerdotal clown,
> On coming to a well-known town,
> Arrested all the rank and file—
> Aristocrats and monks erstwhile—
> And without any rhyme or reason,
> He had them all led forth to prison.
> Each, fearing much the guillotine,
> Made offers to the Capuchin
> (For so it is the story's told)
> Of costly jewels, silver, gold.
> All night they bargained, standing there ;
> At length they yielded to his prayer.
> The prisoners were allowed to go
> For a hundred thousand crowns or so.

Never was contradiction more evident or irrefutable than the letter from Montmorin. Chabot, however, although unprepared for such a blow, did not appear at all moved. Later, more fully informed and apparently convinced that Madame de Lamballe was still in Paris, he merely stated, with very culpable

indifference in the face of so dastardly an accusation
lightly made:

" I was mistaken in saying Madame de Lamballe.
I meant the Princesse de Lambesc.'"

The accusation had no immediate results, but the
blow told, and the princess had to suffer the consequences. The bearing of the wretched woman, her
least acts already watched, and her short absence at
Anet from May 6th to 12th, must have served as a
foundation for the accusation of Chabot. These six
days at Anet were the last which Madame de Lamballe
devoted to her father-in-law.

What changes she found since her last visit! The
poor duke was scarcely able to rise from his sick-
bed and his suffering was frightful. His household,
too, was sadder than ever. His last chaplain, the
Abbé Lambert, whom Monsieur de Juigné, Bishop of
Paris, had sent him, has given in his " Mémoires " an
interesting picture of the life of his penitent. At five
o'clock they entered his room and, shortly after, Monsieur de Penthièvre prayed and meditated; then his
reader read to him, sent off his letters, and finally the
duke breakfasted on a cup of chocolate. He dined at
half-past one, remaining three hours at table. The
afternoon, until six o'clock, was usually given up to
driving. He resumed his correspondence and supped
from half-past ten to midnight. Then, retiring to his

apartments, he read the Scriptures or prayers, and did not go to bed before two o'clock in the morning.

He was so precise and punctual that he would have suffered if any of his habits had been the least varied.

Always very religious, his piety seemed augmented; every day he attended mass and he partook of communion each week. His correspondence with the Cardinal de Bernis shows us how calmly he bore his suffering, which daily became more violent, and the resignation, sometimes joyful and oftener stoical, with which he accepted all the innovations or changes imposed on him.

"There is really nothing," he wrote, "to prevent me from remaining a member of the Order of the Golden Fleece if I will submit to being called a foreigner, and if I will consent to be deprived of the prerogatives of active citizenship. As the king still continues his membership I shall not resign. I thought I had received an insult lately; the good people were pleased to spread a report that I was receiving bishops, aristocrats, arms, horses, and baggage from Monsieur le Comte d'Artois. Fortunately, the municipal officers of Houdan, a town near Anet, where the explosion was ready to burst, were wise enough to say that they would have to be allowed to verify the facts *incognito* before acting against me. They carried out their plan and their return calmed everything."

Under the date of February 16th he complains of his weakness, finding that "the irregular attacks of fever" from which he suffered seem to be "disappear-

ing,'' and laughingly refers to his ''state of imbe-
cility.''

This happy condition could not have lasted long,
for a month later he says:

''I am still in great pain. A cold I caught several
days ago augments the difficulty I have in breathing
and the dizziness with which I am troubled.''

The following letter, in which he tells of the assassination of the King of Sweden, whose host he had
been in 1784, of the death of the Comte de Dillon,
and of the unexpected adventure to his surgeon, is
written with such spirit that we should like to publish
it almost *in extenso :*

''ANET, June 1, 1792.

''Neither my daughter nor myself can sufficiently
thank your Eminence for the manner in which you have
aroused the interest of Mesdames in our favor. We ask
that you continue to do so. It was necessary for me
to be as stupefied as I have been by the suffering which
I undergo every day to have forgotten that you, personally, would mourn the King of Sweden. I am, however, fully aware of the friendship he showed you when
you desired a coadjutor. I imagine that you have heard
of the sad accident of Monsieur de Dillon, and the
story of what occurred at Mons. We hear every day
of the slight skirmishes which take place on the frontier
of the Netherlands. An armed negotiation might be
well, if it is a question of states which would consent
to enter into a parley. But I do not feel the need of
an assembly, the well-known custom of which is not to
treat regarding anything that concerns the Constitu-

tion. He who writes for me, since I am unable to do so for myself, says that I sent to your Eminence an account of a slight discussion we had on this subject. If he is not mistaken, you must be wearied by this repetition. My surgeon had the misfortune to drop in a citizen's house at Anet a glass on which was written ' Vive la Nation,' and the imprudence to say, ' The nation has fallen.' This aroused our citizens. I was obliged to send my surgeon to the justice of the peace, who, finding no serious charges against him, merely imprisoned him for a few hours in the town-hall. But that was not enough; when he came out of prison I had to send the guilty man back to his family in Paris. The Commune afterwards begged me to recall him and he has returned. In spite of having to obey my physicians I am still looking forward to my journey. It is not possible for me to have the travelling companion of whom you speak. Her husband has left, with the last of her children. It is said he has gone to Valenciennes.

" I will say nothing of what is going on in Paris. You know this better than I. How could I forget the proofs of friendship your Eminence has not ceased to show me. They are graven on my heart, which is filled with the truest and most sincere affection. Madame la Comtesse de Joinville says that she shares the sentiments of her father."

A few days later, he relates to the Cardinal an accident, the results of which might have been serious, but at which he was the first to laugh, as he himself tells us:

" We were overturned last Tuesday in an eight-seated carriage as we passed through the gates at the foot of my garden. These are placed so that the turning is very difficult. The coachman could not control the eight horses he was driving. But no one was seriously hurt, thank God; I ran the most risk; my daughter and a chief officer of my household, who is no light-weight, fell on me. I could neither speak nor move for the short time in which I remained in that position. I was almost suffocated.''

In the following letter he declares that, contrary to the advice of his physicians, he will not go to Italy— ''since,'' he adds, '' Madame la Comtesse de Joinville cannot take the trip, as her affairs are progressing so slowly.''

The poor man closes with a remark that shows he scarcely dares to speak of current events:

'' Everything that is occurring is too bad for me to discuss. Moreover, I speak very little of these things, and you know them better than I.''

There is at this point in his correspondence, a lapse greatly to be regretted, for suddenly we jump to the 17th of November. It is unfortunate that we have not the letter in which he describes the sad death of his daughter-in-law.

The last two missives, especially the one dated from Bizi, February 11, 1793, three weeks before his death, show that the condition of the wretched prince was growing worse. He could scarcely utter the following words, yet his mind remained clear enough for him to call the secretary to whom he dictated his letters " the man whose strength replaces the weakness of my hand, or rather of my head."

" I still suffer greatly. There are moments when an intense trembling, which tortures me, completely undermines my strength. If I were not as feeble as I am the gratitude I owe to my citizens would procure me happiness which my overwhelming misery prevents me from feeling. The soldiers who passed through here on their way from France to the army showed me a touching proof of friendship. The Commune of Vernon came to plant a tree of liberty before my door, after having attached an inscription to it which I here enclose, not daring to dictate it to him who by his strength replaces the weakness of my hand, or rather of my head.

" While thanking you for deferring to my wish in the matter of titles, I must ask you not to address letters *en sa maison; à sa maison* is the correct form. I do not usually assume the title of Citizen, because it is not yet in general use. I limit myself to receiving it from those who wish to give it to me, and to using it in return, humbly following the formula by which they address me."

The last letter is heartrending. The duke's trouble had grown worse, and the constant suffering was greatly augmented by a distaste for every kind of food. His weakness was great.

" Increased infirmities compel me to do no more than thank your Eminence for the letter I received from you the 23d of last month.   I was not sure of being able to dictate even these few lines. Three days ago I had an attack of fever which has been broken, but which has increased my distaste for food and consequently my weakness; meal hour is a time of torture.   Besides this I have had a swelling of the feet, occasioned by a night passed in my armchair, because I was unable to bear the pain I felt in bed.   My daughter and I ask you not to omit your custom of recalling our names to the two kind friends living with you——''

CHAPTER XVII

A grave conflict arose between the king and the Assembly, a conflict caused by the refusal on the part of Louis XVI., who had been hesitating for several days, to sanction the two decrees for the deportation of the priests and for the formation of a camp of twenty thousand men in Paris. This refusal, due in part to the firmness of Marie Antoinette, brought on the famous 20th of June, when for the first time we see the Princesse de Lamballe taking part with her sovereigns in an insurrection and showing that dauntless resolution which was so foreign to her nature, but which she knew how to assume.

The Tuileries once invaded by the people, the faithful subjects, in spite of the supplications and the tears of Marie Antoinette, were compelled to oppose her wishes to join her royal husband. "Let me go," cried the queen; "my place is with the king." To this Messieurs d'Haussonville and de Choiseul replied, "Your place is with your children." Then, when the crowd filed by her, abusing her with every sort of insult, the queen took refuge in the council hall, holding the dauphin in a red cap in her arms, and surrounded by her ladies, Mesdames de Lamballe, de Tarente, de la Roche-Aymon, de Tourzel, etc., etc.

Let us now, in regard to the firm and courageous attitude of the princess, quote the passage from the "Souvenirs" of the Comtesse de Lâge, giving the testimony of the Comtesse de Ginestous:

"Madame de Lamballe," said she, "showed great courage, leaning throughout the long scene against the armchair of the queen. She seemed concerned only with the danger surrounding this unhappy woman, and had no thought of herself."

That day with its overpowering heat was a horrible one for the defenders of the court, since the château was not entirely evacuated until eight o'clock in the evening. Shortly after, reports arose concerning the affair. Almost every one accused the Mayor of Paris, whose conduct was variously interpreted.

Roederer decided on the innocence of Pétion[1]; the report of the counsel of the Department of Paris, signed by Germain-Garnier, Leveillard, and Demantort, on the contrary, blamed the conduct of the mayor, that of the Procureur of the Commune, as well as that of the Commander-in-chief of the National Guard, and demanded their suspension. Pétion in turn attempted to justify himself, and had his remarks published in the "Moniteur." He concluded by saying, "No one could ever convince a reasonable man that the entrance into the château was premeditated." Not content with this statement, the following day he had a notice published urging the citizens to be calm.

In spite of these statements, Pétion and Manuel
were suspended from office for having on the 20th
failed to execute the law.   This suspension was however a triumph for the mayor, who was led back to
his home by a " numerous following of patriots."
Moreover, six days later, the every evening of the
fête of the Federation, he resumed his position.   That
day the king was to take the oath and drove to the
Champ de Mars with the queen, their two children,
Madame Elisabeth, Mesdames de Lamballe and de
Tourzel.   Fortunately everything went well; but this
was another real triumph for Pétion, whose name
alone was constantly cheered during the drive of the
royal procession.   This same Pétion, however, was
called on at the close of July to render a signal service
to the royal family.   At the request of the king he
betook himself to a faubourg to quiet the agitation
caused by the report, intentionally spread abroad, that
Merlin, Chabot, and other patriots had just been murdered, and that in the cellars of the château was stored
a large number of guns.   The anxiety of the royal
family was such that Louis XVI., convinced of the
impossibility of defence, decided to report to the Assembly.   This he did a few days later.

Times had now become so exciting that every day
some fresh report caused new alarms.   Once it was
that the king was planning to escape, and this rumor
was so easily believed that the populace were thinking
of attacking the Tuileries.   But there again Pétion

appeared, energetically opposed the idea, and gave positive orders to the commander-general to reinforce every post. We again find Pétion when the people had encamped around the Tuileries.

"It is suggested," he cried to the sections, "to form a cordon about the Tuileries to protect them and to prevent the abduction of the king. I need not tell you that such an idea is wrong. It would be putting pressure on the National Assembly[2] and dictating to it what course to pursue. A simpler and more conciliatory plan would be for all the battalions to hasten to the protection of the king, so that there may be no section which will not have its citizens there. By evening this measure will be partly carried out; therefore, let the sections not act in an isolated, incoherent manner. . . ."

"If it were possible," he wrote again in a lofty style full of moderation, "for these walls to bristle with bayonets, instantly the cries of ill-will would rise to say that there is no freedom and that the people have obtained through fear that which only civism should dictate. I have heard it said that they wish to appoint a day and an hour for the decision. This idea is intolerable. One never says to a judge, ' At such an hour you are to decide my case.' "

Unfortunately these efforts were useless; once again passion won ascendency over the wisest counsel; and while the faubourgs in a turmoil were hastening to arms in order to march against the Tuileries, watch was kept over the château to avoid a surprise, and preparations were going on in silence for a struggle, or at least for forcibly repelling the invaders.

Now that we have given a rapid sketch of the historical side, let us return to our good and gracious princess, and profit by the last days of the unhappy woman's liberty to become well acquainted with her, to analyze her character, her thoughts, or her fears for the future.

Upon the return of Madame de Lamballe the Comtesse de Lâge, we may remember, as well as Madame de Ginestous, had remained at Aix-la-Chapelle. Afterwards the latter, who being a foreigner could serve as a safeguard, returned alone to the princess to resume her duties. The Comtesse de Lâge lamented this formal order, even feeling offended at such desertion, without taking into consideration, poor child, that only the deep affection and the very natural fears of the princess for her had dictated a wish, this time so imperiously expressed and wholly contrary to the conciliatory character of Madame de Lamballe.

Cost what it might, in spite of her impatience she had to remain and await events. However, the health of her mother, who daily grew worse, determined the Comtesse to join her. Going by way of Paris she arrived July 28th, at the same time as the people from Marseilles.

At once informed of her arrival, Madame de Ginestous rushed into her arms, told her of the constant fears of the queen and of her faithful companion, and begged her in the name of the princess not to try to go to the Tuileries, in order to avoid bringing on the two wretched women and their surroundings fresh pretexts for distrust, of which they were already too frequently the objects. The princess especially advised her not to send to the Hôtel de Toulouse because of the ill-will of its inmates, principally that of the concierge.

The anxiety of Madame de Lamballe probably caused her to exaggerate the doubtful sentiments of her house. As proof her outrider was, for injuries to a clerk of the section of 1792, sentenced to five livres' fine, with considerations which at a less sad time would have been positively laughable.

" MAISON COMMUNE OF THE CITY OF PARIS.
"Court of the Municipal Palace.

" *Verdict.*

" Which enjoins the Citizen Girard to show honor and respect to public officers in the exercise of their duty; condemns him to five livres' fine for having injured the Citizen Raffy, Clerk of the District of 1792; forbids him to commit the same offence under penalty of heavier punishment, and orders this printed and published at his expense.

" Friday, December 7, 1792.

" In the name of the Nation, the Executive Provisory Council to all present and future, greeting: The Judges composing the Court of the Municipal Police of the City of Paris have given their verdict, which is as follows:

" Between the Procureur of the Commune, plaintiff for the report of the Commissary of Police from the District of 1792, the 27th of last October, and for the summons made in consequence by Jaffron, Crier in this Court, the 5th of the present month, on the one hand, and the Citizen Girard, outrider to the stables of the late Madame de Lamballe, living in the Rue de Richelieu, defendant for said report and summons, appearing in person and assisted by the Citizen Barré, his legal defender, on the other hand; without injury or prejudice:

" In this case it was a question of knowing if Citizen Raffy, Commissioner of Police of the Section of 1792, bearer of the order of the executive power, went to the Lamballe stables for some harness to be used for carts in the service of the Nation, and if the Citizen Girard refused it and injured him.

" Agreed: Vincent Ollivault, Counsel for the Commissary, Solicitor for the Commune, who has concluded that it must be enjoined to the said Girard to be more circumspect in future, and to show honor and respect to public officers in the exercise of their duties; and because of not having done this, and because of the certificate delivered to the Solicitor by Citizen Raffy to-day, the 7th of December, stating that the said Girard was a good citizen, he is condemned to such punishment as the tribunal may be pleased to inflict, and is forbidden to repeat the same offence under penalty of more severe punishment, with expenses.

" Agreed, likewise, Citizen Barré, Counsel for Citizen Girard.

"Since it is a question of injuries inflicted by Citizen Girard upon a public officer, acting according to the conclusions of the Solicitor of the Commune, the Court enjoins to the said Girard to show honor and respect towards public officers in the exercise of their duties; and for his having injured Citizen Raffy condemns him to pay five livres' fine, forbids him to repeat the same offence under penalty of greater punishment, orders that the present verdict to the number of one hundred copies shall be printed at his expense and posted wherever necessary; condemns him, besides, to the payment of five livres, thirteen sols, six deniers, including those present and the legal notices of the same.

" Done and approved in the public court of the Tribunal of the Municipal Police of the City of Paris sitting in the town hall, in which were present Citizens la Roux, president; Legneux, Favanne, Legrand, Concédille, and Balzac, Friday, December 7, 1792, the First Year of the French Republic.

" All officers are hereby commanded and ordered to put the present verdict into execution ; all National Commissioners in the Tribunal to take the matter in hand, and all officers and commanders of the public force to lend help where they shall be so legally required.

" Given by us, Clerk of the Tribunal of Municipal Police of the City of Paris, to be carried out according to the present minutes, deposited in our Registry, sitting in the town hall of said city.

" BOYENVAL.

" From the Press of C. F. Patrés, Press of the Commune, Rue du Faubourg Saint-Jacques Dames Sainte-Marie.''

During her sojourn in Paris the Comtesse de Lâge saw Madame de Ginestous every day, and often several times a day. But a visit which was valued by her, which was a great surprise to her, and the remembrance of which she could not efface, was that of the princess, the evening of July 31st.

" My unfortunate princess," she wrote, " came at nine o'clock the evening of the 31st, in a cab, with Madame Ginestous; this was probably the first time in her life that the princess had ever gone out in such a way without a servant. She stayed with me far into the night, and that was the last time I ever saw her. Years cannot efface the impression produced on me when I bade her ' Farewell, ' especially as I had to struggle with her determination to leave the next day.'

The conversation then turned upon the situation of the royal family and that of herself. With the latter the princess did not seem to be especially occupied, crediting, as for that matter did all who surrounded her, the wise determination of the king to prevent by arms any attack directed against his dwelling.

Madame de Lâge then observed that at each new episode for the past two years the question had been merely that of the king's energy, and that every time at the last moment he had avoided force under the pretext that he did not wish " to appear armed against the people." The princess was convinced that the king realized his weakness and the evils it had caused.

She thought he would certainly show more firmness in future.

Madame de Ginestous, who saw more clearly than her mistress, was far from sharing her hopes, especially in those which concerned the king. But it was time to part, and the separation was sad and tender.

"The princess," continued Madame de Lâge, "promised to write me often; and, in fact, I received a letter from her dated August 8th, but this did not reach me until after she was in prison."

The next day, August 1st, the Comtesse left.

For several days the agitation in the faubourgs was alarming; the people wanted to precipitate the downfall which they thought could be obtained only by marching upon the Tuileries, and the Mayor of Paris made every effort to calm them. As a last resort, on August 9th, the very evening before the day on which the ancient monarchy foundered, Pétion distributed among the citizens a paper in which he strove to show them that they were being led astray. "The Assembly," said he, "is at present occupied with our greatest interests. Let calm surround its walls, let it discuss matters in a calm and dignified manner, and let us wait with confidence the decree which will emanate from its wisdom. . . . I have heard it said that some wish to set the day and the hour for its edict. This idea is intolerable."

In spite of these wise exhortations recommending

calm, there was no further doubt but that the Tuileries were to be attacked that evening.

At first the Swiss, by order of Mandat, and with the permission of Pétion, left their barracks at Courbevoie and Rueil to join the defenders of the château. These consisted of some battalions of the National Guard, which some courtiers and several officers passing through Paris voluntarily joined.

At midnight the bell of Notre Dame began to ring; this was the signal agreed on. The tocsin[3] then resounded on all sides; everywhere the drum beat.

The friends of the king were intensely anxious. The nobles and the officers, who had been on duty, seemed resolute. The Swiss, well disciplined, confident of their leaders, sacrificed their lives; some of the National Guard seemed animated by the highest sentiments; others, on the contrary, whose hostility was beginning to be evident, waited only the issue of events to declare it.

To cap the climax, Mandat, who had been invested with general command, and who had been given explicit instructions to resist, was assassinated on the steps of the Hôtel de Ville, just as he came to give an account of the measures he had taken.

Deprived of their leader the defenders hesitated; the king did not know what to do. _ Before all else he wished to avoid a rupture.

Throughout the entire night the Princesse de Lamballe remained with the royal family, and when at daybreak the king amid loud cheers reviewed the National Guard and the Swiss, she went for the last time to her rooms.

"Madame de Ginestous," says the Comtesse de Lâge, "told me that about half-past six o'clock in the morning she went with Madame de Lamballe for the last time to her apartments in the Pavillon de Flore, two windows of which looked out from the first story on to the Pont Royal. With Monsieur de Clermont they took a stand before one of these windows to see the movement of the people and the arrival of the troops. For the first time her companion noticed that Madame de Lamballe looked sad and sinister, and to try to keep up her courage she said to the princess, 'Let us hope that we are about to be freed. Do you see the battalion of the Daughters of Saint Thomas? It has come to help us; the king's faction is larger than ever. All goes well, Madame.'"

Whereupon Madame de Lamballe looked sadly at her and replied:

"My dear, my dear, nothing will save us. I think we are lost."

From this conversation it seems clear that our two unfortunate women were not deceived as to the outcome of the struggle; even the princess no longer had in the judgment of the king, in his prudence or in his resolution, that blind confidence which she had been able to inspire in others, or at least of which she had boasted July 31st, in her last interview with the Comtesse de Lâge; for Madame de Ginestous, until then supported by the same belief, seemed greatly surprised at this tardy revelation, and exclaimed:

"Oh, my God! are you doubting the resolution of the king? Is he no longer ready to put himself at the head of his party? Oh, if he weakens, we are indeed lost!"

After the review the king returned to his apartments, but was still undecided as to his course of action.

Roederer, who saw the hostile disposition of the National Guard, who heard the cries of "Hurrah for the Nation! Pétion! The downfall!" given by the troops massed on the Carrousel, in response to the cheers of the Swiss for the king, dared not take it upon himself to affirm that the lives of the royal family were not in peril; therefore he advised Louis XVI. to go to the Assembly.

New and protracted hesitation followed on the part of this weak and incapable monarch, who did not decide until nine o'clock to follow Roederer's suggestion, while the queen begged him in mercy to act with energy and exhorted him to resist.

Seeing that her efforts were of no avail Marie Antoinette, worthy daughter of Marie Thérèse, felt in her veins the blood of the Cæsars, and turning to the deputies said:

"Monsieur Roederer and gentlemen, will you answer for the person of the king and for that of my son?"

" Madame," replied Roederer, " we will promise to perish at your side; this is all we can guarantee."

Beautiful words, truly, and for men determined to do their duty in such a situation the only possible reply to so embarrassing a question. What a contrast between this conduct, full of abnegation, and the eternal hesitation of the king!

In his thrilling account of the struggle at the Tuileries Colonel Pfyffer tells us, on the contrary, that as soon as the review was over a deputation presented itself to the king, who had returned to the château, and that thanks to their persistent efforts they prevailed on him to ask refuge for his family and himself in the Assembly;¹ the remainder of the account confirms the queen's heroic and firm conduct.

" It was then," said he, " that a deputation of the National Guard, led by Monsieur Roederer, Monsieur de Baume, and a third member of the Department of Paris, came to beg the king, who had returned to the château, to go to the National Assembly. Monsieur de Bachman, witness of the instances in which they sought to bring the monarch to some decision, turned to Monsieur de Gibelin, saying, ' If the king goes to the Assembly he is lost.' These were the last words the comrades of this virtuous chief heard from him. The queen made futile efforts to prevent the mournful departure, after which the most heroic resistance, since it had become objectless, could have no good result."

This determination was deplorable from every view-

point; for as soon as it became known the larger part
of the National Guard still occupying the interior of
the château made common cause with the battalions
from the faubourgs.

On their side, the sincere friends of the royal family,
those who had rallied around them out of devotion, ready
to give their last drop of blood, lost courage, and the
confusion became general when the king was seen
going on foot to the Assembly, followed by the queen
holding her two children by the hand. They were
accompanied only by Madame Elisabeth, Madame de
Tourzel, and the Princesse de Lamballe. The latter
as a relative of their Majesties had obtained permission
to follow them.

On his arrival the king sat down near the president;
opposite were the queen, the children, and the royal
suite; but upon the observation of one of the members
that the presence of the king at the meeting was contrary to the Constitution, Louis XVI. and his family
were obliged to take refuge in the clerk's box, behind
the president's chair.[5]

This narrow, half-dark room, which received light and
air only through a thick grating, was intensely hot;
furthermore, the atmosphere was so heavy and overpowering that Madame de Lamballe, who always
fainted easily, became nervous and had to be carried to
the Feuillants.[6] However, this time her indisposition
lasted only a few hours, when in spite of her lack of
strength she insisted on returning to resume her place

beside the royal family, although Marie Antoinette sent word to her not to come back, advising her to go to her father-in-law until she recovered from her nervousness.

To the physical suffering of the unfortunate family was added moral suffering which was much more painful. From time to time in the midst of the stormy deliberations of the Assembly the sinister firing of the cannon, mingled with groans and cries, reached them in a confused way, showing that in spite of the great sacrifice to which the king had at first consented the struggle and the shedding of blood still continued.

In the midst of frightful confusion the Assembly decreed that until order was reëstablished the king and his family should stay in their midst, and gave orders that suitable lodgings be at once prepared at the Fueillants. Commissioners were appointed with power to watch the allotting of these lodgings and to make sure that every one slept in the room assigned to him.

Madame Elisabeth and Madame de Lamballe, says the Comtesse de Lâge, slept in the same room, on mattresses laid on the floor, good Madame Mertins at their feet; the queen, Madame, and Monsieur the dauphin in another room, opening off of this, with the door open; the king in a chamber at the end of the corridor with a valet named Cléry.

The following day Madame Campan went to the Feuillants, and tells us in her " Mémoires " interesting details as to the attitude of the king and the queen. Louis XVI. seemed to her completely overwhelmed.

She found him occupied in having his hair cut. Better understanding the situation, which she considered desperate, Marie Antoinette lost courage only at sight of her children. She could not help saying how much she had been troubled by the resignation of the king since his stay at the Feuillants, adding that he had his usual appetite;[7] that that had produced a deplorable effect on the devoted deputies; but that no remonstrance had been made.

The installation of the royal family at the Feuillants, however, was only temporary. The Assembly was not long in perceiving that its inmates were not perfectly safe. It was absolutely necessary to find a place easy of defence and adapted to resist any surprise.

The ancient house of Monsieur, the Luxembourg, was suggested, but Manuel had no difficulty in showing the danger this would entail, and spoke of the Temple as the place combining the greatest advantages, where the defence and chiefly the guarding would be more efficacious. His advice prevailed and the transfer was made Monday the 13th, at half-past six in the evening, in one of the large court carriages.

The king took a seat at the back with the queen; the dauphin and Madame, Madame Elisabeth, Madame de Lamballe, and Pétion were on the front seat; Madame de Tourzel, whose account is such a valuable help to us, occupied with her daughter one of the side seats, while Manuel and Colonges, the municipal officer, sat on the other.

The procession stopped at the Place Vendôme and proceeded the length of the boulevards, amidst shouts, threats, and cries of " Live the Nation! Long live Liberty ! "

At length, after a drive of no less than two hours and a half, a veritable ordeal for the royal family, they arrived at nightfall before that doleful prison which was to be the final dwelling of the unfortunate sovereigns, and which by the cruelest irony was illuminated as if for a fête day.

The small tower of the Temple, although very incommodious, had been arranged to accommodate the unfortunate family. They had to crowd together, for each floor contained only two small chambers connected by dressing-rooms. The princess occupied one of these, between that of the queen and the dauphin, still feeling herself happy in being near Marie Antoinette, to whom she could give care and sympathy. But it was decreed that she was not to have many hours with her friend: their eternal separation was at hand.

Why this sudden parting ? For what reason? Did the Commune before the large number of friends who in spite of the dangers had decided to follow the king to the end, fear that some method would be arranged outside to facilitate his escape ?

This hypothesis is probable, for it was decided to leave with the king and his family only those absolutely necessary to them.

This order was carried out the night of August 18th. Madame de Tourzel tells us of it in the following words:

"Saturday the 18th," she wrote, " we heard among the municipal guard some talking which made us anxious. One of them who did not dare to express himself openly strove to make us understand that for the time being we were to be separated from the royal family. What he said, however, was so unintelligible that we could make nothing of it. We went to bed as usual, but just as I was falling asleep Madame de Saint Brice awakened me and told me that they were arresting Madame de Lamballe. A moment later we saw an officer enter my room; he ordered us to dress at once, saying that he had received word to conduct us to the Commune to undergo an examination, after which we were to be brought back to the Temple."

There was nothing to do but to obey, and the poor women went down to Madame de Lamballe's room, which the queen was not slow in reaching.

The separation of the two friends was heartbreaking; the princess on her knees was about to kiss the queen's hand, when " they tore her away, saying that such an act was well enough for a slave toward tyrants, but that in a free nation, in the midst of an equal people, it was not to be borne."

CHAPTER XVIII

One may easily imagine the grief of the poor woman who saw herself at so critical a moment separated
from the family for which she had sacrificed her liberty
and even her life.   On the other hand, how touching
a reward for her devotion were the final words of Marie
Antoinette, addressed in a low tone to Madame de
Tourzel:

" If we are not fortunate enough to see one another
again, take good care of Madame de Lamballe.   On
all solemn occasions be spokesman and save her as
much as possible from having to answer troublesome
and embarrassing questions."

After traversing the lower passages of the Temple
by the light of torches, the princess and a few court
attendants entered three cabs, and, accompanied by
officers and gendarmes, set out towards the Hôtel de
Ville.   Arrived there, each prisoner was taken to a
large room where the examination under the direction
of Billaud-Varennes [1] and a secretary was at once begun.
Messieurs Hue and de Chamilly were called first, then
Mesdames Thibaut, Navarre, and Saint-Brice.   Not
until three o'clock in the morning was the princess

sent for to undergo her examination. This was one of the weakest and took only a few minutes.

These absurd scenes, which lasted fifteen hours, threatened to continue forever on account of a discussion which was brought up concerning the taking back of the prisoners to the Temple. Finally the suggestion of Manuel was followed, and it was decided that the princess as well as each of her faithful attendants, except Hue, who had obtained permission to return to the Temple, was to be sent to La Force. The unfortunate women were not yet at the end of their torture. The cabs in which they were to be driven through the Rue des Ballets did not leave the Commune until noon, and in order to reach their destination they had to traverse streets filled with crowds which hurled at them all sorts of invectives. The formalities of the ordeal once over, the princess was locked in a small room.

The good woman was so overcome, and her mind so affected, that on crossing the threshold of her prison she felt neither fear nor emotion. The only pain she experienced was at finding herself separated from Madame de Tourzel and her daughter. Incapable of collecting her thoughts, in the face of the disasters which overwhelmed the royal family, she was indifferent to everything. However, having taken a greatly needed rest, she set herself to work to consider the terrible position in which she was placed.

Madame de Tourzel on her part lamented loudly at

being parted from her daughter. On entering her cell the jailer was witness to her violent despair. This man, who was really human, was filled with pity at sight of so motherly a show of feeling, and sought Manuel, no doubt to explain to him how needless was this excess of cruelty. His eloquence prevailed, for a few moments later the Procureur of the Commune sent Pauline back to her mother, and the joy felt by these two poor victims at being together again was such that Manuel himself, in the words of Madame de Tourzel, was moved and proposed to send them at once to Madame de Lamballe.

The following morning (Monday, the 20th) at eight o'clock, according to his promise of the previous evening, Manuel came to take Madame de Tourzel and her daughter to the princess. The poor women had settled themselves among their surroundings as well as they could, and received from the outside world only what was absolutely necessary. Their days were spent in attending to their rooms, in sewing and in reading. Madame de Tourzel, from whom we borrow these details, gives us a most touching picture of the princess, describing her as "gentle, good, and obliging," always ready to do "the smallest favor in her power."

". . . This kind princess," she says farther on, "wished to be spoken to frankly, and on my saying that one who had acted as honorably as herself must not be childish, for that would harm her, but must begin to lead a new life, she replied gently that she had already formed such a resolution, and that she intended resuming her religious duties, which she had somewhat neglected."

These several arrests had not left Paris unmoved. In his diary, August 20th, John Moore mentions them and gives as a cause " some secret correspondence of which the victims were accused." The " Moniteur " of Monday, August 20th, also refers to the transfer to La Force of Madame de Lamballe, Tourzelle (*sic*) mother and daughter, of three other waiting women belonging to the queen, and of the royal prince, besides two valets who had followed the king to the Temple. The paper gives no reasons; it states, however, that seals were put on their papers.

The most interesting of all these accounts is without doubt that of the " Chronique de Paris," which we give in full. It will be seen that these letters, which apparently frightened the city so greatly, were the only grievances this sheet could advance, and they were purely imaginary :

" THE ROYAL FAMILY IN THE TEMPLE.

" The face of the queen is greatly altered. The king's is in no way changed, and his appetite is unaffected. Madame de Lamballe, Madame de Tourzel and her daughter, Monsieur de Chamilly, and several others are in the Temple with him. Every effort has been made to carry on a correspondence. Already letters have been smuggled between the folds of a chemise, in a child's balloon, in a piece of almond cake, and in a pot of pomade. The municipal officers, informed about these details, on Saturday removed Mesdames de Lamballe and de Tourzel, who left the queen with a show of affection which did honor to their attachment; but they also gave proofs of that servile respect which Asiatic slaves have for despots, and this lessens the sympathy their love should inspire: they kissed the hands of the queen without daring to embrace her. It was two o'clock in the morning; the king awakened and asked what was going on; on being told that they did not want him, he turned over and again fell asleep. He rose as usual with a large appetite, which he promptly satisfied. We give these minute details because they may help to show the characters of the prisoners, and history may some day profit by them.

"Mesdames de Lamballe and de Tourzel and Monsieur de Chamilly have been taken to the Hôtel de la Force.

Let us now return to La Force and to the princess and her companions, whom we find saddened by lack of news. Uncertainty as to the fate of the queen especially affected them. From time to time they ventured to question their jailer, but the latter had orders to tell them nothing definite. For this reason the anxiety of the wretched women was all the greater. However, one day they received a visit from Manuel, whom they at once questioned on the subject uppermost in their minds. At first Manuel refused to answer, giving as an excuse his feelings of hatred against

the royal family; but by degrees becoming softened by
their explanations and the loyal confession of their profound love for every member of the royal family, he
completely reassured them and gave the princess a letter
from her father-in-law.   Then, not content with what
he had already done, and more and more touched
by the gratitude of the victims whom he had been sent
to watch, Manuel gave them permission to write "a few
unsealed words," to receive letters, and—a still greater
favor—ordered the jailer to let them walk in the courtyard.

Another time Colonges brought some coarse linen
and, handing the package to the princess, ordered her
to make shirts, under the pretext that it was customary to work in prison.   "They are for the use of our
brothers-in-arms; you are surely too loyal a patriot,'
said he, "not to sew them gladly."—"Nothing that
can be useful to our fellow-countrymen," answered
Madame de Lamballe gently, "shall be neglected by
us."   These shirts, however, were at once removed,
probably by order of Manuel, and nothing more was
heard of them.

In spite of the change in her mode of life, in spite
of the miseries of the prison, never, in the words of
the governess, had the princess been in better health;
she was not troubled by the slightest nervous attack
and bore her situation with angelic resignation.

Sunday morning, September 2d, the jailer, with face
contorted, entered the cells of his prisoners and told

them he would not take them for their usual walk
because of the agitation caused by the approach of the
enemy's army. Greatly alarmed at this news, the
meaning of which they could not understand, the unfortunate women were beset by various conjectures.
Except for the omission of the walk, that day passed
like the preceding ones. When the prisoners had retired and had fallen asleep, a good-looking individual
with rather a kindly face, whom as yet they had not
seen, entered their room and ordered Pauline to rise
and follow him. The unexpected arrival of this man
and the command uttered in a tone which admitted of
no reply, so filled the poor mother with terror that she
did not even think of rising. Upon the stranger's in-
sisting that no time be lost, Madame de Lamballe in
spite of her fright began to attend to the preparations
for Pauline's departure. The affair was over so quickly
that the door was closed before Madame de Tourzel
fully realized it all; she was completely overcome,
speechless, unable to collect her thoughts. At length,
thanks to the care and the kind words of the compas-
sionate princess, Madame de Tourzel came to herself
and was able to thank Madame de Lamballe for her
thoughtfulness. We can do no bettter than quote the
entire passage from her "Mémoires" in which she
gives high praise to the kindness of her companion in
misfortune:

"I shall always be grateful," she said, "to Madame de Lamballe for all her goodness to me and to my

daughter. It is impossible to be kinder than she was that dreadful night, or to show more sympathy and courage.''

In short, the princess did not lose her presence of mind on that sad occasion, and did not think of taking the few hours remaining for sleep until after she had burned that part of her correspondence which might compromise her or her companions. Towards six o'clock in the morning the jailer suddenly entered to announce that they were to receive a visit.

Scarcely had François given them this warning before they saw six men enter armed to the teeth, who retired after they had asked the names of the prisoners. After the departure of the visitors the miserable women, filled with the greatest anxiety, incapable of understanding the real aim of this sudden visit, threw themselves on their knees and prayed, asking heaven to give them both the strength necessary to meet the danger they feared. At the same time Madame de Lamballe, wishing to see what was going on in the street, climbed to the window-sill; but as soon as she was perceived she was aimed at and had to retire at once. She saw, however, that before the gate of the prison was a dense, tumultuous crowd, the sight of which served only to augment her terror. When she raised the window opening upon the interior of the prison there was not the slightest sound. The courtyard was filled with prisoners, calm and resigned. This was so striking a contrast to the outer agitation that she and her companion waited to obtain an explanation from the jailer. Not seeing him arrive, and in the hope of diverting their thoughts, they took up their sewing.

At eleven o'clock in the morning the door again opened; armed men entered the room, asking for Madame de Lamballe. Madame de Tourzel, whom they had not demanded, was unwilling, however, to abandon the princess, and both at once went out. They were ordered to be seated while the other women of the prison were assembled. Madame de Lamballe, who had eaten nothing since the previous evening, asked for some bread and wine to revive her failing strength and enable her to keep up until the end. Shortly after, they received orders to descend to the courtyard, where they found the attendants of the queen.

Here things looked sinister. Everywhere were men with repellent faces, covered with rags, and for the most part intoxicated. These cowardly brutes had the cruelty to laugh and to heap the most ribald insults upon the unhappy prisoners who were being led out. The arrival of the princess was greeted with redoubled cries and shouts. But weak as she was she succeeded in compelling the respect of the wretches, who recoiled involuntarily to make way for her.

Madame de Lamballe seated herself in a corner of the court, accompanied by Madame de Tourzel, who did not leave until the princess was summoned to appear in court.

According to the account left us by her companion

in misery the princess showed the greatest courage during the farewell scene. But once separated from her friend, overcome by the efforts made to reassure her, the poor creature's nerve gave way, and, completely exhausted, she lost consciousness on entering the clerk's office. This fainting spell was easily explained by the atmosphere of the revolutionary tribunal.[2]

This improvised tribunal was held in the chamber of Bault the concierge. The room was very small and was filled with a crowd of spectators. The air of this frightful place was atrocious. The vapors arising from the drunken crowd made one ill. Furthermore, the sight of the dreadful creatures who lined the public benches, and the moans of the dying, heard from without, were sufficient to shake stronger nerves than those of a woman. The president first plied her with the usual questions, regarding her name and title; then he asked her what she knew of the plots at court, of which she had probably heard, and of that of August 10th in particular.

The princess declared that she had never been informed of these facts.

In conclusion she was called on to take the oath of liberty and equality, as well as that of hatred toward the king, the queen, and the royal family.

At this supreme moment, when she was asked to perjure herself and give up those whom she held most dear, the princess seemed to gather herself together. The story is that some one leaned towards her and whispered that she was lost if she did not swear. But moved as by a hidden spring Madame de Lamballe made a violent effort and cried out:

"I have nothing to answer. Whether I die sooner or later is a matter of indifference to me. I have sacrificed my life."

Under the pretext that she had evaded the question, the president ordered her taken to the Abbaye.[3]

This was the death sentence. At once deafening cries and shouts mingled with cheers burst from all sides. Some of the more courageous ventured to raise their voices and ask the release of the princess, but these were soon deadened by the increasing tumult in the crowd, which was constantly demanding new victims to immolate.

At that moment some men with haggard eyes and bare arms red with blood, rushed towards the poor creature and dragged the princess away. Scarcely had she crossed the threshold when she received, they say, on the back of her head a blow from a sabre. She was covered with blood; her hair was loosened; hands continued to push her; she staggered over corpses with which she was forced to come into contact. She could scarcely stand; at last she fell back exhausted. She was immediately raised; two men seized her by the arms and compelled her to move on.

But human endurance has its limit, and when her strength had completely left her and she had become

inert, the men who supported her threw her on a pile
of dead bodies.

Then these murderers, maddened by the dastardly
crowd around the victims, were pitiless enough to rush
upon this palpitating body and cut off its head.

Having reached this point in the drama, we shall be
very reserved. There are in fact numerous accounts
of the massacres of September, and particularly of the
death of the Princesse de Lamballe. But historians
differ, the most of them yielding to their personal feelings. As none of them were eye-witnesses, their descriptions suffer. Others of still livelier imaginations,
and with the confessed object of interesting their
readers, have added details of such horror that we cannot even repeat them.

Consequently, in the face of their lack of historical
value, we will refrain even from giving the passages
which seem probable, and will merely cite without
comment those which seem to us least known. It is
generally believed that some men took possession of
the head of the princess and carried it to a wine merchant's to drink its health. Furthermore, a hairdresser
was asked to curl the hair, to paint the cheeks—in a
word, to make it beautiful.

It is absolutely certain that this head and this body
were carried through the streets—the one on a pike, the
other dragged by means of a rope—as far as the Temple.
The object was to exhibit the bloody remains to the royal
family. We give an account of the gloomy proces-

sion written by a municipal officer in the service of the
Temple—an account which is, we believe, even if it
has been before published, only slightly known:

"The following day, September 3d, we learned that
there was trouble in the prisons. Shortly after, we
heard of the massacre of some of those connected with
the court; at last about one o'clock we were told of
the death of the Princesse de Lamballe, whose head,
they said, they were carrying to be kissed by Marie
Antoinette; then they meant to drag the bodies of both
women through the streets of Paris.

"In the name of the Council of the Temple I
wrote both to the Consul-general of the Commune and
to the President of the Legislative Body to inform
them of the danger which threatened the hostages confided to our charge. We asked each to send six
commissioners from the bodies which enjoyed most
public favor, repeating that whatever happened we
expected entire devotion to us.

"Yet an orderly sent to reconnoitre announced that
an immense crowd was rushing to the Temple with the
head of the Princesse de Lamballe; that they were dragging with them her body and shouting for Marie Antoinette, and that in five minutes they would be at the
Temple.

"Two commissioners were at once despatched to
find out the intentions of the people and apparently to
make friends with them if circumstances demanded it.
Above all the commissioners were to get possession of
the pike, for carried according to our directions it
would serve as a guide to the crowd, which in this way
would be managed more easily.

"Two other commissioners were charged to go to

the suburbs to inform those who seemed most hot-
headed that Paris could never recover from so atrocious
and needless a crime if it so compromised itself, etc.
Several good citizens joined them, promising us to use
every effort to bring the most obstinate to reason. The
noise increased, and with it the confusion. The Chief
of Police asked our orders, adding that he had four hundred well-armed men for whom he could answer, but
that he would assume nothing himself. We told him
that we intended using force only as a final resort; that
our duty first compelled us to try persuasion; that consequently he must be careful about using arms, etc.
He made his plans accordingly.

" Already the crowd in the street was dense; we
had the great gate opened in order that those on the
outside might become calmed on seeing our peaceful
intentions. A portion of the National Guard lined up
without arms from the outer gate to the next one confirmed our attitude. However, all arms, posts, and
avenues were well guarded, as we feared a surprise.

" Uproarious and prolonged cries of ' Here they are! '
were heard. A tri-colored band hastily fastened outside the gate on the street was the only rampart with
which the magistrate opposed that apparently overwhelming torrent. A chair was placed behind; I
mounted it and waited; the bloody procession arrived.

" At sight of the revered emblem those hearts drunk
with blood and wine seemed to cast aside the fury of
homicide to give place to national respect. Each one
used what strength he had to prevent the desecration
of the sacred barrier. To touch it seemed a crime.
. . . They wanted to seem what they thought they
were—virtuous. So much does opinion, which is the
standard of public morals, hold sway over the very man

who, while insulting it, renders it glorious homage! Two men were dragging by the legs a naked, headless trunk slit open to the breast, its back on the ground. They halted before the swaying platform, at the feet of which the body was laid with a show of solemnity, the limbs arranged carefully, and with an indifference that gives to the philosopher much room for thought.

" At my right, on the end of a pike, was a head which at the gesticulations of the bearer often touched my face. At my left another fiend, more horrible still, was holding in one hand pressed against me the entrails of the victim, and in the other a huge knife. Behind these a great coal-heaver was waving, suspended from a pike above my forehead, the fragment of a chemise soaked in blood and slime.

" My right arm had been extended since their arrival, and without making any sign or movement I awaited silence; I obtained it.

" I told them that magistrates chosen by them were charged with a trust by the National Assembly, a trust for which they must render account to this Assembly as well as to the whole of France, and that they had sworn to give back this trust in the condition in which they had received it; that we had been told in vain that complaints had been made against the prisoners as a pretext for the use of arms against them; that this measure had been rejected with horror, persuaded as we were that Frenchmen had only to hear the language of justice to listen to it. I made them realize how impolitic it would be to get rid of such valuable hostages just as the enemy was master of our frontiers. On the other hand, would not the innocence of these hostages be proven by the fact that we dared not try them? How much more worthy of a great people it was, I added, to strike on the scaffold a king guilty of treason! This wholesome example in carrying just terror into the souls of the tyrants would impress on that of the people a sacred respect for our nation, etc. I concluded by inviting them to fortify themselves against the advice of some merchants who wished to lead the Parisians into excess in order afterwards to calumniate them in the minds of their brothers in the departments. To testify to them the confidence the Council had in their wisdom I told them that it had decreed that six of them should be admitted to a tour of the garden, the commissioners at their head.

"The gate was at once opened and about a dozen of them entered with their spoils. We conducted them with courtesy as far as the tower, but because of the workmen among them, it was difficult to restrain them. Some called Marie Antoinette to come to the windows; others said if she did not show herself they must ascend and make her kiss the princess's head. We threw ourselves in front of these madmen, assuring them that they should carry our their frightful ideas only after they had passed over the bodies of their magistrates. One of these wretches said that I was playing the part of tyrant and came at me with his pike with such fury that I must certainly have fallen under his blows had I shown weakness, and had not a citizen thrown himself between us, saying that in my place he should have been obliged to act as I had done. My calmness impressed him, and on leaving he was the first to embrace me, saying that I was a fine fellow. However, two commissioners had hurled themselves in front of the first gate of the tower, to defend its approach with the courage of devotion. Then, seeing that they could obtain nothing from us, the ruffians swore

terrible oaths, giving vent to dreadful shouts in the
most obscene and disgusting terms. This was the final
gasp of fury, and we let it pass. However, fearing that
the scene might lead to a climax worthy of the actors,
I undertook to harangue them again. But what could
I say? How reach those unfeeling brutes? I gained
their attention by gestures; they looked and listened.
I praised their courage, their deeds. I made heroes of
them. Then seeing them soften, by degrees I mingled
reproach with praise. I told them that the spoils they
brought were the property of all. By what right, I
added, can you alone enjoy your conquest? Does it
not belong to all Paris? And should you deprive the
city of the pleasure of sharing your triumph? Night
will soon be here; hasten therefore to leave this place,
which is too narrow for your glory. At the Palais
Royal, in the Garden of the Tuileries, where so many
times has been trampled under foot the sovereignty of
the people, you should place this trophy, an everlasting
monument of the victory you have just won.

"Shouts of 'To the Palais Royal!' showed me that
my absurd harangue had told. They departed, leaving
us covered with blood and wine from their horrible
embraces.

"However, the Legislative Assembly sent the six
commissioners we had asked for. They learned with
pleasure that the reports already spread abroad were
false, and showed us in the name of the legislative
body their satisfaction at the way we had acted.

"Scarcely were the commissioners gone before
Mayor Pétion arrived. He seemed in despair because,
as he thought, we had let the people force Marie Antoinette to kiss De Lamballe's head. 'Never should
magistrates,' said he, 'have allowed such a dreadful

thing.' He was delighted to learn not only that no one had entered the tower, but that the commissioners who were near the prisoners had not even permitted them to approach the window to see what was the cause of the noise they heard in the garden, but had sent them at once into a rear room. The Commander-general Santerre also came to us." [6]

CHAPTER XIX

Some historians say that from the Temple the procession passed to the Palais Royal and then to the
Hôtel de Toulouse. It is positive that the body of the
unfortunate victim was taken to the district of the
Quinze-Vingts. The official account of this, written
hastily in the midst of the confusion, unfortunately does
not indicate the time, while that concerning the head
gives the exact hour. It was seven o'clock at night.
This second report alone, which is more explicit,
proves to us that that beautiful head, covered with its
marvellous hair, rests in the cemetery of the Enfants-
Trouvés.

We append both accounts. They are fuller than
those given by any historian so far, and contain the
description of the famous ring of hair which Marie
Antoinette sent to her friend during the stay of the
latter at Aix-la-Chapelle:

" DEATH OF THE CI-DEVANT PRINCESSE LAMBALLE.

" [Extract from the official reports of the district
of the Quinze-Vingts.]
" On the 3d of September, in the year 1792, the
fourth year of Liberty and Equality, there appeared

before the Permanent Committee of the district of the Quinze-Vingts Sieurs Jacques Charles Hervelin, drummer of the gunners of the district of the Halles, former battalion of Saint Jacques de la Boucherie, dwelling number 3 Rue de la Savonnerie, opposite the little street of Avignon au Cadran Bleu; Jean Gabriel Quervelle, cabinet-maker, at the corner of the Rue du Fauxbourg Saint-Antoine and the Rue Saint Nicolas, Maison à Bouneau; Antoine Pouquet, gunner of the district of Montreuil, number 25 Rue de Charonne, at Sieur Vicq's; and Pierre Ferrie, dealer in fancy goods, number 39 Rue Popincourt. These men were bearers of the headless body of the ci-devant Princesse de Lamballe, who had just been killed at the Hôtel de la Force, and whose head was carried by others on a pike through the principal streets. They stated that in her clothes they had found the following articles—namely, a small volume bound in red morocco with gilt edges, entitled ' Imitation de J.-C.'; a red morocco portfolio; a case containing eighteen national assignats' of five livres each; a gold ring with a bezel of changeable blue stone, in which was some blond hair tied in a love-knot with these words above it: ' Whitened through misery '; an English bulb; a small ivory pencil-holder containing a gold pen with two small gold rings; a small two-bladed knife, the handle of tortoise-shell and silver; a corkscrew of English steel; a small pair of pincers of the same metal; a small card attached to a vignette bearing undecipherable words; a bit of paper on which was written a laundry list; two small glass flasks used for inkstands, with gold tops, and some sticks of different colored sealing-wax; a sort of double-faced image, on one side representing a bleeding heart surrounded with thorns and pierced by a dagger, with

these words below: ' Cor Jesu, salva nos, perimur,' on
the other a bleeding heart with a fleur-de-lis above,
and below the words: ' Cor Mariæ unitum cordi
Christi '; a medallion on light blue cloth, on which
was painted a bleeding heart pierced by a dagger, embroidered in blue silk. These articles were verified by
us in the presence of the above-named and the undersigned to whom we gave them all, in order that they
might be laid before the National Assembly. This the
undersigned promised and swore should be done. All
this having been arranged they gave us a written receipt and signed with us, commissioners.

" CAUMONT, BORIE, SAVARD, Commissioners.
" RENET, Clerk of the Secretary.

" The same day at seven o'clock a citizen named
Jacques Pointel, living in the section of the Halle
au Bléd, number 69 Rue des Petits Champs, appeared before the Committee from the district of
the Quinze-Vingts. He asked us to be kind enough
to use our authority to have the head of the late
Princesse de Lamballe buried, as he had succeeded
in obtaining it. Unable to do otherwise than approve
the patriotism and the humanity of the aforesaid citizen,
we, the undersigned commissioners, went at once to
the cemetery of the Enfants-Trouvés and had the aforesaid head buried there, drawing up for future use the
present official account of the burial, which said Pointel
signed with us.

" DESESQUELLE and SAVARD, Commissioners.
" POINTEL.
" RENET, Secretary.

" At the same time were presented Messieurs
Hervelin, Quervelle, Pouquet, Ferrie, and Roussel,

named in the above account. They showed us a receipt for all the effects mentioned in the present report, with the exception of ninety livres in assignats, of which no mention is made; consequently we commissioners of the district, because of this omission of the bills, say that one of us accompanied by the Clerk of the Secretary from the district will go at once to the Committee of Vigilance of the National Assembly in order to learn the reason for this omission, and we have signed ourselves

" SAVARD, DESESQUELLE, Commissioners.
" RENET, Secretary.

" The attestation of the Committee of Vigilance given to the Commissioners and to the Clerk of the Secretary in the presence of the above-named. The Committee of Vigilance declares that it was not bound to account for the ninety livres in assignats, because the citizens had kept them—after having shown them, as three of those present testified immediately in the presence of the Commissioner from the district of the Quinze-Vingts. The Committee sent to the district to find out and judge of the reason for this retention. At the Committee of Public Safety, September 3d, fourth year of Liberty and Equality.

" BERNARD, President.
" BASIRE, Secretary.
" CLAUDE, FAUCHÉS, MOSSON, VARDON, LOMONT."

It may not be wholly useless to know the opinion of the newspapers on the subject of this frightful crime. Their attitude is curious indeed. The papers which dared, deliberately drew a veil over this dreadful page of the Revolution.

The " Thermomètre du Jour" merely related the facts without comment; the " Chronique" did not venture to speak of the event until five days after. Moreover, it was uncertain as to the exact date of the death.

" Louis XVI.," it says in the article entitled " Variétés," " shows a sort of forced composure: he translates Horace and teaches his son verses of tragedy. On the afternoon of the 2nd he was told that he must consent to see Madame de Lamballe's head, which a few men from the immense crowd surrounding the Temple had brought to show him. Marie Antoinette and Louis XVI. showed some emotion. The king advanced without hesitation. He has had a good supper and the entire family always have fine appetites."

The " Courrier Français" is trying to exonerate Manuel, and attributes the massacres to the fear felt by the people at leaving their relatives in the midst of the brigands of the capital while they rushed to the frontier:

" What a night! What a day! The Procureur of the Commune tried in vain to bar with his body the door of the Abbaye. He succeeded no better than did the deputies of the National Assembly. The people made it a duty to purge the city of all criminals so that while they are away fighting the Austrians they need not fear an exodus from the prisons against the women and children.

" There is no longer at the Châtelet any one but the concierge. They have liberated the innocent and those imprisoned for debt. Twenty-four women also have been spared. Madame de Lamballe has lost her life.'

Thus the paper does not enter into details but merely states that Madame de Lamballe lost her life. Nor is the matter referred to again. Three days later, on the 7th of September, the '' Courrier '' gives a few details of the events that took place that afternoon before the Temple. This was no doubt intentional or in accordance with instructions, followed through fear, not to dwell on the dreadful butchery in the Rue des Ballets.

'' The 3d of September the commandants of the posts were informed that an immense crowd was rushing to the Temple with the head of Madame de Lamballe. Only a tri-colored band impeded their mad rush. This band bore the following inscription: ' Citizens, you who to just vengeance can join a love of order, respect this barrier; our care and our responsibility make it necessary.' The people respected the barrier, but they demanded that some commissioners accompany them in order to carry the head of Madame de Lamballe around the tower. ' We desire,' said the spokesman, ' that those who have caused so much trouble may see the sad and fatal result of their conspiracies and their infernal plots.' The commissioners thought they ought to yield to the wishes of the people. Messieurs Chardier, Guichard, an officer of the National Guard, and the patriot Palloi determined to warn the king and his family. Madame Elisabeth showed some fear; Louis XVI. appeared at once. ' *You are wholly in the right, Monsieur*,' said he to the speaker.'

The following account is no more explicit than the rest :

" PARIS, September 4th.

" It was absolutely impossible for us yesterday to give an account of the events of the previous evening, the affairs which must have engrossed every good citizen. The difficulty of giving positive details in the midst of so many contradictory reports prevented us from so doing, and our readers will prefer us to defer the account which they consider due rather than that it should be inexact.

" Madame de Lamballe's head was cut off and her body borne through the streets. We are told that Mademoiselle de Tourzel was respected on account of her youth, but her mother was subjected to the same fate as Madame de Lamballe."

Now that we have indicated the sources from which our readers may find details of the massacres and have given the tone of some important papers of that time, let us name various accounts less known, and absolutely fictitious, which seem to have been written merely to render this atrocious crime still more odious.

We will commence with M. W. Lindsay, a phlegmatic Englishman, who knows nothing because he saw nothing, but who feels so much horror in relating such infamies that he prefers to keep silent. This is a fine way to write history and one which fortunately for us has not always been followed.

The account of the Abbé Barruel is a tissue of blunders written for the needs of the cause which he defends with a tendency towards intentional exaggeration:

"At the feet of those piles of corpses," we read in his work, "another kind of experience was awaiting an illustrious victim. Madame de Lamballe, that princess so justly celebrated for her attachment to the royal family, preferring danger near her king and queen rather than a place of safety and the homage of London, was at first taken to the prison of the Temple and then to that of La Force. The Jacobins had to punish her for her fidelity.

"This victim was a choice bit for their rage. She would have been the first sacrificed, but the massacre had begun at La Force early in the night and it was in broad daylight that they wished to immolate her. About three o'clock in the morning she saw the first signs of her ordeal. One of the murderous duumvirs, the so-called judges of the people, went to the prison of the women shouting to the executioner and to the guards in the courtyard: 'Citizens, the people have sent me to put the Princesse de Lamballe through a first examination; I will return in a moment and tell you the result.' He did return but was silent as to the result. The courage of the princess had covered him with confusion, although it had in no way lessened his rage. About seven o'clock the duumvir, followed by twenty men bearing pikes or bayonets, came back again and shouted: 'Citizens, we are going to get the Princesse de Lamballe.' Before long the princess, dragged by the hair, appeared in the courtyard where the prisoners were awaiting their sentences. Until nine o'clock she saw crowds coming and going, but preserving a noble dignity she stood, awaiting sure death, refusing even the comfort of a chair which was offered her.

" At nine o'clock she was called to the court of the ferocious duumvirs. They reproached her with having been an accomplice in the crimes of the queen against the nation. She replied, ' I know of no crimes of the queen against the nation.'—' You were informed of the conspiracy of August 10th against the people.'—' I still protest that I am ignorant of any such conspiracy against the people.'—' You have corresponded with the *émigrés* and you have received from the Prince de Condé this letter which is before you.'—' To receive letters from a relative is no crime; this letter contains nothing against the nation.'—' Swear with us hatred against the king, the queen, and royalty.'—' No such feeling is in my heart. I cannot swear it.'

" At this reply the duumvirs pronounced the fatal word ' Discharged.' The princess was dragged toward the gate.

" At sight of her shouts of savage joy run along the double line of executioners. Her death is decided on, but it will ill satisfy their rage if they cannot add to it the pleasure of having humiliated her.

" As she passes the line stretching out to the heap of corpses some executioners rush forward and bar her way; with ferocious smiles on their lips, with brutal sarcasms in their mouths, with monstrous pride in their hearts they strike with bloody hands the cheeks of their august victim. The plaything of these atrocious bandits, she summons all her strength. She does not lose it even at the sight of the horrible trophy. At the place where the chief of the brigands was accustomed to demand the oath of Liberty and Equality he orders the Princesse de Lamballe to kneel and to ask pardon of the nation.

"' I have not sinned against the nation. I have no pardon to ask of it.'—' Your forgiveness depends upon your obedience.'—' I do not ask mercy from brigands such as you who dare to call yourselves the nation.'—' Once more if you value your life, obey, kneel, and ask pardon.'—' No, I will not kneel; no, I have no mercy, no pardon to ask.'

" Thus this generous soul showed herself firm, unwearying, determined. A thousand voices from the maddened crowd cried in vain: ' On your knees and ask pardon.

" She remains standing. Two enraged executioners, one on each side, seize her by the hands and twist with sufficient force to dislocate them. She gathers all her remaining strength and says: ' Pull, hangmen. Never, never will I ask pardon.'

" With all the madness of fury other executioners spring upon her and with redoubled blows from their sabres slit her open and disembowel her. Her head, remarkable for its long hair, soon appeared on the end of a pike; her heart torn by the teeth of a brigand was thrown into a basin.

" This head and heart were carried in triumph through the streets of Paris as far as the Temple, and even before the eyes of the king, who was compelled to look at them. Fortunately the queen had fainted from horror and so was spared the frightful sight.

" The least of the outrages done to the body of the princess was to strip it and throw it on a heap of corpses. It remained there until the end of the horrible massacre, feet and back turned toward the prison. It was still there on the night of the 3d of September, when Monsieur Flaust, curate of the Maisons, was led to the place by the executioners.''

We have not yet finished with exaggeration, as is shown by the following account:

" . . . At last the 2nd of September arrived, the day on which the massacres became general in Paris. All the prisons were broken into and all found there, even though they were for the most part good patriots and zealous partisans of the Constitution, were inhumanly massacred and cut to pieces. The number reached twelve thousand. Monsieur Louvet even stated on the 29th of October, before the National Convention, that twenty-eight thousand had perished. The streets ran with blood.

" The murder of the charming Princesse de Lamballe, the intimate friend of the queen, excited general pity. The monsters dragged her from prison, stripped her, maltreated her, insulted her, committed infamous outrages on her, forced her to kiss bloody corpses, cut off her breasts and various other portions of her body, slashed her with swords, severed her head, which they carried on a pike through the principal streets of the capital, and dragged her mutilated body through the bloody mire.

" Truly she died an heroic death. Having obtained permission to make her will she wrote it with the greatest calmness, handed the document to an urchin who stood near by and cried, ' Almighty God, receive my soul! Come on, tigers, I am ready. Kill me!' One of the brigands carried on the end of a pike that head from which hung a mass of blonde hair soaked with blood. He was followed by another, who carried in his hand the bloody heart of the princess while her entrails were twisted around his arm. In this way they passed under the windows of the Duc de Penthièvre, whom they forced to gaze on the mutilated members of his daughter-in-law. From there they proceeded to the Temple, to the royal family. The queen fainted at the horrible sight. All the carriages in the streets were stopped and their occupants compelled to kiss the head of the princess. One monster boasted of having made his dinner on the heart of Madame de Lamballe.

"At the murder of the princess there was in the crowd of spectators a man of some feeling. Seeing the infamous insults which the assassins heaped upon the naked body of the princess, . . . he cried out in his indignation, 'Shame, you wretches! Remember that you have wives and mothers!' Instantly he was pierced by a thousand blades and his mutilated body was torn to pieces."

Finally we will quote the version of the Comte de Fersen,[2] who had been abroad since the journey to Varennes.

"Madame la Princesse de Lamballe," he wrote, "has been tortured most horribly for four hours. My pen refuses to write the details. They tore out her entrails with their teeth and afterwards gave her every possible restorative for two hours to resuscitate her that she might more fully realize the torture of death."

We will conclude with Rétif de la Bretonne, an authority seldom consulted perhaps, yet of use in regard to the customs of the end of the eighteenth century. In his work Rétif refers three times to these events. First, in "L'Année des Dames Nationales" in the

xi. *hors-d'œuvre*, in which he says in substance that he has sought eye-witnesses: " I have found them," he continues. " I state nothing of which I am not sure. I am unlike many others who far from seeking the truth ignore it when it does not tally with their preconceived ideas."

Then in " Monsieur Nicolas," in which he attributes to Tallien the honor of having saved Madame and Mademoiselle de Tourzel.

The third and most interesting account, in which Rétif assumes the position of eye-witness and in which at the supreme moment he fainted away, shows us the difficulty experienced by *this friend of facts* in relating an episode which with writers of the Revolution is one of the strong points:

" I arose dazed with terror. The night had not refreshed me, but had inflamed my blood. I went out. . . . I listened. I was among those running to the scene of the disasters, for such was their expression. Passing in front of the Conciergerie I saw an assassin who they told me was a sailor from Marseilles, his wrist swollen from fatigue. . . . I passed on. Before the Châtelet lay piles of dead. I started to flee. . . . Yet I followed the crowds. I reached the Rue Saint-Antoine, at the end of the Rue des Ballets, just as a wretched victim, who had seen how they were killing his predecessor, instead of stopping overwhelmed on passing through the gate, started to run at full speed. A man who did not belong to the butchers, but who was one of those numberless unthinking machines, stopped him with his pike. The miserable wretch was attacked by pursuers and murdered. The man who had stopped him said to us coldly, 'I did not know that they wanted to kill him.' This prelude was enough to make me turn back when another scene met my eye. I saw two women come out; one whom I have since known through the interesting Sainte-Brice as lady-in-waiting to a former royal princess, a young person of sixteen years, Mademoiselle de Tourzel.

" There was a cessation of the murders: something was taking place within. . . . I flattered myself that all was over. At last I saw another woman come out; she was as pale as her linen and was supported by a jailer. They shouted to her roughly, ' Cry *Long live the Nation!* '—' No, no! ' said she.

" They made her mount a pile of corpses. One of the butchers seized the jailer and thrust him aside. ' Oh! ' cried the unfortunate woman, ' do not hurt him.' Again they bade her cry '*Long live the Nation!*' She refused with scorn. Then a butcher seized her, tore off her clothes and ripped open her stomach. She fell and was finished by the others. . . .

" My imagination had never pictured such horrors. I strove to flee, my limbs gave way, I fainted. . . . When I came to myself I saw the bloody head. . . . I was told that they were going to wash it, curl the hair, put it on the end of a pike, and carry it beneath the windows of the Temple. Needless cruelty! It could not be seen from them. . . . This unfortunate creature was Madame de Lamballe."

We have now reached the most critical point in our work. Expected to give a decision that we know in advance must be somewhat uncertain because of the numerous lapses in the history of that time, our mind hesitates; it seems unjust, even cruel to the memory of certain individuals to throw the opprobrium of this crime on one rather than on another.

By their numerous researches some conscientious writers have thought it possible to fix the part of each of the instigators and actors in these terrible scenes. But none of them has entirely succeeded in this undertaking. History is not content with simple suppositions, and as it is impossible to find any document whatsoever absolutely compromising the accused we do not intend to follow them. Moreover, this impossibility has already been recognized doubtless because of the substitution and even of the disappearance of all compromising documents, since at the time of the trials of the authors of the September massacres, of which we are about to speak, they did not follow those who gave the orders, but only those who executed them.

On the other hand we will give the famous circular sent the 3rd of September by the Committee of Vigilance of the Commune to all it departments:

" The Commune of Paris hastens to inform its brothers and all the departments that some of the ferocious conspirators shut up in the prisons have been put to death by the people, an act of justice which seemed necessary to terrify, and so to restrain those legions of traitors hidden within the walls at the moment when they themselves were about to march against the enemy; and no doubt the whole nation, after the long continuance of the treacherous acts which led it to the brink of the abyss, would hasten to adopt this means so essential to the public safety, and all Frenchmen would cry out as the Parisians had done:

" ' We are marching against the enemy, but we will not leave behind us brigands to cut the throats of our wives and children. . . . ' "

What are the signatures to this address? In the first place Danton, who as Minister of Justice countersigned it; the ten members of the Committee of Vigilance: Panis, Sergent, P.-J. Duplain, Jourdeuil, Leclerc, Lenfant, Cally, Duffort, Guermeur, Deforgues (*sic*).

These were the men who consented to shoulder the responsibility of the deed.

But no! Desforgues, the thirteenth Thermidor, the third year (Monday, the 17th of August, 1795), protested against the affixing of his signature to the incriminating circular, because the twenty-sixth Thermidor he was under arrest.

"I can," said he, "with one word render powerless all the shafts of calumny. I swear that I never signed the celebrated circular in question. ' "

And he strives to prove that he was not really elected until the 14th of September, and that for this reason he could not be prosecuted on account of the massacres, which began on the 2nd.

On the other hand, we give below a document which relates to the same matter, and in which the name of Desforgues occurs on the margin:

" DEPARTMENT OF THE POLICE AND THE NATIONAL GUARD, MUNICIPALITY OF PARIS.

" We, the undersigned, appointed by the Mayor on the Police and Vigilance Committee by a decree of the Commune which states that one of us (Panis) shall choose three colleagues who with him shall constitute the Committee—we have resolved, considering the crisis of affairs and the various and important works to which we must attend, to appoint as associate administrators our six citizens: Marat, the friend of the people; Desforgues (Chief of the Bureau of the Mayoralty); Lenfant, Guermeur, Leclerc, and Duffort, who shall sign with us under our inspection, since we the four undersigned are responsible for the whole. At the Mayoralty, September 2nd, '92, the first year. Administrators of Police and Vigilance Committee, " PIERRE DUPLAIN, PANIS, SERGENT, JOURDEUIL."

In this document, dated September 2nd, the name of Marat appears, and on September 14th it is replaced by that of Cally.

Does not this circular tend to prove that the Com²mittee appointed members without consulting them?

And what would then become of the Collot-d'Herbois, the Billaud-Varennes, the Stanislas-Maillard, Tallien, and others?

The first as president of the section of the Biblio-

thèque signed August 18, 1792, the following decree
stating that " as Monsieur Vesbre (for Weber), *foster
brother of the wife of the king*, was about to send away
his furniture and go himself, two commissioners went
to his home to put it under lock and key and make
sure of his person."

Panis, the brother-in-law of Santerre, in a half-
sheet leaflet in-8, 1814, also protested against his
having been implicated in the massacres. This pamphlet was without the name of any printer and was
signed " Panis, Attorney for Parliament and Deputy
from Paris to the National Convention."

" The author," says Monsieur Barthelémy Maurice,
" died in 1827 poor and unknown, as did most of the
Revolutionists. Replying to an article in the ' Gazette
de France' October 13, 1814, he attempts to prove
that it was the same with Danton and several of
his colleagues on the Committee. This is wholly
contrary to the contents of this circular. He adds that
it was exclusively the work of Marat, who wrote and
signed it for all the others and who, when the latter
ventured some remonstrances, calmly replied: ' Yes,
I have signed it for all of you, and if there is a *j—f—*
that is not satisfied I will have him strung up to a
lamp-post this evening.' "

For the second, here is what Fabre de l'Aude says:

" Billaud-Varennes, that monster who the 3rd of
September mounted a pile of the dead bodies of victims, thus harangued the murderers:

" ' Brave men and good citizens, you are immolating the enemies of liberty; our grateful country will reward you for the sacrifices you are making for her; the Commune will recompense you in a manner proportionate to your services. No doubt the booty and the spoils of these wretches (the victims) belong to those who have delivered the owners into our hands; but you will take into consideration the scarcity of the funds of the Commune: *whoever* will have *worked in a prison* will receive a check for a louis payable at the bank. Good citizens, continue your work and the country will revere you.' "

As to Stanislas-Maillard, following is the document he wrote; it is without date, but the editor of the " Catalogue " assigns it to September 2nd or 3rd:

" Gentlemen, the tribunal of the people is final; the head of the accused is desired; if he is not guilty we will prove his innocence to the people; if he is guilty they have sworn his death.

" On the part of the people,

" Signed: MAILLARD. "

Thus is Panis absolved; but we give a document tending to prove that at least he was informed of the intention of the murderers. It consists of an autograph order signed and dated September 2, 1792:

" The Concierge of the Abbaye will set free at once, in order to withhold him from the vengeance of the people, who in their fury might forget themselves, and who they say are at this moment approaching, Thuillier, etc., . . . all the seven gendarmes of Paris. "

In his " Mémoires " Sénart boldly accuses Tallien of complicity, stating that the Secretary of the Commune signed with Panis and Sergent compromising documents, which were found at Maillard's after his death.   He adds that this Maillard, " leader of the cut-throats of Paris, known under the name of Tappe-Durs," was a dangerous sharper, a tool wholly in their pay.

In a pamphlet on the real perpetrators of September 2nd, Mehée de la Touche, who hides himself under the pseudonym of Felhemesi, affirms that, besides Marat, Panis, and Tallien, Billaud-Varennes must be included amongst those most guilty :

" Let us render to Cæsar that which is Cæsar's, and to Billaud the things which are Billaud's."

He goes so far as to claim that the morning of the 3rd Billaud-Varennes entered the council chamber of the Commune, holding amicably by the hand a murderer covered with blood whom he introduced as " a brave fellow who has worked well."   But Mehée de la Touche, because of his various callings the nature of which he could not acknowledge, cannot be taken seriously; therefore we have cited him only as a matter of interest.   We are fortunate to be able to offset the manifestoes of the Commune of Paris by the following document from the National Assembly :

" Address from the National Assembly, September 3, 1792, fourth year of Liberty and first of Equality.

" Citizens: You are marching against the enemy; glory awaits you; but beware perfidious suggestions. Your zeal is led astray; you are robbed in advance of the fruit of your efforts, the price of your blood. You are being set at variance; hatred is being sown. There is an attempt to kindle civil war, to excite disorder in Paris. Your enemies flatter themselves that they will spread throughout the empire and throughout your armies; they flatter themselves that, invincible if you are united, you can by intestinal dissensions be delivered without defence to the foreign armies.

" Citizens, there is no longer strength where there is no longer union; there is neither liberty nor country where force takes the place of laws.

" Citizens, in the name of country, humanity, liberty, be wary of men who arouse discord and provoke excess; listen to the voices of the representatives of the nation who were the first to swear Equality. Fight Austria and Prussia; within a few days the Convention will lay the foundations of public happiness. Work to make them secure by triumphs; show by your example that the law should be respected.

" The National Assembly decrees that the present address shall be at once published and posted; that the municipality shall have it proclaimed to the sound of a trumpet, and that it shall be sent to every department and to the army.

" Compared with the original by us, the President and the Secretaries of the National Assembly.

" Paris, September 3, 1792, fourth year of Liberty.

" Signed: HÉRAULT, President; MARANT, Secretary; G. ROMME, Secretary.

" Paris: National Press.''

Furthermore, a reaction could not have been long in making itself felt, and on the 6th the Mayor of Paris addressed a letter to the National Assembly. It reads as follows:

" Permit me," wrote Pétion, " to draw a veil over the past to hide from your eyes the scenes which sadden the soul; let us hope that they may not be repeated; let us hope that the harmony which is to exist among the authorities will guarantee the public tranquillity."

Not content with this, Pétion, who desired order, wrote again September 18th, when the excitement was scarcely calmed, to exhort the inhabitants of Paris to put an end to the repeated disturbances which were disorganizing everything, driving peaceable citizens from the capital, and tending to prevent the National Convention from establishing itself there. " Let those," he continues, " who wish order come forward; let them have the courage to speak boldly; then this handful of agitators who are upsetting everything will be reduced to nothing. '

Following is the substance of a curious letter relating to the massacres and addressed, September 26, 1792, by Roland to the President of the Convention:

" The bills presented to his predecessors for the expenses of the prison of L'Abbaye Saint Germain were inconsiderable; but the one given him to-day by the Concierge of this house, from July 1st to September

5th inclusive, reaches the sum of nineteen thousand and nineteen francs, and he does not think he should authorize the payment of so enormous a sum. He thinks he should wait for orders from the Convention, especially as the greater number of the prisoners named were taken to the Abbaye on simple warrants from the municipality.''

On the margin of this letter Camus, the Secretary of the Convention, had written:

'' Returned to the Committee of Six to show the condition of Paris.''

In this way Roland, by calling attention to the flagrant abuses, hoped to provoke charges against the Commune. But calm and indifference were not reëstablished in spite of the exhortations of Pétion, and it was not until three months later that the Convention dared at last to fix officially the blame for these crimes by ordering the prosecution of their authors. Finally the decree demanded by all honest men was promulgated. It was as broad as could be desired, and accorded to the Minister of Justice every latitude so that none of those guilty might escape:

'' Decree relative to the events of September the 2nd and August the 10th, 1792.
'' The National Convention decrees as follows:
'' Article 1. It is enjoined on the Minister of Justice to prosecute before the tribunals the authors, accomplices, and instigators of the massacres and outrages committed during the first days of September.

MADAME DE LAMBALLE

" 2. The Minister of Justice is also charged to prosecute those who, the night of the 9th and the day of the 10th of August, had gathered together in the Château of the Tuileries armed against the people.

" 3. The Minister of Justice is also charged to prosecute the public officers who left their posts to conspire in Paris with the tyrant and his accomplices. He will give an account of the progress of these various proceedings during the eight days.

" In the name of the Republic the Executive Provisory Council commands and orders all administrative bodies and tribunals to enter the present law on their registers; to read, publish, and post it, and to execute it in their departments and respective courts; in token of which we have hereto affixed our signature and the seal of the Republic.

" Paris, January 23rd, 1793, second year of the French Republic.

" Signed: GARAT, President of the Executive Provisory Council.

" Countersigned: GARAT; and sealed with the seal of the Republic.

" Certified as conforming to the original."

The sane portion of the population began to breathe more freely, hoping that, thanks to this decree, the bandits of September would leave the capital. But this hope was not of long duration, for on the 8th February, 1793, the Convention retracted, recoiling before its self-imposed task, and issued a new decree suspending the proceedings which were already begun.

CHAPTER XX

At the close of 1794 a violent reaction took place and from all sides was demanded the condemnation of those accused of the crimes of September.

In support of this we give the address from the section of the Fraternity to that of the Unity to thank it for having denounced the criminals; for " it is necessary for the whole world to know that those days of mourning and of blood belong not to France but to a faction paid by the foreigner."

" Address from the section of the Fraternity to that of the Unity, pronounced décadi 20 Frimaire, the third year of the French Republic, one, indivisible, and imperishable, by Citizen Franconville:

" Citizens, Brothers, and Friends:
" In paying, as you did, last primidi the tribute of our gratitude to the National Convention for its glorious work, we were witnesses of your triumph; it was worthy of you, brave Republicans, to be the first to demand the denunciation of the criminals who took part in the massacres of the 2nd and 3rd of September, 1792.
" In yielding to your demand the Convention has just proved that in its eyes nothing can excuse the crime of assassination, and that the voice of the

public will not ask in vain the vengeance of the
law on the heads of the cannibals who in their bloody
rage immolated thousands of victims.

" We swear to you in the name of the *Section of the
Fraternity* that it shares your generous sentiments and
that if it succeed in discovering the murderers it will
follow your example.

" We, like you, wish that the pages of history
which record to posterity the massacres of the 2nd
and 3rd of September may also record the punishment
of the assassins; the honor of the French people demands this; the whole world must know that those
days of mourning and of blood belong not to France
but to a faction paid by the foreigner.

" Incorruptible sentinels, ever ready to cry in unison
Qui vive ! at rogues and assassins; we shall no longer
see flowing the precious blood of innocents; we shall
no longer see our laurels mixed with cypress; united
by the same feelings, we will declare war upon the
Terrorists and Scoundrels; we shall reduce the shouters
to silence; we shall establish between us an active
correspondence; thus we shall unearth all the liberticidal
plots. *Unity, Fraternity, and Liberty will triumph.*

" Long live the Republic ! Long live the Convention ! ''

We wish to rectify certain errors committed by Monsieur Mortimer-Ternaux in his excellent '' Histoire de
la Terreur.''

According to him the trial of the September murderers
began as soon as the decree of January 30, 1793, was
issued, while the Convention, as we have already said,
suspended proceedings the 8th of the following February.

He commits still another error when he speaks of only sixteen accused, for we give below a warrant of arrest from the Committee on General Safety of the Convention, signed by the Secretary Colombel, and dated Fructidor 16th, the third year, which mentions " seventeen, and there will be still more.''

" According to information from the section of the Jardin des Plantes (formerly des Sans-Culottes), *seventeen citizens* of that section, detained in the prison of Port-Libre, were sent to the criminal court in Paris as accused of having taken part in the massacre of September 2nd.''

In support of other proofs we will give some extracts from a letter addressed to the Minister of Justice by one of the defenders; then the order for the arrest of one of the most guilty in connection with the death of the princess, which does not come up again until the fifth complémentaire of the third year (Monday, 21st September, 1795). The accused, Gonnord, does not appear among the seventeen prisoners of Port-Libre. Furthermore, Monsieur de Vieil-Castel cites sixty-six prosecuted for that crime.

" Extract from a letter from Pepin Degrouhette, 25 Rue du Santier, one of the defenders of the accused, to the Citizen Minister of Justice:
" The events of September were tolerated by the Government. They were inspired by the fanaticism of liberty and by the fear of falling under the blows of the

royalists who were determined against national representation and the people, and who were allied with the Prussians and the Austrians then investing and invading our territory.

" Should one after three years seek the authors of past events and thus give a cause of triumph to the enemies of the country ? "

It concludes thus :

" I beg you to remember, Citizen Minister, that in the month of February, 1793, when the Convention was still undivided, when no faction had made any attempt upon its integrity, it issued a decree forbidding prosecution to be made because of the deeds of the 2nd and 3rd of September, and that it ordered the discharge of all those under arrest because of those deeds. This law was never put into execution. Could it have been annulled by a decree issued during the mournful reaction which almost overthrew the Republic and caused the massacre of the legislators and all the Republicans ? "

Gonnord, whose name is not found on the list of the seventeen accused, since his arrest did not take place until September 21st, was denounced in May by two citizens, one of whom actually charged him with having taken part in the murder of Madame de Lamballe.

" Copy of the reasons for the arrest of Gonnord, the 5th Prairial, the third year, by a decree of the section of Unity :

" Citizen Burel of the School of Public Works, Rue

Taranne, at the house of Citizen Maignien, institutor, states: That the said Gonnord, sub-lieutenant of the 16th company of the army force, in speaking with him of subsistence said that he *f*—— the government as much as a *m*——, that those who were at the head of the government were *f*—— scoundrels.   He declared that on his observing to Gonnord that he did not think he spoke seriously, the latter replied: 'You do not know what I am; I am *f*—— for opening the body of a man and eating his heart.'   It seems that these expressions were repeated several times by Gonnord, who was still vociferating against the existing government. This document was signed.

"The same day the said Citizen Maignien, institutor, declares that he overheard Gonnord say that he had taken part in the massacres at La Force the 2nd and 3rd of September, and that with another he had led the woman Lamballe by the arm, without specifying this place.   This statement was repeated several times and was signed.

"(Conforms to the extract.)

"Signed: FAYARD, Clerk of the Secretary.

"(Conforms to the copy.)

"GONORD."

Citizen Maignien returns to his first declaration and now affirms that he considers Gonnord a brave man and that he knows nothing bad about him.

This curious letter deserves a place here:

"Literal copy of a letter written to Gonnord by Maignien, the 15th Fructidor, the third year:

"Citizen, I repeat that if it is on my declaration that they have imprisoned you I am surprised, for that proves nothing. I thought that it would serve merely to make them inquire after you and that was all; furthermore I am ready to give the most favorable testimony in regard to you. I should even like to have an opportunity to shorten your imprisonment; as a good citizen I have declared what I know about you; as a good citizen I declare that I regard you as an honest man. I should not be one myself were I to say the contrary. Were I convinced of the contrary, and above all were I sure that you had taken part in any massacre whatsoever, I declare to you that I would never communicate with you directly or indirectly; but I have no such idea, for I recall that you never spoke to me of the affairs of September except with expressions of disapproval. This, so far as I am concerned, is what I have to say for you. I like to think that all the witnesses who may be called for you will be no less favorable; I hope so. I tell you again not to spare me. I am angry enough that you have been so long imprisoned, even should it prove only temporary; you would have been more useful in a shop and justice would have lost nothing.

" Greeting and fraternity,

" Signed: MAIGNIEN.

" This 15th Fructidor, in the year 3."

On the address was written: " To Citizen Gonorre at the Bourbe."

" This copy conforms to the original, which is in the hands of my wife.   GONORD."

This letter, which fear dictated, nevertheless succeeded in obtaining Gonnord's release; for fresh information concerning him derived from a reliable source necessitated a new inquiry, which a new and perfectly legitimate order of arrest was to close:

" Extract from the Registry of the Clerk of the Prison of La Force, the fifth complémentaire of the year III. of the Republic.

" In virtue of a warrant of arrest issued by Citizen Faure, Public Prosecutor in the Criminal Court of the Department of Paris.

" To be confined in said prison Jean Pierre Gonord, aged thirty-eight, a native of Paris, a wheelwright, living number 528 Rue Taranne, Faubourg Germain.

" The said Gonord is accused of having taken part in the massacres of September 2 and 3, 1792 (old style).

" The copy conforms to the registry in said prison. Paris, this 6th Vendémiaire, third year of the French Republic.

" Signed: LEGÉ,
" Employé in the Registrar's Office."

The verdict was not rendered until the 22nd Floréal, fourth year.

The trial was very long, if we accept the version of Monsieur Mortimer-Ternaux.

According to the same author only one man was condemned and, thanks to extenuating circumstances, merely to twenty years in chains. This was Raigné, called Nicolas, to whom, moreover, after his execrable work a certificate was given proving his perfect honesty.

This civil warrant was taken by us in the city library from the copy of the Revolutionary Tribunal issued by Ledru-Rollin:

" The 5th Pluviose, third year of the French Republic one and indivisible.

" Citizen Pierre Nicolas Raigné, called Nicolas, living number ——, Rue des Prêtres Paul, Maison du Boulanger, when asked to go to the committee named in execution of the law of the 13th Frimaire in order to give it information which would satisfy the law, presented himself there and, besides aiding the commissioners by his information, gave the following document :

" ' Paris Commune, September 12, 1792, fourth year of Liberty and first of Equality.

" ' We the undersigned municipal officers certify that the said Pierre Nicolas Raigné and Charles Nicolas Michel have been employed in the prison of La Force to transfer the corpses to places indicated, for which service they were paid at the rate of fifty sols a day; we certify moreover that they behaved in such a way as to leave no doubt of their honesty and loyalty. Given in the Prison of La Force, September 12th, fourth year of Liberty and first of Equality.

" ' C. JAMS, Municipal Officer; DANGÉ, Municipal Officer; LESGUILLON, Municipal Commissary; VA, Clerk of the Committee.'

" Seen and read in the General Assembly of the Section of the Arsenal, which has never believed in the evil accusations made against Citizen Pierre Nicolas Reinier, whose patriotism it well knows.

" This September 13, 1792, fourth year of Liberty and first of Equality.

" CONADIEU, President.

" HANY, Assistant Secretary.

" J. P. LE DRU, FÉLIX, COLLIN, PETRO DEPERORIAN, VINCENT.

" NOTE.—This document was copied in toto from the Registry of the Committee number four, page 314, dated September 13, 1792.

" (Copy conforms to the original presented and delivered on aforesaid day, month, and year.)"

He was not the only one sentenced, however, if we are to believe the " Décade Philosophique

" As to the murderers of September several have been convicted, but a greater number have been acquitted. Only inferior and blind agents are detained, and although their crime may be atrocious, possibly their sentences will be lightened in favor of extenuating circumstances. However, none of those who took part in the massacres can return to society. They would excite horror; they would arouse a desire for vengeance, and hence would be driven again to crime."

In spite of all these researches, others escaped prosecution at the time, and a general amnesty was promulgated fourth Brumaire, year IV. (Monday, September 26, 1795). A year later one of the butchers of the poor princess was condemned to death for murder.

" Grizon, convicted of having been one of the murderers of Monsieur de l'Aunay, Governor of the Bastille, and for having cut off the head of Madame de Lamballe to please the Duc d'Orléans, who was her next heir, has just been condemned to death at Troyes as leader of the brigands who robbed the Department of the Aube. Emery, one of his accomplices, a native of Lyons, received the same sentence.

The latter was the bearer of several letters from Couri-
oilles, punished in Paris as assassin of the courier from
Lyons.'

This to our knowledge was the only justice done.

Let us quote the lines of Lebrun apropos of the massacres of September:

LINES WRITTEN SEPTEMBER 3, 1792.

" Thou, whom I adored, O, sad Fatherland !
Thy poet, in tears, turns sadly from thee.
Indignant because of thy fair glory's brand,
Perjured king and his murderous subjects I flee."

Was it a question of banter, of derisive verses ?

In vain have we read the patriotic ode of Lebrun;
we have not found this passage there.

As one must always seek a motive for a crime we
wonder why the Princesse de Lamballe was one of the
first victims of the Terror.

Harmand (de la Meuse) claims to know the cause,
and tells us that upon his entrance into office the Legislative Assembly had resolved to take charge of the
education of the dauphin and to give him a tutor of
his own choice.   In the meantime the Constitutional
Monarchists, in order to attach to the court the most
influential and the most popular man of the time, had
thought of Robespierre in this connection.

According to the deputies of the Right everything
depended on the way the matter was presented to the
king; hence they sought a person of some influence

and of well-established credit who might with some chance of success suggest the idea.

They turned their eyes upon the Princesse de Lamballe. The latter was incensed at such an overture and refused positively. But when they explained to her the value of the combination and the good which might result therefrom for the royal family, she consented to speak to the king.

Louis XVI. stopped her at the first word, saying: " You are not thinking of such a thing, cousin! "

But Madame de Lamballe it seems knew how to be eloquent, and induced the king to consent to the nomination of Robespierre under the following conditions, imposed by the Constitutionalists themselves:

Robespierre was to be chosen tutor; he was not to fulfil the duties of the office but was to be contented with the title and was to draw the salary. On his part he engaged to establish a paper on the side of the monarchy, to speak in favor of the king at the club of the Jacobins, and finally to hand in his resignation as public prosecutor.

The result of this arrangement was the founding of the " Défenseur de la Constitution " by Robespierre, who carried out his promise to the letter until the princess informed him that the king could not keep his word in the face of the hostile attitude of the queen. At this unexpected news Robespierre realized that he must regain his popularity. Therefore he changed front, suppressed his paper, and fled August 10th.

Later he must have arrested the princess and organized the massacres in order to destroy all evidences of his ambition.

This opinion is somewhat confirmed by the Abbé Georgel,[1] who claims that "if Robespierre had been elected tutor of the dauphin, a position with which he would have been modestly contented, perhaps there would not have occurred those scenes of horror of which we were the sad witnesses, although Robespierre might have edited the ' Défenseur de la Constitution,' a paper started to deceive the court by masking the projects of the faction." He adds that if in his hatred Robespierre did drive the royal family to the scaffold it was from " mortification at not having been elected."

So according to him there was no nomination, while Harmand affirms that there was. But that is not the only error we wish to correct, for Robespierre did not start his paper until June 1st, and Madame de Fleurieu was appointed governess of the dauphin April 18th.

Following is another version of the causes of the death of Madame de Lamballe. We give it only as a matter of interest, without attaching more importance to it than to that of Harmand.

" SECRET CAUSE OF THE DEATH OF THE CI-DEVANT PRINCESSE LAMBALLE.—TERRIBLE ANECDOTE ABOUT HER HAND.

" Every one knows that the ci-devant Princesse Lamballe was one of the first victims of the execrable days of September; that after her death her bloody corpse was dragged through the streets, a target for the most horrible outrages; but that which is not known is the invisible hand that directed the blows of the butchers. The murder has generally been attributed to her successor, d'Orléans; motives of interest seem to justify this presumption, but positive information has come to us on this subject, leaving no further doubt as to the true cause of this tragic death.

" Three members of the National Assembly, who later at the Convention assumed the leading rôles on this revolutionary theatre, some months previous to August the 10th, had coveted the places of the Ministers. R—— aspired to the position of Minister of Justice; P—— to that of Minister of the Interior; D—— to that of Minister of Finances. They knew that in order to succeed it was first of all necessary to obtain the consent of the queen; their names alone were for her a reason for refusal and execration; what should they do ? The Princesse Lamballe had great influence with Marie Antoinette; they resolved to make her an instrument for their ambition.

" The three candidates took care to present themselves. B——, who was negotiating for the 10th of August, undertook to make the proposition. He showed the princess the advantage that Louis XVI. and the court would derive from the nomination of these men of the people; he dwelt particularly on the advantage of arresting all monarchical movement. ' Do not let their names frighten you,' said he; ' they are all the more fitted to serve in the cause of the king; their popularity is the surest safeguard of the monarchy; Mirabeau at first undermined the foundations of the throne in order to make it all the stronger later.'

" The Princesse Lamballe listened to his arguments,

although she felt the same aversion for the solicitor as for the candidates; she promised to propose them to the queen. Scarcely had she suggested their names before Antoinette, turning on her a furious glance, exclaimed, ' Do you wish to give us for ministers our executioners, to introduce into the council of the king the authors of the massacres of the early days of October ? Are they not trying to draw nearer to us in order to deal us surer and swifter blows ? ' The princess did not insist, but far from delivering the actual answer of the queen she said to B—— that the king had already made his choice and that on no condition whatever could he revoke it. The manner in which she expressed herself seemed to indicate that she had managed the affair with some indifference. They took this refusal as the result of a lack of good-will on her part, and from that moment her death was determined on.

" The name of this unfortunate woman headed the list of the massacred; the murderers of September received their instructions from the triumvirate; these instructions were carried out beyond the wildest hopes of their authors. The assassins of the forest contented themselves with immolating and stripping their victims; those of La Force in the middle of the bloody streets disputed over pieces of flesh torn from the princess, which aroused in them at the same time feelings of cannibalism and something worse. How many times before her last breath did this princess die! In her everything that the sex holds most sacred was shown least respect, and a few days after the murderers still showed publicly in the inns bloody remains which modesty will not even allow us to mention.

" It was not enough to have hacked the princess to pieces alive, to have divided her body among them, and to have dragged it by bits through streams of blood: the assassins had not yet offered a proof of their barbarity to those who were paying for the massacres. The triumvirs were gathered together with some other leaders in a house adjoining La Force. They were at supper; four of their agents arrived and placed on the table the right hand of the princess. They looked at it, passed it from one guest to another; they made about her fingers jokes as atrocious as they were lugubrious. R——— examined the token attentively and said with the coolness of scorn: ' It was pretty.'

" These accounts, which we publish with hesitation, solely in the interests of history, were given us by two persons still living who, although they did not dip their hands in the blood, were nevertheless closely connected with these three men, one of whom has been fêted as a martyr of the Terror."

The memory of the good princess and of her worthy father-in-law was religiously preserved by their faithful servants; the anniversary of their death was celebrated by a mass even during the darkest days of the Revolution.

We give in full the funeral oration pronounced in the Church of St. Paul at the beginning of these touching ceremonies:

" Funeral Oration delivered by Monsieur Sevray, who acted for the institutors of the religious ceremony held in memory of the unfortunate Princesse de Lamballe in the Church of (*sic*) Rue Saint-Antoine near the Place de Bastille, and since held in the Church Saint Leu:

" O cruel memories, let our hearts beat for one moment! O days of misery and terror, days, alas, as deplorable as frightful, depart forever from our eyes! From the midst of this lugubrious scene which recalls to us a sweet and well-loved face, rise sublime virtues which impose on us important duties.

" O plaintive shade of the purest of mortals! Now that we are gathered together to celebrate her memory her sweet and gentle soul has returned to the bosom of the God of peace whence it came; it is more affected by our tender regrets than by the horror imposed on it by those cannibals who usurped the name of men only to dishonor the race by the blackest and most cowardly of barbarities. Such is the horror they inspire that we would not breathe the same air, would not live in the same place; and if a legislation imperfect until now has withheld them from the just punishment that they deserve, the scorn which we forever feel for them will make of what is left of their lives an eternity of remorse and torment, limitless, endless.

" O virtuous and worthy princess, were you still here among us you would compel us to suffer; and by this example you would teach us to respect and submit ourselves to the will of the strongest, as do your worthy relatives, rich heirs of the love which we bear you. But what am I saying? Alas! you exist only in our tender regrets and sad memories.

" Sensitive Souls! deplore, and let us all deplore the fate of the unfortunate princess who, escaping for a few instants from my care, saw herself in the midst of a crowd; frightened and paralyzed with terror, deserted and pitiably abandoned, even by those who loved her, to the ferocity of scarcely a handful of wretched murderers, who in order to kill her subjected her to the cruellest and most dreadful torments—torments so dreadful that pencil and pen refuse to describe them and decency will not allow me to explain.

" Nobles! and People! learn from this horrible illustration to what shameful excesses those who wickedly wish and aspire to act and govern themselves without sovereigns and without laws are capable of yielding.

" O Almighty God! O God of kindness, divine Providence! O Holy Trinity for all eternity! Believing fully in the immortality of the soul we humbly beg Thee to reward Louise de Savoye, the unfortunate princess, with the brilliant crown of the martyr, and to admit her into the shining company of the elect, where in her eternal resting-place she may sing forever to the glory of the Father, the Son, and the Holy Ghost. Amen. De Profundis. '

The commemorative masses were continued during the revolutionary and imperial periods,[2] but probably in secret, while from the time of the Restoration they became semi-official in character, for the " Moniteur " newspaper mentions them :

" Acts of piety leave deep impressions on the heart. The service and the mass for the dead which a faithful servant of Monseigneur le Duc de Penthièvre had celebrated during the Revolution on the anniversary of the death of this prince and of that of Madame la Princesse de Lamballe attracted a large number of the faithful. From the Restoration these two pious ceremonies were much more largely attended under the auspices of the worthy successor to the name and the virtues of the Duc de Penthièvre. Her royal Highness the

Duchesse-dowager d'Orléans went yesterday to the Church of Saint-Leu to attend the mass which was celebrated at noon for the repose of Madame de Lamballe's soul. The high altar and the door of the church were draped in mourning and bore the coat-of-arms of the princess. In accordance with the wish of the founder only low mass was celebrated."

The funeral services celebrated respectively the 4th of March and the 3rd of September were kept up until 1819. From the beginning of 1820 the "Moniteur" makes no further mention of them.

Does this mean that the health of the Duchesse d'Orléans, who was soon to die, did not permit her to attend them?

The Restoration thought at one time of giving Paris a monument in memory of Madame de Lamballe. A proposition to this effect was made at a meeting of the Chambre des Pairs, Saturday, January 13, 1816. The project was never carried out; and indeed no monument or effigy, were it from the chisel of the most skilful master, would have been able to withstand the political troubles.

The poet Delille wrote the following epitaph for Madame de Lamballe:

> " Lamballe has succumbed, Lamballe whose great zeal
> For her queen, by dying, she strove to reveal.
> And her beautiful hair, her low graceful brow,
> Ah, Heaven ! in what a sad state are they now !
> Shocked Nature cries out, and friendship so dear,
> Before those loved features recoils as in fear ! "

We will conclude this biography of our unfortunate princess by quoting from the work of Francis Girault— " *Le passé, le présent et l'avenir, ou Prédictions, vérifications et explications de quelques prophéties remarquables de Michel Nostradamus.* Paris: Hivert, Gaume, Dentu. Pamphlet in-8, 43 pp., 1839 "—a prediction ingeniously dedicated to Madame de Lamballe:

" DEATH OF THE PRINCESS DE LAMBALLE. CENTURY II,
SIXTH, 55.

" Sooner or later shall pass from earth
A lady of high degree.
Her spirit to God, her body to man,
By many regretted shall be.
All her relations shall mourn her loss,
A younger woman shall bear the cross,
And two others the misery."

" The manner of death, the regrets of the Duc de Penthièvre and of all the Carignans, the tears of Madame Royale, and the grief which the king and especially Marie Antoinette felt in their hearts—do not all these facts clearly show that this referred to the beautiful and unfortunate Princesse de Lamballe ? "

The prediction, although perhaps not containing every evidence which our author was pleased to attribute to it, nevertheless deserves to be noticed because of its historical interest.

It is for this reason that we have given it, adding in conclusion only one thing, namely, that the sad privilege of those who suffer greatly, because of the important place they occupy in the great human drama, is to lend themselves admirably to sombre predictions and very often to realize them. Never, perhaps, has a more sinister prophecy from this point of view had a more gloomy fulfilment.

THE END.

Translator's Notes

CHAPTER I

[1] "Among those who came about me was the bridegroom himself, whom I had never yet seen. So anxious was he to have his first acquaintance *incognito* that he set off from Paris the moment he was apprised of my arrival in France and presented himself as the prince's page. . . . What was my surprise when the Duc de Penthièvre presented me to the prince, and I found in him the page for whom I had already felt such an interest! . . . This was really love at first sight."—" Memoirs of the Princesse de Lamballe."

[2] The King of Sardinia, as the head of the house of Savoy and Carignan, said there had been some conversation as to the Princesse de Carignan's becoming a member of his royal family ; but as she was very young at the time, many political reasons might have arisen to necessitate a change in the projected alliance. " If, therefore," said the King, " the Prince Carignan be anxious to settle his daughter's marriage by any immediate matrimonial alliance, I certainly shall not avail myself of any prior engagement nor oppose any obstacle in the way of its solemnization."— " Memoirs," p. 82.

CHAPTER II

[1] Mesdames Mackau, de Soucie, the Comtesse de Noailles (not duchesse, as Mademoiselle Bertin calls her in her " Mémoires ") claimed that the Princesse de Lamballe was the most beautiful and accomplished princess at court, adorned with all the grace, virtue, and elegance of manner which so eminently distinguished her through life. Although she had no particularly shining talents, her

understanding was sound and she seldom gave her opinion without mature reflection, and never without being called on, or when she distinctly foresaw the danger which must accrue from its being withheld.

The Princesse de Lamballe was so uniformly eager in contributing to the peace of mind and happiness of every individual who sought her mediation that she was as well known by the appellation of " the peace-maker " as she was by her title.

CHAPTER III

[1] Afterwards Duc d'Orléans and the celebrated revolutionary Philip Égalité. His son, the grandson of the Duc de Penthièvre, was afterwards Louis Philippe.

In her diary and letters the Princesse de Lamballe dates her misery and grief from the marriage of her beloved sister-in-law Mademoiselle de Penthièvre to the Duc de Chartres. In revenge for his unrequited passion for the princess, the latter enticed away her young husband, who soon became the prey of every dissipation and debauchery.

The Duc de Chartres was never a favorite of the queen. He was tolerated only on account of his wife, and because of the great intimacy which existed between him and the Comte d'Artois. Louis XVI. had often expressed his disapprobation of the duke's character, which his conduct daily justified.

" The infamous and recreant Duke of Orleans "; and, again, " Philippe, Duke of Orleans, born in 1745, was one of the most infamous personages of the Revolution. This prince combined in himself all that was most depraved and bad in the old noblesse, and all that was most odious in the ambitious mob leaders."—See Morris, pp. 24–25, 35.

[2] " The Duc de Chartres then possessed a very handsome person and most insinuating address."—" Memoirs of Madame de Lamballe."

[3] The queen had been attached to the Princesse de Lamballe long before the sledge parties took place. But see Madame de Campan, vol. i., p. 129.

[4] " In her (Marie Antoinette's) happier days of power, the great Gluck was brought, at her request, from Germany to Paris. He

cost nothing to the public treasury, for her Majesty paid all his expenses out of her own purse. . . . She heard all his pieces, at Gluck's request, before they were submitted to the stage."—" Memoirs," p. 110.

CHAPTER IV

[1] The Prince de Lamballe was the son of the Comte de Toulouse, himself a natural son of Louis XIV. and Madame de Montespan, who was considered the most wealthy of all the natural children in consequence of Madame de Montespan's having artfully entrapped the famous Mademoiselle de Montpensier to make over her immense fortune to him as her heir after her death, as the price of liberating her husband from imprisonment in the Bastille, and herself from a ruinous prosecution for having contracted this marriage contrary to the express commands of her royal cousin, Louis XIV. —*Vide* " Histoire de Louis XIV.," par Voltaire.

[2] The deposed court oracle, the Comtesse de Noailles, had been succeeded as literary leader by the Comtesse Diana Polignac. She was a favorite of the Comte d'Artois, and was the first lady in attendance upon the comtesse his wife. The Comtesse de Polignac had a much better education and considerably more natural capacity than her sister-in-law the duchess, and the queen disliked her merely for her prudish affectation. The Comtesse d'Artois grew jealous of the count's intimacy with the Comtesse Diana. . . . But making a merit of necessity she submitted at length to retaining the comtesse, who remained in the family up to the 17th of October, 1789, when she left Versailles in company with the Polignacs and the d'Artois, who all emigrated together from France to Italy, and lived at Stria, on the Brenta, near Venice, for some time, till the Comtesse d'Artois went to Turin.

[3] The Duchesse de Chartres had complained to her father, the Duc de Penthièvre, in the presence of the Princesse de Lamballe, of the very great ascendency Madame de Genlis exercised over her husband, and had even requested the queen to use her influence in detaching the duke from this connection. It was generally understood that the duke had, by Madame de Genlis, a daughter who later was married to the late Irish Lord Robert Fitzgerald.

[4] An obsolete office was revived in favor of the Princesse de

Lamballe. In the time of Maria Leckzinska, wife of Louis XV., the office of superintendent, then held by Mademoiselle de Clermont, was suppressed when its holder died. The office gave a control over the inclinations of queens by which Maria Leckzinska was sometimes inconvenienced ; and it had lain dormant ever since. Its restoration by one who it was believed could be guided by no motive but the desire to seek pretexts for showing undue favor, was eyed askance, and before long openly calumniated.

CHAPTER V

[1] At this time Comte de Mercy was Austrian Ambassador to the court of France. For Mercy, see "Marie Antoinette," by D'Arneth and Geoffroy, ii. 223.

[2] Tutor, secretary, confessor, and unfortunately in many respects the ambitious guide of Marie Antoinette.

Louis XVI. had no prepossession in favor of the Abbé Vermond, and merely tolerated him in order not to wound the feelings of the queen. Marie Antoinette was conscious of this, and is said to have frequently stated the fact that she did not remember the king's ever having held any communication with the abbé during the whole time he was attached to the service, though the abbé always expressed himself with the greatest respect towards the king.

Neckar's opinion of Vermond was that he was quite as obnoxious to the people as the Duchesse de Polignac ever had been.

Vermond enjoyed much influence with regard to ecclesiastical preferments. He was too fond of his situation ever to contradict or thwart her majesty in any of her plans ; too much a courtier to assail her ears with the language of truth ; and by far too much a clergyman to interest himself but for mother church. In short, he was more culpable in not doing his duty than in the mischief he occasioned ; for he certainly oftener misled the queen by his silence than by his advice.

[3] One of the popular objections to the revival of the office of superintendent in favor of the Princesse de Lamballe arose from its reputed extravagance. This was groundless. The etiquette of dress, and the requisite increase of every other expense, from the augmentation of every article of the necessaries as well as the

luxuries of life, made a treble difference between the expenditure of the circumscribed court of Maria Leckzinska and that of Louis XVI.; yet the Princesse de Lamballe received no more salary than had been allotted to Mademoiselle de Clermont half a century before. And even that salary she never appropriated to any private use of her own, being amply supplied through the generous bounty of her father-in-law the Duc de Penthièvre.—" Memoirs of Madame de Lamballe."

[4] The laughable title of Madame Etiquette which the dauphiness gave Madame de Noailles clung to her through life ; and though conferred only in merriment, it was never forgiven.

[5] There was an eccentricity in the appearance, dress, and manners of the Prince de Conti which well deserves recording.

CHAPTER VI

[1] The queen's favorite brother. It was he who on leaving Italy and coming to Paris interested himself in causing Louis XVI. to settle the differences then subsisting between the court of Naples and that of Spain ; and it was his opinion which some time afterwards influenced the Queen of France to refuse the offer of the Queen of Naples to affiance her daughter, the Duchesse d'Angoulême, to the son of the Queen of Naples, and to propose as more eligible a marriage which after the Revolution took place between the house of Orleans and that of Naples.

It was said that the French treasury, which was not overflowing, was still more reduced by the queen's partiality for her brother ; but the finances of Joseph were at that time too superior to those of France to admit of such extravagance or even to render it desirable.

For further account of Joseph see Madame Campan.

[2] Comte d'Artois, afterwards Charles X., one of the first to desert the king and the royal family.

[3] The splendid fêtes, balls, and entertainments indiscriminately lavished by all ranks throughout the kingdom on this occasion augmented those of the queen and the court to a pitch of magnificence surpassing the most luxurious and voluptuous times of the great and brilliant Louis XIV.

TRANSLATOR'S NOTES

The following verses on this occasion written by Metastasio are
of interest:

> " Io pudei: l'augusta figlia
> A pagar, m'a condemnato
> Ma s'è ver che a voi somiglia
> Tutto il mondo ha quadagnato."

[4] Baron de Besenval, one of the seconds at the well-known duel
between the Comte d'Artois and the Duc de Bourbon.

CHAPTER VII

[1] Venerable is a title of the Master in French lodges, equivalent
to Worshipful in English and American lodges.

Venerable Brother, a title given to each officer of the Grand
Orient.

[2] The Masons of Europe are much more addicted to the use of
this method of contracting masonic writing than American Masons.
The abbreviations among our foreign brethren are usually distinguished by the use of three periods, placed in the form of a
triangle—thus .'. or thus '.', as the writer may prefer. This
peculiar form of contraction was first introduced by the Grand
Orient of France in 1774.

[3] Among them were the Duchesse de Bourbon, the Empress
Josephine, Lady Montague, Duchess Elizabeth Chesterfield, and
the Empress Eugènie.

[4] Adoptive Masonry was a name given to certain degrees resem-
bling masonry and masonic in spirit which have at times been invented for ladies who have claims upon the Order of Freemasonry
through relatives who are members of it.

Adoptive Masonry first made its appearance in France in the
early part of the eighteenth century, and there is still a legal and
regular branch of the institution in that country.

The Adoptive Lodges were at first rapidly diffused throughout
all the countries of Europe except the British Empire.

[5] Écossais-e (French), *Scotch*. A term applied to the Ancient and
Accepted Rite, and the name of the fifth degree of the French sys-
tem.—"General History of Freemasonry," by Robert McCoy, 33°.

TRANSLATOR'S NOTES

Écossais—a French word usually translated Scottish Master or Mistress, and first introduced by the Chevalier Ramsay, whose theory was that Freemasonry originally came from Scotland in the general form it is now practised. For further reference see " The Royal Masonic Cyclopædia," edited by Kenneth R. H. MacKenzie, ix°.

CHAPTER VIII

[1] Palace of La Muette, situated in the Bois de Boulogne, very near Paris.

[2] To this intimacy of the queen with the governess of her children may be referred the first direct blows at the royal dignity.

[3] On the death of Louis XV. the entire court had gone to La Muette.

[4] The Duchesse de Gramont was one of the confidential friends of Louis XV. before he took Du Barry under his especial protection. She was noted for her independence and dignity.

[5] The Duchesse de Guémenée having been obliged to leave her residence at Versailles in consequence of the duke's dismissal from the king's service on account of the disordered state of his pecuniary circumstances, the situation of governess to the royal children became necessarily vacant and was immediately transferred to the Duchesse de Polignac.

[6] " At this time their majesties were adored. Marie Antoinette, with all her beauty and amiableness, was a mere cipher in the eyes of France previous to her becoming the mother of an heir to the crown; but her popularity now arose to a pitch of unequalled enthusiasm."—" Memoirs."

CHAPTER IX

[1] The Duc du Nord was afterwards the Emperor Paul. It was during the visit of himself and his wife at court that the Cardinal de Rohan again appeared on the scene.

CHAPTER X

[1] Duc de Normandie, afterwards the dauphin.

TRANSLATOR'S NOTES

CHAPTER XI

[1] In her " Mémoires," tome ii., Madame de Campan says the necklace was intended for Du Barry. The exact date of its manufacture, however, is not known. Du Barry went into " half pay" May 10, 1774, the day her king died.

"Abbé Georgel, who has given a long solemn narrative of the necklace business, passes for the grand authority on it, but neither will he, strictly taken up, abide scrutiny. He is vague, writing in what is called the 'soaped pig' fashion. There are hardly above three dates in his whole narrative. He mistakes several times; perhaps . . . misrepresents a little."—Carlyle.

[2] Bette d'Etienville's description of De Rohan is as follows : A handsome man of fifty, with high complexion, hair white-gray and the front of the head bald; of high stature, carriage noble and easy, though burdened with a certain degree of corpulency. (First " Mémoire pour.") " On May 31, 1786, sentence was pronounced; about ten at night the Cardinal escaped from the Bastille; large mobs cheered him, angered at the court." See Georgel. See also " Mémoires," note, p. 166 et seq.; also Marquis de Valfous, " Mémoires," 60; De Levis, 156; and Madame d'Oberkirk, i. 127, and ii. 360.

[3] See " Vie de Jeanne, Comtesse de Lamotte " (by herself), vol. i.; also four " Mémoires pour " by her in this " Affaire du Collier "—Carlyle says, "like lawyers' tongues turned inside out." Afterwards one volume, " Mémoires justificatifs de la Comtesse de," etc. (London, 1788), with appendix of " Documents " so-called and misdated as to day of month. Also two volumes, " Vie de Jeanne," etc., printed in London, by way of extorting money *from Paris*. The latter was bought up by French persons in authority. It was the burning of this *editio princeps* in the Sèvres Potteries, May 30, 1792, which raised such a smoke that the Legislative Assembly took alarm and had an investigation about it, etc., till the truth came out. Copies of the book were speedily reprinted after August 10th.

Compare Rohan's four " Mémoires pour" in the " Affaire du Collier " with Lamotte's four.

See also Georgel, who dates the affair in 1785; also Comte de Lamotte's narrative in the " Mémoires justificatifs."

TRANSLATOR'S NOTES

In regard to the accounts of above by Madame Campan, Carlyle says: "Madame Campan, in her 'Mémoires,' generally, does not seem to *intend* falsehood. She rather, perhaps, intends the producing of an impression, which may have appeared to herself to be the right one. But, at all events, she has . . . no notion of historical rigor; she gives hardly any date, or the like ; will tell the same thing, in different places, different ways, etc. There is a tradition that Louis XVIII. revised her 'Mémoires' before publication. She requires to be read with scepticism everywhere, but yields something in that way."—From Carlyle's "Diamond Necklace."

[4] See Lamotte's MS. songs in the "Affaire du Collier," etc.

Carlyle says : "Nothing can exceed the brutality of these things; which nevertheless found believers—increase of believers in the public exasperation, and did the queen incalculable damage."

[5] "The princess, though disappointed in some of her main objects with regard to influence and information, became so great a favorite at the British court that she obtained full permission of the king and queen of England to signify to her royal mistress and friend that the specific request she came to make would be complied with. She visited Bath, Windsor, Brighton, and many other parts of England, and managed so judiciously that the real object of her visit was never suspected."—"Mémoires," p. 280.

[6] Baron de Bréteuil, a sworn enemy of the Cardinal de Rohan.

[7] Loménie de Brienne, Archbishop of Toulouse and Sens, born 1727, died 1794. As minister of Louis XVI. he exiled the Parliament of Paris to Troyes in 1787, and compelled it to register edicts of the king which it had opposed.

Marie Antoinette persisted in upholding every act of Brienne till his ignorance and unpardonable blunders drew down the general indignation of the people against her Majesty and her protégé, with whom she was identified.

"The monarchy was seldom guilty of acts more arbitrary, violent, and iniquitous than those sanctioned by Brienne."—Morris, "French Revolution."

[8] Abbey of Fontevrault. In this connection it will be of interest to the reader to consult "Architectural Studies in France," new edition, revised by Edward Bell.

TRANSLATOR'S NOTES

CHAPTER XII

[1] "The French Revolution may date its epoch as far back as the taking of the Bastille."—"Mémoires."

[2] For journey from Versailles to Paris, see Campan, vol. ii. 313 ; also Bertrand de Molleville.

CHAPTER XIII

[1] "Le Gazette de France" was the first French newspaper. It was published in 1631 by Théophraste Renaudot. It appeared once a week, contained the news and gossip, and was very popular.

CHAPTER XIV

[1] For card-playing, see "Mémoires," p. 143.

CHAPTER XV

[1] Only the children of the king and the heir-apparent were called "Enfants de France." It was for centuries later the rule that only the Enfants de France might ride or drive into the Louvre, Palais, Hôtel St. Paul, Tournelles, or any royal palace. Princes of the blood must get down at the door, nobles in the street. See De Sareval.

[2] The Duc d'Orléans was the first to abandon the royal family.

[3] Barnave was conspicuous among the reformers of the National Assembly.

See Morris, p. 56. Also "Mémoires," pp. 221, 228, 283, 302.

[4] "Ci-devant" means former. It was a term constantly used by Republicans during the first revolution in France, in regard to a noble attached to the former régime by his position.

CHAPTER XVI

[1] For this "favorite pastime," which was hunting, see "Journal de Louis XVI.," published by Nicolardot. Also De Luynes, ix. 75, 79,

105 ; Madame Campan, i. 147; Taine's "Ancien Régime"; Duc
de Lauzun, " Mémoires," 51; and Madame de Genlis, " Mémoires,"
chapter xiii.

² For Versailles, see Châteaubriand, " Mémoires," i. 221.

³ An eye-witness of many stirring scenes. Her husband was the
bravest of the royalist generals whom he commanded in La
Vendée, 1793-94.

CHAPTER XVII

¹ A false and artful popularity seeker.
See Morris ; also " Mémoires," p. 375.

² See Burke's " Reflections on the Revolution in France,"which
remain the best and most profound commentary on the work of the
National Assembly.

See also Professor Von Sybel's " History," book ii., chap. iv.

For life and conduct of the royal family at this crisis, see " Letters of Louis XVI., Marie Antoinette."

³ It may be of interest to note that the word tocsin in the seven-
teenth century was spelt *tocquesin*, notably by Ménage, and is com-
pounded of two words—*toque* (act of striking) and *sin* (a bell).

⁴ This was a desperate step, and equivalent, under the circumstances, to an abdication of the throne.

See " Souvenirs de la Terreur," by George Duval, quoted by M.
Feuillet de Couches, vol. vi., p. 285.

See also M. Mortimer Terneaux's " Histoire de la Terreur."

⁶ The royal family were placed in a small box or chamber called
the *logographe*.

⁶ So called from the club which was held in the convent by the
Feuillants, a branch of the Order of St. Bernard. The club was
set up to counteract the power of the Jacobins.

⁷ So at another critical moment on the arrival of the delegates at
Varennes, Louis seemed, it is said, "to have been most anxious
about finishing his morning meal."—*Morris.*

And again, " the chief of the illustrious race of Bourbon, in sight
of the falling throne of his sires, ate, it is said, with seeming content, a dish of peaches ! "—*Morris.*

TRANSLATOR'S NOTES

CHAPTER XVIII

[1] Billaud Varennes was afterwards prosecuted and sent beyond the seas.

[2] The so-called mock judges at the tribunal were Thibaudeau, Hebert, Simonier, etc.

[3] For graphic description of Lamballe's execution, see p. 380 *et seq.* of " Mémoires."

" The Duc de Penthièvre set every engine in operation to save his beloved daughter-in-law." He promised Manuel half his fortune if the princess could be rescued ; and this might have been accomplished had it not been for a misunderstanding in the matter of orders.

See also M. Thiers' "Histoire de la Révolution Française," vol. ii., p. 335, edit. 1842.

[4] Santerre, "who so cruelly ordered the drums to beat, to hasten the execution and prevent the dying king's last words from being heard."—" Memoirs," p. 393.

Santerre was originally a brewer in the Faubourg Saint Antoine, at Paris. He first made himself conspicuous in the revolt of the famous 14th July, 1789, which ended in the taking of the Bastille. In 1793 he was given command of some battalions sent against La Vendée, but showed himself a worthless general. He was routed by the Royalists before the walls of Coron. He was reported to have been killed, and the following epitaph was composed for him at Paris:

" Ci gît le général Santerre,
Qui n'eut de Mars que la *bière*,"

a pun on the word *bière*, which means both *bier* and *beer*, and Santerre, as we have said, was originally a brewer. *Bière de Mars* was a very light beer brewed in early spring.

CHAPTER XIX

[1] Paper money, the emission of which was decreed on the 1st of April, 1790, and annulled February 19, 1796. The creation of these

assignats was the cause of fearful disasters to the commerce, industry, and credit of the nation.

² For Comte de Fersan, see pp. 148, 212, 217, 290 of the "Mémoires."

³ In the matter of the journey to Varennes, had the king been guided by the Comte de Fersan he would have succeeded.

It is at Varennes that Madame Campan places the beginning of Barnave's sentiments in favor of the royal family. Other historians differ on this point.

For Varennes, see also Morris's "French Revolution" and Watson's "France."

CHAPTER XX

¹ "A most assiduous, ever-wakeful Abbé."—*Carlyle*.

"The factotum, principal agent, and secretary of the Cardinal de Rohan." And again: "To the Abbé Georgel may be attributed all the artful intrigues of Rohan's disgraceful diplomacy."

See also Madame Campan: "The Abbé Georgel in his 'Mémoires' justifies the conduct of his superior with great ability; and it was very politic in him to do so, because he thereby exonerates himself from the imputation he would naturally incur from having been a known party, if not a principal, in all which has dishonored the Cardinal."

² "It was reported that Napoleon when he became Emperor of France, respecting the virtues of this illustrious sufferer, ordered in commemoration of this event the funeral rites to be performed in the parish where she had been butchered, on the 3d day of every September. Her birthday would have been on the 8th of the same month."—"Mémoires."

Printed in Great Britain
by Amazon

82587629R00215